AF615567

"Except"

Presented to ______________________________

On this ______ day of ________________ 20 ______

City ____________________________ State __________

By ____

ALSO BY PRESTON BRADLEY

THE FINAL WARNING

THE LOUDEST ALARM

GOSPEL OF JUDGMENT

www.visionpublishers.com

"Except"

Divorce Guide For Christians

(and all human beings)

Instructions from the Holy Bible

VISION-*publishing*

Huntsville, AL USA

Published by
Vision Publishing
3801-22 Triana Blvd. SW
Huntsville, AL 35805-5386

Library of Congress Control Number: 2005928229

Bradley, Preston

"Except" Divorce Guide For Christians and all Human Beings

ISBN 0-9669709-1-8

1. Religion—Current Affairs—Literature
2. Divorce—Religious Aspects—Christianity
3. Marriage—Religious Aspects—Christianity
4. Reconciliation—Religious Aspects—Christianity

248.846

Much appreciation is extended to Dr. Dionne Felix for her caring assistance in the preparation of the manuscript.

Manufactured in the United States of America

Dedicated to the reader who is looking forward to his or her first marriage, have been married, and is married. . . .

CONTENTS

“Except”

Divorce Guide For Christians

(and all human beings)

1

Divorce: Episode One

THE mean scowl on her face could scare a vulture away from a carcass. Adon had seen that awful contortion of countenance before—across the dinner table, on family outings, even in church when the choir sang accompanied by cymbals and drums. "Drums are for the jungle, not Christian worship," he had heard his mother-in-law say.

But the present occasion was out of the ordinary, since she had just arose from off her knees and giving the sacred prayer to open the seventh-day Sabbath. Jewel was sitting on the love seat next to Adon, her husband, in their comfortable suburban home, when the words that accompanied the scowl escaped from her lips. "Adon," his mother-in-law said, sitting six-feet away, and looking directly at him, "I don't care if you're lost!"

Adon had heard every word of her seemingly sincere prayer to Jesus for His blessings and guidance, but then, after hearing the scathing words of loathing that had bruised his discipleship, he wondered who his mother-in-law could have been praying to. Where did that damaging remark originate from? He felt as though he had been shot, but he was still living, and trying to figure out from which direction the bullet had come, in case another one was speedily on the way. He managed a look to his right at Jewel, and he saw that her face was expressionless, and not appearing to be affected by what her mother had blatantly said to her husband. A remark so cruelly adverse to Christian principles of love, especially directed at a family member, that Jesus must have turned His face in shame. But Jewel never said a word in defense of her husband, and Adon was too wounded to speak.

Indeed, this was three weeks before Jewel left the house with all the furniture that the busy movers could cram on an empty Mayflower van, and her BMW anchored to the bed of a transport truck for the trip to the East Coast. Princess, Adon and Jewel's fifteen-year-old daughter, had preceded her mother and grandparents to the east to reside with her mother's friends so that she could register on time for high school. Legal separation was imminent; but divorce, Adon thought, was out of the question since they had agreed that for them, being Bible Christians, divorce was not an option.

Adon and Jewel had been married for seventeen years, and his in-laws were practically daily members of his household. The time Jewel's parents spent with their daughter and Adon, now that Jewel's father had retired from full-time Christian ministry, seemed to Adon to be beyond the call of common sense. They were his house guests on every holiday for at least a full week on each side of the day the banks were closed, and not less than a month before and beyond Christmas. They had their separate residence out of state, but at Adon's they also had their own bedroom and private bath.

In the beginning, Adon was happy to have his in-laws as frequent guests in his home since he knew it greatly pleased Jewel to be in such close proximity to her parents. Jewel felt that a good two-week vacation was one spent with her parents. She was an only daughter, with an older and a younger brother, and she and her parents shared every nuance of one another's lives.

Adon soon learned after their marriage that whatever he said to Jewel in private would ultimately get to her parents for their input, and suggested course of action. Because of this leak in confidentiality, Adon began to guard what he said to Jewel since whatever input Jewel shared back with him was not born of her own reasoning, but it was an agreement she had arrived at from secret counseling with her parents. This made Adon feel as though he could have been sleeping with Jewel and her parents, in the same bed, since they were privy to everything that occurred in his household.

The impact of Jewel's involvement with her parents became more troubling when Adon learned from his mother-in-law, a brief year after the ceremony, that she never wanted Jewel to marry him, or anyone else. She was looking forward to Jewel being her close confidant, and private nurse, in her older years. Adon couldn't share this with Jewel because she would never believe such a thought could occur to her mother.

A matter that upset Adon a great deal, too, was that Jewel was a constant source of his private information to her parents, but she would never share a tidbit of their family business with him. Indeed, Adon didn't learn that they were married on his mother-in-law's birthday, until after the divorce. He had often wondered why his and Jewel's anniversaries seemed to occupy second place to something else her family was buzzing about behind closed doors.

Adon was a guarded conversationalist when it came to his and Jewel's family affairs, never whispering a word to anyone that might place "their business in the street." But Jewel was very talkative, a virtual newsreel: on the phone for hours every day after she had arrived home from work. Her habit was to keep in touch with her parents and brothers by telephone, whether they called her, or she called them. She had new church friends since relocating after marriage, old college girlfriends spread across the country, and girlfriends she had known from childhood growing up in her church. Jewel had them ranked according to the importance of the news she shared, with her parents being on top. Adon suspected that they all knew more about his private family matters, from Jewel's point of view, than he did. His suspicions were confirmed when his and Jewel's pastor informed him, several months before it actually occurred, that Jewel was planning to relocate to the East Coast—probably without Adon. Jewel told Adon, after their separation, that her church friends were surprised when she told them, a week before it happened that she was leaving her husband. But Adon knew, from recalling some of the small remarks that Jewel's friends had made to him, that they must have known her plans many months before he did—and were careful to guard their secret. Back then, Adon wondered, with so much going out from Jewel regarding their family affairs, how anyone would ever become aware of even a minute portion of the circumstances within their marriage that affected him the most.

After Princess was born, and she was less than a week old, Jewel took herself and Princess by non-stop air to her parent's home for eight weeks, while Jewel recuperated from her pregnancy and sought help with Princess. Adon regretted that he had given in to Jewel, and agreed to let her leave with his baby girl. Those were lost hours of bonding with his newborn daughter that could never be reclaimed; and his daughter continued into her teen years to identify more with her uncles and grandparents than with her father. Adon wondered if that mistake he had made was a calculated maneuver by his in-laws. He should have insisted, on this occasion, that Jewel's mother come to his home to help out, which was the usual and sensible custom for a mother desiring help with a breast feeding infant. But Jewel was adamant that she retire to her mother with Princess, and she did, for two long months—four weeks longer than they had agreed upon.

Soon after they were married, Adon found it difficult to advance to a better paying position at the TV station where he was employed (he sought on-air talent) or even to find better employment in another field since most new positions he qualified for required that he work on the seventh-day Sabbath, a concession that he and Jewel had agreed he could never make. For this reason (and deep entrepreneurial tendencies) Adon sought out self-employment opportunities where he could set his own hours, and begin with little money. He became deeply involved in several multi-level marketing ventures, which was fashionable at the time, where he spent a lot of time and lost a great deal of money. During this period, he would have gone under completely were it not for Jewel keeping the family alive from her steady employment as a registered nurse.

Jewel was good at making their one dependable income go a long way toward covering all of their high expenses of living in Southern California. She spent many hours clipping food coupons, and searching out used but like-new baby clothes for Princess. She never overly spent on anything for herself, which most of the time was simply buying white shoes and white nurses uniforms that were required for work. Adon recalled that those white uniform days were when hospital personnel looked like professionals, rather than scrub wearing ne'er-do-wells as they do today.

Adon used his weekday mornings dressing and feeding Princess, taking Princess to her babysitter, and then picking her up in the evening. He kept their garden apartment clean, so that Jewel would not have that chore to perform after she arrived home from work. He spent most nights meeting with his multi-level marketing associates, even traveling long distances to encourage and motivate his "down-line." But the money that he should have been using for his family kept pouring out, and not much coming in. Jewel complained, but she never faltered in keeping the family afloat.

Adon finally found a steady, good paying job at a state university where he counseled during the day and taught evening classes two nights a week; and he had every weekend off so that he could observe the Sabbath according to his and Jewel's religious beliefs. During this fruitful four-year period of steady employment, he and Jewel scrimped and saved enough money to invest in a tract of unimproved real estate. Adon had some knowledge of construction and land development, and they planned to subdivide their view property into lots for custom homes. They spent many thousands of dollars on engineering services, and environmental studies, but later on, in a sacrificial state of mind to please God, they decided to sell their property to their church administration's real estate department, which they in turn would sell to Adon and Jewel's local church who was seeking desirable property to build on. After a required vote by the local church membership, and 90 days of careful consideration by Conference personnel, whose job it was to purchase real property for all the churches in their district, the sale was consummated.

Adon used the proceeds from the sale to pay off thousands of dollars that would have been paid to contract engineers after the property was developed, but became immediately due when the property was sold. Then he paid off his and Jewel's many monthly bills, and student loans, and bought much needed furniture for their home. Adon used the balance of the proceeds to start up a conventional, commonplace business.

Jewel continued to work full-time in her chosen profession, and eventually landed a marketing position with a large multiple hospital firm. Adon worked long hours at the new business, covering all the bases that were required to keep the business running and growing. The business grew, until he found himself constantly begging Jewel to quit her marketing (employee) position with the health care company and perform the same type of duties in her own company which, after all, was where their lucrative financial future rested. Taking on this management role in her own company would take a great burden off of Adon, and he could concentrate his hearty efforts in other areas that needed his attention. His dream had always been for him and Jewel to be in business together. He drew a great deal of his motivation for working so hard from his desire to prepare relevant circumstances, surrounding the business, to make it much easier for Jewel to eventually join him. Some of his favorite magazine articles were ones where husbands and wives ran successful companies.

Jewel promised on many separate occasions to quit her job, usually after a flagrant argument with Adon over the matter, even setting several convenient dates in the near future which would be her definite departure time. He tried desperately to make her understand that making big money involved repeated risk. But Jewel never terminated her employment to assist Adon—not until she quit two weeks before she abandoned him for good. Adon's father-in-law "accidentally" let some information slip to Adon that only Adon and Jewel had discussed that told Adon that Jewel's parents had counseled her *not* to quit her job to join him in their business.

After rightly determining that Jewel would never choose him over her family and long friendships, and realizing that Jewel would never be his close associate in their business, he felt his high enthusiasm for obtaining financial independence slip away. And the heavy work load from running the business, plus the constant upheavals with Jewel and her parents, began to take its adverse toll on Adon. He developed an annoying peptic ulcer in a short space of time.

He knew in his heart of hearts, by then, that she would eventually leave him, but he had always discarded the evil thought, placing his sole assurance instead in her Christian upbringing that utterly discouraged divorce. He assumed that because of their faith, no problem was too large to overcome. Even after he had found a love letter in the mail to Jewel from another man he refused to believe, because of her Christian upbringing, that she could ever be unfaithful. He never was, and he had never wanted to because he loved her very much. To him, she was the most beautiful woman in the world, and his desire for her never waned. He had gladly married her, to spend his whole life with her. His greatest desire, after pleasing God, was to be with Jewel.

But Jewel must have had long-awaited other plans that she had frequently discussed with her parents, and siblings. Adon was not sure how they managed it. How Jewel herself could want a divorce and her mother could want a divorce for jewel, and her brothers and father had their own selfish reasons for wanting Jewel away from Adon, but they were all careful not to appear to one another as conniving, and *unchristian,* while seeking the other's support to wreck his marriage.

Adon didn't know if Jewel had subtly used her parents, or her parents had manipulated Jewel, to end his marriage. It could have gone either way since they both secretly wanted the same thing, but had to be discrete about it. He suspected that in the beginning, early in his marriage, his mother-in-law was afraid to let Jewel know that she was against her daughter's marriage. After all, Jewel had sought her parent's approval before saying, "Yes," to Adon's proposal. At the time, Adon thought very highly of Jewel for seeking her parent's approval before taking such an important step as marriage. (Little did he know!) Jewel had informed him, in a flippant moment, after their union, that she would not have married him if her parents had said no. Then, in a more beneficial mood, she said that more first marriages would be successful if good parents provided good advice, which was heeded, to their children before marriage. Some marriages should not take place, and good parents need to advise their children accordingly.

But Jewel's parents had given their ardent blessings for their daughter's marriage to Adon. His in-laws had even paid all of the expenses for a large, expensive church wedding that Adon never provided one ounce of input for the planning of—not even the type of tuxedo he would wear. Adon was naive, back then, and thought that he didn't know anything about weddings anyway, so why ask him. (He preferred a small, inexpensive church wedding with family and a few friends.) Jewel and her mother were on a dizzying seven-month high planning it: flowers, bridesmaids dresses for seventeen bridesmaids, invitations, gift registries, bridal shower, singers, pictures, food, the whole potato for a wild display of ritual matrimonial celebration.

Divorce: Episode One

Adon couldn't prove it, but he greatly suspected that his mother-in-law felt that it would be much easier, and less revealing of her true nature, to break up his marriage than to prevent it. Besides, over the years, she had put the money aside for an enviable wedding for her only daughter. If she had prevented it, Jewel could have gone for life without a husband, and forever blamed her parents for refusing to sanction her marriage. The prevention route to achieve her goal was much too risky, and likely to damage her ultra-close relationship with Jewel; better to approve the marriage, even pay for it, then clandestinely help cause it to fail, placing most of the blame on an unsuspecting, love-struck husband.

Then, after the ceremony, and the marriage had progressed into years, Jewel's mother had observed that Jewel didn't dissuade her from probing into the inner sanctum of her marriage. Even from the first week, when she called *every* morning from the East Coast, where it was 8:00 A.M., her time, but 5:00 A.M. in the early morning for Jewel and Adon. Adon complained to Jewel about the calls, thinking that she was just as annoyed as he was, but Jewel didn't seem to mind, and told Adon just to ignore it—her mother would stop calling when she tired of the long distance phone bill.

It took six months, of constant calling, for the phone bill to discourage Jewel's mother! Then Jewel began to set the radio alarm, to wake up early, to call her mother before she dressed for work, and again in the evening, after she had arrived home. Adon loved early morning sex with Jewel, and Jewel loved it too, but she would call her mother after they were done, and talk about, among other trivial things, what bra she should wear to work.

As time went on, and even until Jewel left seventeen years later, the sheer enjoyment that her family received from their involvement with one another continued to be a deep mystery to Adon. He was from a large family—four brothers and three sisters—and they loved one another too, but not to the point of warm shivers at the mere mention of a family member's name.

As Jewel's mother continued to involve herself in Jewel's marriage, without any apparent objection from Jewel, and to a considerable degree unknown to Adon, Jewel's mother became less apprehensive concerning Jewel being aware of her dislike for Adon. Her overt remarks about the low condition of Adon's character ("Worse than an infidel," was one of her favorites), although he was a respected member (elder) of their church and morally faithful to his wife, became more frequent and disparaging.

Then, recognizing her mother's willingness to be a party to hearing gossip, Jewel realized that she, too, had an outlet for criticizing Adon that could eventually lead to uncompromised support for divorcing him. Indeed, if Jewel shared enough bad news about Adon to her mother, her mother would have to side with her regarding any decision Jewel made to separate from Adon. This revelation from Jewel was blessed news to her mother, but she couldn't let Jewel be completely aware that she wanted a breakup too; that would ruin her Christian image and her vocal advocacy of permanent marriages. She herself had been "happily" married for nearly fifty years, and any reliable advice she gave to Jewel regarding "sticking it out with Adon" had to be perceived as being solidly in support of married couples bearing the bruises to maintain their marriage.

Inwardly, however, she was overjoyed at being able to switch roles with Jewel, and now become the shocked mother at the very idea that Jewel could entertain the wickedness of leaving Adon. Jewel, on the other hand, couldn't let her mother know that she was methodically gathering support from her to leave Adon, even with lies about him. That would ruin her persona as a loving, sacrificial wife and daughter that was attempting everything she could to save her marriage—just as her parents had raised her to do.

So the jostling for justification went on, with Jewel playing the role of the damaged wife who desperately needed room to breathe, away from her husband, and her parents playing the role of objecting counselors who were forced, by the welfare of their sweet, innocent, ever-giving daughter, to provide their loving assistance in helping her to achieve her goal. Near the end, truly, what else could they do? Their only daughter was on strong antidepressant medication resulting from her desperate need to get away from Adon. However, role playing demanded that divorce was out of the question.

Adon recalled that the method by which Jewel had obtained her divorce, without any involvement or objection from him (in fact, he knew nothing about it, until nine months after it was final!), was a stroke of genius, on someone's part.

The day that the movers were loading their 55-foot moving van, Jewel approached Adon in his lower-level office, in their home, with a legal separation document that she had received from her attorney. By then, Adon had relinquished all future interest in the business, and it was practically a complete loss; the business bill collectors and taxing authorities were biting at his heels from every corner.

His mental state at watching Jewel, for the past three weeks, assisted by her parents, coldly clearing out the house of every conceivable item, preparing for the movers, had stressed him near to the breaking point. His mother-in-law had even asked him to help! (Someone, Adon had his strong suspicions, had put out the rumor among some senior members of their church that the real reason Jewel's parents were in her home, helping her move, was to protect Jewel from Adon. Adon had never spanked his daughter, let alone laid a hand on Jewel!) Jewel had, over a full year previously, moved out of their bedroom to the sofa-bed in the family room, and now her parents were covering *his* bedroom mattresses on both sides with form-fitting sheets for the movers to take away.

When Jewel approached him to sign the legal separation, the reason she gave was that she didn't want to be affected by any subsequent collection actions, as a result of the failure of the business. That made good sense to Adon, since he didn't want his wife to suffer in any manner or fashion, either. Besides, she unequivocally assured him that the document was simply a precaution, and in no way would she ever (ever) use it for anything else—especially not a divorce. So, Adon signed the legal separation to protect his family, feeling confident, even in his reduced mental state, that her heartfelt objections to divorce would eventually bring them back together.

Then Adon left in his truck because he couldn't bear to witness any longer, that last day, the morbid spectacle of his wife leaving him, and she seemed much happier, and relieved, since he had signed her document.

When Adon returned, the living quarters of the house was completely silent, and totally empty, except for the carpet on the floor, the custom drapes on the windows, and the blue kitchen telephone sitting on the tile counter with the little dependable answering machine still attached to it—$150,000.00 worth of cars, furniture and appliances packed—and gone. They had even cleaned the dust out of the corners!

Two months went by and Adon was still living in the empty house, sleeping on the floor in his lower-level office, when he received a letter from Jewel. It was a short letter, quite direct and to the point, mainly giving him her new address on the East Coast, at her brother's home. There was no hint of desiring any type of reconciliation.

Before the letter, during the first week of her absence, she had tried to reach Adon by telephone. But Adon was much too confused, and angry, to talk with her, so he just listened to "I hope you're okay," on the answering machine. The answering machine became for him a source of closeness to Jewel. Many times, when he keenly wanted to hear her voice, he listened to the response tape, where Jewel had recorded her voice telling the caller that their call would be returned. He missed Jewel all over his body, from the inside out.

Adon had spent some of his adult life, before he met Jewel,

living in New York City, and he felt that returning there to the hectic pace of metropolitan life would help him to withstand the length of time it would take Jewel to come to her senses. Indeed, Jewel and Princess now lived on the East Coast and he would be closer to them, in case of an emergency, and he needed to get to them in a hurry, or he was wanted for *anything.*

Nine months after Jewel had left, and he was on his way to New York, after calling to let her know that he was in her town, he stopped in to see Jewel and Princess at Jewel's brother's home. The reception he received from Princess was terse, as if she had seen him only a few hours ago. Jewel was stand-offish, and appeared not at all glad to see him. She told him, later that evening, that her stomach starting hurting as soon as she arrived home and saw him standing in the driveway, waiting to greet her.

Jewel's parents were "visiting" their oldest son, and Jewel's mother was the friendliest to Adon, sitting on the long couch in the family room, keeping him company, until Jewel came downstairs. Everyone else in the home, brother-in-law, nieces, nephews, including Princess and her grandfather, stayed out of sight. Shortly, Jewel's talkative mother retired for the night, going towards the basement where, Adon assumed, there was fire or her sleeping quarters were. Then Adon removed himself to the living room to wait for Jewel.

Adon spent twenty-five minutes, alone, in the dimly lighted living room anticipating the arrival of Jewel. When she finally did come downstairs they sat on the sofa in the living room to talk. She offered no apology for taking an usually long time to place herself in his company. To Adon she was as attractive as she ever was, and he could feel the old flame of passion for her resurrecting in his members. He had remained celibate since they last slept together in their home, almost a year ago, and he would have paid a million dollars right then if he could have taken her to a hotel, or even the back seat of his car.

They talked for ten minutes before Jewel said that she was

tired, and wanted to see her parents before they left that night on their return trip home. Adon was reluctant to leave since, to that point, their conversation had been cordial, and seemed to him promising for another meeting the next day, if he didn't appear too anxious. Jewel handed him a single sheet letter that she had recently attempted to send him over the business Web site, but the email had been undeliverable. He folded it in half, to read later.

Standing at the door, on his way out, he stole a quick kiss on her forehead with his arms around her waist, and he could feel her body stiffen in resistance. He was slightly discouraged, but they were still married, he thought to himself, and that reality revived his hopes. Then he said he would call her tomorrow, and he left, going toward his car. On the way, he recalled how he had spent over an hour in the house, and no one had inquired about his overnight sleeping plans, or offered him anything to eat—not even a drink of water—and knowing that he was fresh on their doorstep after a long drive across country. But he looked forward to seeing Jewel, tomorrow.

The next day, about an hour before he assumed that her lunch break would begin, he called Jewel at work. For some reason, he had expected to hear a happy response to his phone call, but Jewel only sounded annoyed that he had called. He invited her to have lunch with him. She said no, she was taking a late lunch that day. He said he would wait, and eat whenever she did. She said she might not eat at all, that day. He asked if he could see her that evening, at home. She said she didn't plan to leave work until late, probably very late. He said to give him a time, and he would be there. She said—

"Adon, this is not going to work!"

He replied, "What do you mean?"

Her next words were a blur to Adon, but he knew that she had clearly rebuffed him, and shattered all hope that they could have a happy reunion on that occasion. She hung up. Right then he couldn't understand her actions, which were much harsher than the night before at her house. They had lived together for seventeen years, so he knew not to push her, and call her back. Maybe she was just under pressure at work, and he had called at a bad time. He supplied himself with many rationales for her rejection of him, so that he could function for the rest of that day. "But they were still married," he kept telling himself. "As long as they were married, there was still hope!"

After the Sabbath, on Sunday morning, he called Jewel again at home. He informed her that he was considering relocating to New York City—or the state where she now lived. She said the state was not big enough for the two of them to live in!

Adon wandered for a long time, sleeping in his car and eating out of tin cans. "As long as they were married, there was still hope."

His faith in Jesus and his desire to remain married to Jewel, even if they were separated, helped him to maintain his health and stay in his right mind. He eventually found a job and residence in another state, and a year and three months after he had last seen Jewel he received a letter in the mail from her California attorney—stating that their divorce was *finalized* nine months earlier. He had been divorced for nine months, and didn't know it! It wasn't difficult for him to figure out what Jewel had done with the legal separation, which she had vowed not to use for a divorce.

Recounting the time, considering that California requires six months for divorces to finalize, he knew that Jewel must have submitted her document within a few days after his last visit with her. The short letter she had given him at that time hadn't, at all, mentioned divorce, but regret for the bad circumstances they then found themselves in. He had been divorced for nine months, and didn't know it!

2

The Conflict

Note: From this chapter forward, events in the lives of Adon and Jewel are *fictionalized* to emphasize facts on divorce in the Holy Bible.

ALTHOUGH the true story of Adon and Jewel (not their real names) was told primarily from Adon's point of view, one can imagine that Jewel had just as much reason to want out of the marriage as Adon did to stay in it. Nothing is altogether one person's fault, especially in a physically non-abusive marriage such as theirs. However, the story is typical of a great many Christian marriages: there was no provable adultery by husband or wife. And, although there could have been, adultery was not the main cause for the failure of the marriage. Usually the non-adulterous parties to the divorce just don't get along anymore, and decide to call it quits.

At the outset, as with Adon and Jewel, Christian couples ordinarily have much higher expectations for success than couples where religion is not a primary factor in their relationship. Christian couples place a great deal of faith in God to see them through the many problems that can arise in any marriage. And this is where their problems begin—placing their faith in God to get them through their many difficulties, without having a clear knowledge of what God requires of them.

To God, according to the Bible, marriage within the human

family is the most important and sacred connection between individuals for the commandment "Thou shalt not commit adultery," Exodus 20:14, applies not only to Christians but to the whole human race. Indeed, Bible believing Christians will pay particular attention to Christ's stand on marriage when He said "What therefore God hath joined together, let not man put asunder," Matthew 19:6; which means that for persons who intend to live by His commandments there are no marriages where human laws end the marriage.

Divorce for Christians is a nonexistent recourse! If this is the case, why do so many Christian marriages "end" with divorce? The answer to this question is, again, many Christians do not know what God requires of them, or they know, and refuse to totally surrender themselves to His will. The Bible uses the term "hard-hearted," to describe Christians in the refusal state of mind. When directing His reply to the Pharisees, who had asked Him why Moses permitted them to divorce their wives, Jesus said, "For the hardness of your heart he wrote you this precept." Mark 10:5.

Never did Jesus put anyone in the hard-hearted category who was willing to obey His commandments on divorce. When His disciples asked Him "of the same matter," He said to them, without equivocation, "Whosoever shall put away his wife, and marry another, committeth adultery against her. And if a woman shall put away her husband, and be married to another, she committeth adultery." Mark 10:11, 12. Whatever the case the commandment is unchangeable, and not subject to varied interpretations to lessen its impact. The Bible is very clear and repetitive regarding God's stand on marriage and divorce.

It appeared that Adon and Jewel, who were Bible believing Christians, thought they knew God's stand on their voluntary union of marriage. Adon, seemingly, more so than Jewel since he was dreadful of divorce and aware that through marriage God had deemed them to be one flesh. "Therefore shall a man leave his father and his mother, and shall cleave unto his wife:

and they shall be one flesh." Genesis 2:24. He had married Jewel to remain with her for a lifetime, which is the only right motive for marriage involving time, and the only longevity factor that pleases God for "one flesh" demands a permanent, unbreakable relationship.

However, Adon had to look to the future after he was informed that his severed marriage to Jewel, at her insistence, was a fact of life. He was aware that he was still a fairly young man desirous of female companionship, and he knew that the only way he could truly forget Jewel, the love of his life, was to invite another woman to take her place. He believed what he interpreted the Bible as saying about adultery being the only valid grounds for divorce. But he *was* divorced, and, as far as he knew, there was no adultery involved. What was it? Was he Biblically divorced, or not? He was definitely sure of one thing, Jewel was no longer his wife, and a loving God couldn't expect him to remain without a woman for the rest of his life—that didn't make sense!

Jewel never mentioned it to Adon, only to her dearest old girlfriend who had divorced her own husband, but she did have a brief interest in another man whom she had met at a medical convention which involved her work. He was a physician, subjectively attractive, and it was a near-intercourse experience during the convention, where intercourse didn't happen, but it would have, had she not started her period. The affair stayed in her mind, and bothered her, being convinced that under the right circumstances she could let herself be unfaithful to Adon.

She didn't believe that she had committed adultery, since no intercourse had taken place, but she knew after that that she was susceptible, if the right man came along. She loved Adon, and had married him with every intention of having a happy, lifelong marriage. But the unexpected affair made her fearful that someday she might go "all the way" and she didn't want to be married to Adon, and be guilty of adultery in God's sight, when the inevitable finally occurred. So, over the years, she arranged it, with exaggerated tales about Adon—seeking the approval of her parents—and divorced him.

Everyone assumed that Adon, being the man, tall, handsome and outgoing, had provided Biblical grounds for their divorce. Besides, she truly believed that during the time when she was the only one supporting the family, and Adon regularly spent several nights a week away from home with his "down-line" that he had been unfaithful to her—with intercourse! Her dear mother told her that every man, except her father, cheated on their wives at some point during their marriage.

So Jewel felt assured, if she ever wanted to, that she could remarry with the approval of her church since most everyone agreed that the Bible said the innocent party, in a case where adultery was involved, could divorce their spouse and remarry. It was in all the printed Bible studies she had seen, even in her denomination's church manual, and everyone was doing it, so it had to be true. She had read it for herself—"Whosoever shall put away his wife, *except* it be for fornication, and shall marry another, committeth adultery: and whoso marrieth her which is put away doth commit adultery." Matthew 19:9.

She had come close—but she had not committed adultery! Adon was the real guilty one, she believed, so she was free to remarry with everyone she cared about supporting her decision. Truly, she was following the Bible so God couldn't condemn her if she remarried. Anyway, she knew of dedicated Christian couples who had divorced and remarried without even claiming there was adultery by either husband or wife. Some of the men were deacons and elders. The epidemic was *widespread* in her church! What must God think of that? At least, she told herself, she had Biblical grounds for remarriage; she was much better off, in God's sight, than those who didn't care *what* the Bible said!

Oh! what fearful webs we must weave, when Satan clouds the Scriptures, to deceive! Is Jewel innocent of adultery? Do the Scriptures say the innocent, divorcing party is free to remarry?

What about Adon, may he remain single and sleep around to forget Jewel, and then remarry if he finds someone he loves?

The common-sense advice to Adon and Jewel, in present day civilized society, from professional marriage counselors and pastors alike, would be to select a new spouse—and try again. Indeed, in today's society second and third marriages are commonplace; so common that first marriages are seen by many as just a practice run for subsequent marriages, where the lessons learned in the first marriage will help to shore up the second marriage, and so on, lesson upon lesson into the third and any later marriages that may come along.

It is inadvisable for Christians—looking forward to eternal life—to follow the customs of the world. But in many cases this is what Christians are doing. Some think heaven will be populated with folks who, in their opinion, were good people:

"Otis and Maxine were never married, but they lived happily together, and took in and raised homeless kids, and gladly fed any hungry person who came to their door. Fred and Peggy boozed it up a little, and didn't care much for church, but they did the most good in the neighborhood. They were always a joy to be around. Heaven will be a better place with those two decent couples there."

"Ooh! I don't think so!"

Some who read the previous quotes will immediately run to the Bible and misunderstand what Jesus said about judging others. He said, "Judge not, that ye be not judged." Matthew 7:1. This statement by Jesus, like so many statements that He also made concerning divorce and remarriage, is usually taken out of context. Many people have gotten in the habit of reading the Bible by verses rather than by chapters—and the whole Bible.

What if, in our daily conversations, we based most of our decisions on single words rather than words formed into sentences? Without considering all of the words in a sentence, one would come away from important interactions with a great deal of misinformation. Yet, this dangerous approach to gathering information is the method many people use when reading the Bible. Considering Jesus' statement on judging others one must read and understand all of the verses relating to verse 1, which are verses 1 through 5. Jesus is *not* saying never have an opinion of what constitutes sin in oneself and in others—and if you do, keep it to yourself! This is what sinners (all the human race) want the verse to say, so that they can be left alone to flourish in their wrongdoing without having their conscience seared in the process. This is human nature. In fact, He's saying just the opposite: to recognize sin in all its forms, then when the sin is removed from one's own life, then one can receive the blessing of God to help remove that sin from someone else's life.

Consider the context: "For with what judgment ye judge, ye shall be judged . . . why beholdest thou the mote that is in thy brother's eye, but considerest not the beam that is in thine own eye. . . . *first* cast out the beam out of thine *own* eye; and then shalt thou see clearly to *cast out the mote out of thy brother's eye*." Matthew 7:2, 3, 5. The rule on judging is: it is very dangerous to righteously criticize a sin in others until one has put away that sin in his own life!

Persons who have prayerfully discovered truth, and overcome sin, have an honest obligation to assist others to discover truth and overcome sin. A trustworthy admonition that all believers in the Bible should remember is one offered by Elder Charles E. Bradford, a respected evangelist and church leader. He said it often in his pulpit sermons, "A Bible text without a context is a pretext!"

Considering the Bible story of Absalom and David, one could make an informed judgment with respect to the eternal fate of Absalom without being guilty of falsely judging others.

Absalom was the third son of David, a handsome creature with no physical faults. "For in all Israel there was none to be so much praised as Absalom for his beauty: from the sole of his foot even to the crown of his head there was no blemish in him." 2 Samuel 14:25.

However, Absalom came into sore conflict with David, eventually seeking to usurp David's throne, thus making himself king over Israel. He was successful in undermining David until he had a great number in Israel who considered him their king. His nefarious plan was to take complete control by killing his father, David. Ahithophel was the revered counsel to both David and Absalom, "as if a man had inquired at the oracle of God," but his passion was to kill David in a conspiracy with Absalom. "And I will smite the king only . . . and the saying pleased Absalom well, and all the elders of Israel."

After Ahithophel had taken his own life for giving bad advice to Absalom, Absalom took the men of Israel and went to war against the servants of David. "So the people went out into the field against Israel: and the battle was in the wood of Ephraim." Absalom and the men of Israel fought a hard and desperate battle against the army of David but in their heart they feared David, "for all Israel knoweth that thy father is a mighty man, and they which be with him are valiant men," and David mightily prevailed over Absalom with Absalom coming to his death in a fierce battle to end his own father's life. "And a certain man saw it, and told Joab, and said, Behold, I saw Absalom hanged in an oak."

Anyone familiar with the Decalogue, without falsely judging, could certainly predict the eternal fate of Absalom seeing that he was killed while in the headstrong process of breaking the fifth commandment, which says, "Honour thy father and thy mother." Exodus 20:12. This is not judging Absalom, but understanding the holy commandments of God, and making an accurate assessment of the circumstances under which he died and arriving at a logical conclusion based upon the evidence. Indeed, he is an eternally lost man! Further, one could rightly assume, concerning the fifth commandment that Absalom falls into the class of the hard-hearted in Israel.

So it is with persons who die willfully breaking the seventh commandment, "Thou shalt not commit adultery." Exodus

20:14. Persons who are living in an unscriptural marriage relationship, where one or both has a previous spouse who is not dead, is committing adultery, and unless they repent their fate is commensurate with Absalom's. Indeed, eternal life is denied to them. "For the wages of sin is death." Romans 6:23.

Although God surely hates divorce, "For the Lord, the God of Israel, saith that He hateth putting away," Malachi 2:16, divorce is not a sin—another marriage while a previous spouse is living is what brings about the sin of adultery. "So then if, while her husband liveth, she be married to another man, she shall be called an adulteress: but if her husband be dead, she is free from that law; so that she is no adulteress, though she be married to another man." Romans 7:3.

Christians must grasp Biblical truth while there is still Holy Spirit power willing to provide light, for Christ says, "Behold, I come quickly, and my reward is with me, to give every man according as his work shall be." Revelation 22:12. Soon, the mesmerizing power of the fashions of the world will make it next to impossible to distinguish truth from error. Worldly customs are rapidly causing Christians today to wholly obscure the Biblical truth about divorce so that they may not appear odd, and out of touch with the rest of society.

The Christian church should be the "salt" of the world and the leader in lasting marriages—not the example of failure. Salt is odd of its own self, and no other food approaches its taste. Likewise, Christ says to Christians, "Ye are the salt of the earth: but if the salt have lost his savour . . . it is thenceforth good for nothing . . ." Matthew 5:13.

There is a reason the divorce rate among Christians equals the rate of the worldly. A correctable reason—which is a willingness to follow all the commandments of God regarding divorce and remarriage. This will quickly resolve the divorce problem within the Christian church. However, first, one has to clearly see the correctable error.

GOD'S LAW *of TEN COMMANDMENTS*

I am the Lord your God . . .

I. You shall have no other gods before Me.
II. You shall not make for yourself an idol in the form of anything that I have made. You shall not bow down or worship them.
III. You shall not misuse the name of God. You will not go unpunished when you misuse My name.

IV. Remember the Sabbath day, to keep it holy. Six days you shall labor and do all your work, but the seventh day is the Sabbath of the Lord your God: in it you shall not do any work, you or your children, your male or female servant, or your animals, nor the visitor who shares your company. For in six days God made the heavens and the earth, and everything associated with them, and rested on the seventh day. Therefore God blessed the Sabbath day and made it holy.

V. Honor your father and your mother.
VI. You shall not murder.
VII. You shall not commit adultery.
VII. You shall not steal.
IX. You shall not bear false witness against your neighbor.
X. You shall not covet your neighbor's wife, or your neighbor's husband; nor anything that belongs to your neighbor.

Holy Bible (author paraphrased) Ex. 20:1-17

3

Matthew 19:9 (Context)

DIVORCE was not instituted by Jehovah God. The first commandment on holy marriage was, "And they shall be one flesh." Genesis 2:24. And, again, Christ magnified His original commandment when He told the Pharisees—"What therefore God hath joined together, let not man put asunder," stating the fact that God's purpose for the human family is not altered by man's laws.

Sincere Christians find themselves in the unenviable position of attempting to live Bible-based Christian lives, in a grossly sinful world, according to secular laws. They behold the world on television, in the movies, rented videos, car radios, computer websites, and gradually, almost imperceptibly, slip into the practices of the world while continuing to expect God's blessing upon their apostasy; and look forward to receiving eternal life with those who barely enter in prayerfully, and humbly, keeping all of God's commandments. "Enter ye in at the strait gate: for wide is the gate, and broad is the way, that leadeth to destruction, and many there be which go in thereat: because strait is the gate, and narrow is the way, which leadeth unto life, and few therebe that find it." Matthew 7:13, 14. Hence common sense Biblical principles (learned during serious study) are slowly bent to conveniently conform to secular society. This is especially true where divorce is involved.

“Except”

Modern society allows for divorce for practically any reason, so Christians, wanting to “fit in,” seek out what appears on the surface to be an ambiguity in the Bible’s teaching on divorce and make it apply to them, thereby providing a seemingly justifiable reason for divorce. This was the great transgression of ancient Israel—wanting to fit in.

The Hebrew people were not satisfied with being different, having the eternal God to rule over them. They wanted to be akin to all the heathen nations around them, and have a visible king to dominate their daily lives. Their constant cry was, “Now make us a king to judge us like all the nations.” But God knew that desiring a king was just the outward manifestation of their real problem: submission to Him—“But they have rejected Me, that I should not reign over them.” 1 Samuel 8:5-7. Many modern Christians are no different than Biblical Israel. They don’t want to be any different in their obedience to God and in their lifestyle, with respect to divorce and remarriage, than the people around them.

The most misapplied Holy Bible text that is quoted to justify divorce and remarriage is Matthew 19:9, which reads, “And I say unto you, whosoever shall put away his wife, *except* it be for fornication, and shall marry another, committeth adultery: and whosoever marrieth her which is put away doth commit adultery.” In the common and acceptable understanding many Christians interpret this text as giving them Biblical permission for divorce if a spouse has committed adultery—and the innocent spouse (who did not commit adultery and filed for divorce) is free to remarry whomever they please.

Another interpretation is: while the marriage is intact, the discontented couple decides to divorce without adultery playing any role in their reasoning. The couple legally obtains a divorce and takes up separate households. At some point in time, after they are divorced—it may take years—the *first* one to remarry has committed provable adultery and the other spouse is at liberty to remarry with a clear conscience, and absent of the sin of adultery. The one who married first, which committed provable adultery, simply asks God to forgive him/her and continues on in his or her second marriage.

In today's society married couples expect to change marriage partners at least once in a lifetime, thereby, reducing marriage to a temporary experiment in lifestyle. And some Christians, thinking that they understand the rules of divorce, according to Matthew 19:9, purposely commit adultery to Biblically void their marriage so that they may remain in good standing with God (in His promise to forgive realm) and then begin another marriage commitment with someone else.

Jehovah is not so easily fooled as to allow a persistent sinner (from one connived divorce to the next illicit marriage) to be free to commit a subsequent sin—with God's blessing—simply by dissolving a marriage with adultery and then marrying again. God cannot bless sin by allowing a person to be relieved from sin—by committing a sin. Jehovah forgives sin that is confessed and forsaken. He does not reward the sinner who sins by forgiving the first sin, so that He may bless the sinner's need to satisfy his carnal desire to be in another marriage relationship. God does not forgive sin, to *allow* sin. To do so would violate His character, and make void His Word.

But these misapplications of Scripture for divorce and remarriage are just other, modern, variations of the hardness of heart mentality that Christ repeatedly upbraided the Pharisees about. "Moses because of the hardness of your hearts suffered you to put away your wives . . ." Matthew 19:8. Christians who strut in the company of the hard-hearted place themselves in a minefield of presumption, assuming that God will forgive their sin when they are not repentant enough to forsake their sin. The wily devil is keenly aware and overjoyed when he has gained a foothold to cause Christians to willfully stumble into sin, and gladly remain there. Satan knows that sin is like a contagious disease: once contacted, it will spread on it own.

The noxious disease of divorce had infected the Jewish

culture, exemplified by the Pharisees, to the point where they had discarded with the concession that Moses had made allowing them to simply find "some uncleanness in her . . . write her a bill of divorcement . . . and send her out of his house." Deuteronomy 24:1. Uncleanness, used here, is synonymous with fornication. Paul makes the clear comparison, saying, "For this is the will of God . . . that ye should abstain from fornication . . . For God hath not called us unto uncleanness, but unto holiness." 1 Thessalonians 4:3, 7. The Pharisees had gone beyond keeping the Mosaic law to putting away their wives for any number of reasons; one of which could be that she would rather bathe the camel than wash his feet. Or, she never sweeps out the tent on preparation day. The absurdity of their claim for cause to put her away did not matter. The only portion of the Mosaic law that they arrogantly adhered to was, "write her a bill of divorcement, and give it in her hand, and send her out of his house."

Their hard-hearted refusal to obey the law of Moses, a concession made in the original Law that did not permit divorce for any reason, "but from the beginning it was not so," Matthew 19:8, could be compared to Christians today, who have made for themselves a concession for divorce and *remarriage* based on adultery, and are not even sticking to their own false interpretation of the law but are, too, divorcing for any reason. The modern vernacular that hard-hearted Christians use to divorce for any reason is "irreconcilable differences." To satisfy secular laws, which have Godly jurisdiction over joining in marriage and awarding *legal* divorces, this clause covers just about any excuse anyone can think of to divorce. Hence, Christians today follow in the steps of the hard-hearted Pharisees.

An important point to remember, in Matthew 19:9, is that Christ is directing all of His statements on divorce to the hard-hearted Pharisees, while intending for His disciples to overhear His words and, thereby, be educated with respect to the highest standards of the Law. The Pharisees had made up their minds individually and collectively that they were not going to obey the original commandment, forbidding divorce for any reason, nor Moses' commandment permitting divorce only for sexual immorality. Their purpose for asking, "Is it lawful for a man to put away his wife for every cause?" was to trap Jesus into saying something to contradict the law of Moses. "The Pharisees also came unto Him, tempting Him." This, in their mind, would prove to everyone that He could not possibly be the awaited Messiah, the Son of Jehovah God, as He claimed, and give them justifiable grounds to kill Him for blasphemy.

In another confrontation with His enemies, He is charged with blasphemy: "The Jews answered Him, saying, For a good work we stone thee not; but for blasphemy: and because that thou being a man, makest thyself God." John 10:33. Jesus, of course, could not be guilty of blasphemy since He was God, but the Pharisees continually probed Him to discover any reason to take His life. And their aim in questioning Him on divorce, on this occasion, was to trap Him.

Jesus answered their question truthfully regarding cause for divorce by providing them with the history behind the original commandment. However, in His first reply, He answered only part of their question, the part which asked, "is it lawful for a man to put away his wife?" leaving off their question of cause for divorce until his next reply. "Have ye not read," Jesus first said, "that He that made them at the beginning made them male and female, and said, for this cause shall a man leave father and mother, and shall cleave to his wife: and they twain shall be one flesh. Wherefore, they are no more twain, but one flesh." Matt. 19:4-6. Then Jesus pointedly provided the answer to their question of: Can a man divorce his wife? No! "What therefore God hath joined together, let not man put asunder." Saying to them that what Jehovah has done with a male and a female through the act of marriage (which includes first, married sexual intercourse) cannot, under any circumstances, be *undone* by man.

The Pharisees beamed with pleasure at His answer because

now they thought they had Him on the ropes, and their next question was intended to set Him up for the knockout punch. He had made an unequivocal statement that they knew had to contradict Moses. Indeed, any Hebrew who made a claim contradicting Moses could not possibly be the Messiah, thereby guilty of blasphemy, and totally worthy of death. They eagerly questioned Him further, following up on His answer of, No! it's *not* lawful to divorce your wife. They asked, "Why did Moses then command to give a writing of divorcement, and to put her away?"

Jesus' answer to why, Moses had permitted them to divorce their wives, was intended to reveal to them the low state of corruption their obedience to the law of Moses had degenerated to. He continually hoped that they would recognize their evil adultery in repeatedly divorcing their wives, and remarrying, while claiming to uphold the highest standards of the Mosaic law. He went to the deep root of their problem, saying, "Moses because of the *hardness of your hearts* suffered you to put away your wives," then He reminded them, again, "but from the beginning it was not so."

Now Jesus had sufficiently induced them to hear His answer to the second part of their question, what *cause* was sufficient for divorcing their wives? Their ears were perked up, in sure anticipation that He would most certainly make a statement that would contradict Moses. His words to them revealing the motive for their feigned obedience, their hard hearts, had "gone in one ear and out the other" because they were not seeking a reason for obedience, but grounds for murder.

At this point Jesus had dealt with the Pharisees on a daily basis for nearly three years, pointing out their sins, and giving them ample opportunity to repent. But He well-knew that their hearts were forever hardened against Himself and the highest standards of the law of God forbidding divorce, for any reason, so He repeated to them the concession in the law that was written by Moses. A severe concession intended to assuage their hard hearts, but which they had also forfeited. And hoping to bring them back to at least obedience to the law of Moses—a single cause for divorce—and to nullify their plan to entrap Him with doctrine by agreeing with Moses, He said to them, "And I say unto you, whosoever shall put away his wife, *except it be for fornication,"* thus firmly answering their cause inquiry. Then He went on to say what would be the result of their putting away, if they made the foolish decision: *"and shall marry another."* This would be the outcome of *that* foolish decision: *"committeth adultery."* And, finally, this is what happens to the person you've divorced, and the person she marries: *"and whoso marrieth her which is put away doth commit adultery."*

The final words of His reply was to drive home the fact that if trying to prove sexual immorality, *"except it be for fornication,"* in the Jewish culture was not enough to discourage them from divorcing their wives that adultery surely would, if they insisted on marrying again, *"and shall marry another, committeth adultery."* And if it were not enough ruin in their lives if they remarried, and daily lived in adultery, Jesus pointed out the stumbling-block they had become for the one who had been put away, causing her to become a carrier of the disease of adultery, inescapably spreading it to anyone she may marry: "*and whoso marrieth her which is put away doth commit adultery."*

Matthew 19:9 FMA Formula

Fornication . . .only cause for divorce (either spouse).
Marry . . . . . . .foolish move after divorce (both spouses).
Adultery . . . . .outcome of foolish move (both spouses).

Nowhere in Jesus' conversation with the Pharisees does He imply that He is sanctioning divorce and remarriage—quite the contrary—He is totally discouraging divorce and remarriage! Considering Christ's final admonition, "and whoso marrieth her which is put away doth commit adultery," a good rule today for Christians to follow is to look upon any Christian who has been previously married, with a currently living spouse, as a carrier—a carrier of the awful sin of adultery—susceptible to infection if they marry the carrier. The carrier's symptoms are a previous marriage with a *living* spouse. The wise will ponder: Which is most important, God's commandments, or romantic bliss? A mistake in judgment could lead to dying in sin

Admittedly, Jesus was in a bit of a dilemma: In His public speaking He was continually faced with spiteful spies from the Pharisees searching for ways to charge Him with blasphemy. They mercilessly, disrespectfully, tested Him. No public speaker since Jesus has had to daily face the kind of mean audience that He faced; on every occasion, when He taught in public on the subject of divorce and remarriage, He had to uphold the law of Moses while at the same time teaching His disciples to reach higher, beyond the Mosaic law, to the original law of God, which totally forbade divorce.

In private conversations with His disciples, truly, He could not appear to have a double standard: one liberal law for the Pharisees, which permitted divorce, and another strict law for them, which denied it. There is one God, and one unchangeable law that equally applies to every man. He had instructed His disciples in the Sermon on the Mount that, "Till heaven and earth pass, one jot or one tittle shall in no wise pass from the law, till all be fulfilled," and this law of Ten Commandments and law of Moses He Himself had to keep as an example of obedience, and teach as the authoritative Word of God. In order to obey the unchangeable law of no divorce, and uphold the law of Moses, which permitted it, Christ re-enacted the law of *no remarriage,* except upon the death of a spouse. This permitted Him to preach the law of Moses, which allowed divorce, and the law of God, which forbids adultery and divorce.

His disciples, and all true followers of Jesus, are expected to aspire to the creation law of no divorce by remaining married to their creation spouse (their first husband or wife) until one of them has died. By permitting divorce, and not remarriage, this allows the creation marriage to spiritually stay intact, even though a divorce may have occurred. A loyal follower of Jesus who remains unmarried, after a divorce, is still faithful to the original law of God, which forbids divorce for any reason. One who divorces and remarries with a living spouse is committing public and/or spiritual adultery; it matters not the least why the divorce occurred. There are leeways for divorce—but no spiritual grounds for remarriage, except death!

"For the woman which hath an husband is bound by the law to her husband so long as he liveth; but if the husband be dead, she is loosed from the law of her husband. So then if, while her husband liveth, she be married to another man, she shall be called an adulteress: but if her husband be dead, she is free from that law; so that she is no adulteress, though she be married to another man." Romans 7:2, 3. (It is understood this text applies equally to women and men.)

Jesus could never be evilly charged with blasphemy by the Pharisees because He upheld the law of Moses which allowed divorce for a single cause, sexual immorality, and He upheld His own law forbidding adultery by forbidding remarriage—*because a creation marriage can never be broken, except upon the death of husband or wife.* This is why, in His instruction to the Pharisees and His disciples, He prefaced his statements on divorce with, "But/and I say unto you," because He was about to introduce a higher standard of obedience to those who were willing to hear and follow His commandments, not a different commandment, but a higher standard, one that allows obedience to the law of Moses *and* the law of God. The true emphasis He makes after this alert is not providing grounds for divorce, but *disallowing remarriage after divorce*—"And I say unto you, whosoever shall put away his wife, except for fornication (permitting divorce for a single cause), *and shall marry another, committeth adultery: and whoso marrieth her which is put away doth commit adultery* (forbidding all remarriages subsequent to a divorce for any cause)."

To rely on the text to provide Biblical grounds for divorce *and remarriage* one has to, as many Christians do, drastically alter what Christ said and introduce a vast arena of unfairness. Many read it as: And I say unto you, whosoever shall put away his wife, for fornication, and shall marry another, *[does not]* commit adultery: and whoso marrieth her which is put away doth commit adultery.

This is not a true interpretation because the emphasis is on one spouse being free of adultery, and not prevention of remarriage as it is throughout the Bible. The Word of God cannot controvert truth—it has to reconcile in every respect—because its source is God. If one accepts the latter, false reading of the text, one makes Jesus a liar because He will have contradicted Himself by being in opposition to the rest of the Bible.

The correct reading of the text is understood thus: And I say unto you, whosoever shall put away his wife—[the only cause is fornication]—and shall marry another, committeth adultery: and whoso marrieth her which is put away doth commit adultery. This rendering is in agreement with the whole Bible, and fair to both spouses since they remain spiritually married; and neither can remarry without committing adultery.

In Matthew 19:9 the word "except" is intended to exclude all other causes for divorce but fornication, and not to exclude a spouse from adultery should they remarry. This vital distinction is paramount to a correct understanding of the text. Also, with respect to a false interpretation, the word "except" must create an innocent spouse—the one doing the putting away, which is free to remarry. This cannot be so since the Mosaic law, which instituted divorce, does not sanction the one who initiates the divorce to remarry. The Mosaic law permits remarriage only if the *guilty divorces the innocent.* So, Matthew 19:9 cannot produce a spouse who is *innocent* and *divorces the guilty* because the Holy Bible does not, anywhere, endorse this concept of one who is eligible for remarriage.

4

Putting Away in Israel

ADON, like King David, adored women, not as sex objects, but for the beauty in the subtle uniqueness of their creation that lent great satisfaction to the ways of loving them. Had he the power and resources at his disposal to attract any woman that he desired, as David had, he, no doubt, would have observed beautiful Bath-sheba and immediately sent for her, too.

In Adon's church there were many beautiful women, married and unmarried, and he had to be aware of where he attended worship services to mitigate his attraction to those who sometimes dressed too provocatively for church. He often said that the first Adam had no problem naming Eve. Indeed, when he first saw her, fresh from the hand of God, in all of her radiant beauty, dressed in her invisible birthday suit, the first words out of his mouth must have been—Wow! Man!

Through daily, humble prayer, the grace of God, and a growing awareness, through God's holy law, of what constitutes adultery he was gaining the victory over that sin. He had read the words of Jesus to His church, saying, "Remember therefore from whence thou art fallen, and repent . . . To him that overcometh will I give to eat of the tree of life, which is in the midst of the paradise of God." Revelation 2:5, 7. This meant to Adon that when Jesus' followers discover sin in their life that they, through His grace, should strive to overcome it. Jesus said that

He had given His followers the power to discard sin from their lives and "blessed is the man that walketh not in the counsel of the ungodly, nor standeth in the way of sinners, nor sitteth in the seat of the scornful. But his delight is in the law of the Lord; and in His law doth he meditate day and night." Psalm 1:1, 2.

According to the seventh commandment, he could not remarry, so long as Jewel maintained life, and he had the additional responsibility of remaining sexually blameless, which for him consisted of resisting adultery since he was still spiritually married to Jewel. He didn't mind remaining celibate since doing so circumvented varied pressures and unnecessary problems. What bothered him, though, because of the cruel way that Jewel had divorced him, slandering his name, this made it difficult to foster new relationships in his adopted city.

He was deeply impressed, now, how vitally important it was that his fellow Christians see the fairness of God in disallowing all marriages after divorce, and for his church to refrain from attempting to determine who the guilty party was. Only God knows in marriage who is guilty; therefore, in His wisdom He does not continue to leave it up to man to establish guilt (Mosaic law), usually from a misinterpretation of Matthew 19:9. God's re-enacted rule is: there is no innocent party in a divorce where spouses are violating His moral law forbidding remarriage.

Everyone who was made aware of his and Jewel's divorce assumed, because he was the active male and Jewel came from a respectable ministerial home, that he had committed adultery. Then benefiting from her plan to place moral uncleanness on Adon, Jewel could remarry with the full support of her church and not bring reproach upon herself, and her ministerial parents. Indeed, Adon was the one to face disfellowship, should he remarry although it was highly probable, considering Jesus' higher standards for adultery, even though no intercourse had taken place, that she was an adulteress. And had he not become timely aware of God's requirements for broken marriages, knowing that he was innocent of adultery, he would have actively been seeking to remarry, probably before Jewel, and thereby receiving the misapplied punishment from his church of mistakenly removing him from church membership, causing a serious void in his social relationships.

To avoid this miscarriage of church justice, he felt that his church should come to understand the true doctrines of Jesus on divorce and remarriage, and change their rules accordingly: which must include disallowing remarriage for anyone who has a living spouse—it matters not why the divorce occurred. God's intention is to renounce Moses' law permitting remarriage for blameless women, thereby, saving them from spiritual adultery.

When Jesus had finished His reply to the Pharisees, in agreement with Moses, with the stipulation that one can only divorce his wife for sexual immorality, and if a man remarries after such divorce he commits adultery, His answer was so pungent to His disciples (He had made a similar statement in the Sermon on the Mount, but with a vastly different meaning for them) that they immediately made the worried observation: "If the case of the man be so with his wife, *it is not good to marry,"* because they, too, were susceptible, if they had not in fact practiced it, to the widespread custom of divorcing their wives for any reason.

Jesus had recruited His disciples from among the day-to-day people with day-to-day sins and His straightforward answer had applied to them too, and, like the Pharisees, would equally affect them if such a strict rule was actually obeyed. They then had selfish, grandiose plans of soon governing Israel, occupying the throne next to Jesus. Indeed, a new, strikingly beautiful wife would certainly complement such an enviable, exalted position. However, if sexual immorality was the *only* cause for divorce it would practically wipe out their easy divorces—and remarriages—and, truly, cause a drastic reduction in any lasting traces of polygamy that existed in Israel (less available women).

Jesus' succinct reply to their heartfelt concern was, "All men cannot receive this saying, save they to whom it is given." His response was directed at their deepest fear—only *one* cause for divorcing their wives, and no remarriage! Then Jesus tactfully summed up His message with an extreme example of persons who should *not* get married—if they couldn't stay married in a lifelong commitment. "For there are some eunuchs," Jesus said, "which were so born from their mother's womb, and . . . some which were made . . . of men: and there be eunuchs which have made themselves eunuchs for the kingdom of heaven's sake. He that is able to receive it"—If you can go without sex and marriage; "let him receive it."—Whatever your circumstances, you should do it.

Sexual immorality, as the sole grounds for all divorces, was openly despised by Israel but impressed upon the nation by the Pharisees, though they themselves did not observe the Mosaic law. It was next to impossible to prove unless the wife, in a male dominated society, was caught in the act—with witnesses. A wife certainly would not admit fornication, since for her being a non-virgin, and divorced, placed her in the formal position of being an outcast and a disgrace in Israel.

Example: Amnon, king David's first-born son and Absalom's half brother, defiled his half sister, Tamar, Absalom's sister, by raping her. Though she begged him to marry her rather than force her prized virginity from her, saying, "Now therefore, I pray thee, speak unto the king; for he will not withhold me from thee," he refused to marry her, and raped her anyway. After he had robbed her of her pearls he hated her, "so that the hatred wherewith he hated her was greater than the love wherewith he had loved her," and angrily ordered her away from him.

Tamar desperately pleaded with him not to send her away, knowing that her new condition in Israel—a non-virgin without a husband—placed her in a lower class of unrequited whores, with no future respectability as a woman. Though she begged, "There is no cause: this evil in sending me away is greater than the other that thou didst unto me," Amnon summoned his servant, and said, "Put now this woman out from me, and bolt the door after her." Tamar's tolerable future in Israel had abruptly ended—and she sorrowfully "remained *desolate* in her brother Absalom's house." 2 Samuel 13:1-20.

Jesus, in His omniscient wisdom, sought to remedy this blatant abuse and prejudice against women who, through no active fault of their own, were assigned a subservient role in Jewish culture, at the mercy of unscrupulous men, mainly led by the Pharisees. Though they were created to perform different roles in His creation, Jesus endeavored to return to women equal footing with men, the position wherein He had created them. "And the rib, which the Lord God had taken from man, made He a woman . . . and Adam said, this is now bone of my bones, and flesh of my flesh." Genesis 2:22, 23

In order to face Israel back toward the highest standards of obedience to His unchangeable commandments Jesus began with the intact family, the foundation of every civilized society, to stop the decline into adultery in the most intimate of human relationships, holy matrimony, by re-enacting no remarriage after divorce—for anyone! Thus He sought to amply discourage the covetous heart which pants after affairs outside of marriage by removing the basic incentive to divorce—remarriage to someone else. He desired three special classes of people included with those who obey all of His commandments: those who make up widowhood, those who are pure virgins—men and women—and those who are guiltlessly married. By refraining from marriage subsequent to divorce, while a former spouse is alive, and remaining chaste, His divorced true followers, too, could obey the eternal law of no adultery, and face the judgment blameless and without sin.

Although refusing to remarry, to avoid adultery, would cause a present, and disproportionate hardship on women in Israel it was imperative that they obey it, since their eternal life was at stake, for "if thy right eye offend thee, pluck it out . . . and if thy right hand offend thee, cut it off . . . for it is profitable for thee that one of thy members should perish, and not that thy whole body should be cast into hell." Matthew 5:29, 30.

"Except"

The Samaritan woman who met Jesus at the well was caught in the quagmire of seeking a permanent and respectable place in society, and by the time she met Jesus she had been repeatedly used by men, and to stir her conscience to convict her of her sin (of adultery through sequel marriages), and see Him as her only Savior, Jesus pointed her condition out to her, saying, "Thou hast well said, I have no husband: for thou hast had five husbands; and he whom thou now hast is not thy husband." John 4:17.

She was not a despicable prostitute, requiring quick payment for her favors, but a decent mature woman, wanting a husband, who was forced to deal with lawbreaking men who put her away and married her time after time. However, even though she was cruelly used, the responsibility rested upon her, whatever the cost, to stop her adultery and never marry again so long as *any* of her previous husbands were living. This prevalent cycle of divorce and remarriage was the hard-hearted state of mind that Jesus was addressing when He replied to the Pharisees, saying, "Whosoever shall put away his wife, except it be for fornication, and shall marry another, committeth adultery: and whoso marrieth her which is put away doth commit adultery."

This is not a kind statement giving permission to remarry, but a stern rebuke to the hard-hearted Pharisees who were steeped in the sin of adultery, and because they refused to repent, were hell-bent on killing the Messiah. This is not good company for Christians to be in, thinking that Jesus is speaking to them—giving them permission to divorce and remarry. His intent was to reveal the Pharisees lifestyle of sin, and narrow down their wild hast to divorce to one, practically un-provable, cause.

When Jewel and Adon read "*except* it be for fornication," they were certain that Christ was providing them with Biblical grounds for divorce and remarriage, their reasoning being that what Christ offered to the Pharisees He was teaching to all Christians. This is true, but one has to *know what Christ is teaching,* and what He wants Christians *to learn from what He taught.* Paul urgently wrote for believer's admonition, "All scripture is given by inspiration of God, and is profitable for doctrine, for reproof, for correction, for *instruction in righteousness."* 2 Timothy 3:16. Everything that Jesus taught was not meant for Christians to imitate. Indeed, many things were spoken to be avoided.

Christ, through the Holy Spirit, is the Author of the whole Bible. When He brought to light the lesson of the hard heart of the prophet Balaam, by including in the Scriptures that Balaam conversed with a jackass, He didn't intend for Christians to go about talking to jackasses—and expecting jackasses to talk back to them. There is a sound lesson to be extracted from the story of Balaam, and it's not talking to jackasses.

So it is with Jesus' response to the Pharisees, "except it be for fornication," there are lessons to be learned. First, He was agreeing with Moses in order to set aside their cunning trap of blasphemy; then He meant to convict them regarding their hard hearts that forced Moses to make a concession in the Law that, "from the beginning," forbade divorce for any reason.

Because of the ancient, male children of Israel's unwavering demand for the concession, they presumptuously took the next step and remarried after divorce (Mosaic law placed all fault for divorce on the promiscuous dominant husband and presumed all wives to be innocent of any wrongdoing, therefore divorced wives could remarry but not husbands i.e. *guilty divorced the innocent.* Deut. 24:2, 4), and as a result since they remained spiritually married to their spouse they were, by default, living in adultery, for the concession did not change the law of "Thou shalt not commit adultery." And because of their hard hearts—divorcing and choosing to remarry—they forfeited eternal life.

Christians should learn not to run in the company of the hard-hearted, such as the wily Pharisees (who dishonored, too, the law from Moses to govern their conjugal sins), with blissful expectations of pleasing God with contrived obedience born from their own hard hearts in refusing not to remarry.

5

Sequel Marriages

JEWEL divorcing Adon without cause made it difficult for him to start over in another city, in another church, by moving his membership within his denomination, since she had successfully implanted in the minds of Christians in their church body, by her subsequent silence on the matter, that he was an abusive adulterer, and an unrepentant womanizer. Pastors unwittingly discouraged him from moving his membership to their church, subconsciously inclined that they could brush aside the problems he was likely to cause. Women were reluctant to befriend him, suspecting (falsely) that he had a quick temper, and may injure them if they became closely involved with him. Married men discouraged his friendship, protecting their wives from his inevitable advances. Parents looked suspiciously, protectively, when he was kind to their children (he loved children, as Jesus did), their worried thoughts recounting that he may have been abusive to his own daughter, since she was sent away before her innocent mother was forced to leave—under the protection of her parents.

Adon would be judged by God for his own actions resulting from his divorce, but Jesus said that Jewel must share in any of his guilt; the aroused sins regarding the matter in the minds of all the persons with whom he may come in contact were upon Jewel, and she must face those sins in the judgment, for the ninth commandment says, "Thou shalt not bear false witness against thy neighbor."

Jewel must thoroughly seek Adon's forgiveness for he held a troublesome grudge against her for her ill-treatment of him. Though he included her in all of his prayers, and sincerely hoped for her happiness, the thought continually nagged him that she seemed not to see a need to seek his total forgiveness. He had apologized to her for any emotional or financial injury he had caused, but she wouldn't, or didn't recognize a need to apologize to him. Jesus taught His disciples, saying, "Therefore if thou bring thy gift to the altar, and there rememberest that thy brother has aught against thee; leave there thy gift before the altar, and go thy way; first be reconciled to thy brother, and then come and offer thy gift." Matthew 5:23, 24.

By neglecting to pursue forgiveness from Adon, her "one flesh" that she had spent seventeen years with, for knowingly, selfishly maligning his character, Jewel's worship and participation in the holy sacraments of Communion was an offense to God, and could cost her eternal life. God will not forgive hard-hearted sinners who purposely disregard the feelings of others, and do not confess and repent of their sins. Sincere confession and repentance are twin sisters, acting together. "If we confess our sins, He is faithful and just to forgive us our sins," 1 John 1:9, and, "I tell you, Nay: but, except ye repent, ye shall all likewise perish." Luke 13:5. If Jewel confesses and repents in all sincerity, including her divorce, she must never marry again while Adon is living and if she does remarry, while he is living, it must be to him, to avoid adultery.

After becoming aware of the spirit of "Thou shalt not commit adultery," as Jesus taught, Adon was readily cognizant by observation and personal experience the adverse effects of his church's misapplication of the Scripture, "And I say unto you, whosoever shall put away his wife, except it be for fornication, and shall marry another, committeth adultery: and whosoever marrieth her which is put away doth commit adultery."Mat. 19:9

In his previous church, where he had attended before his divorce, in the choir alone there were two sequel marriages—two "innocent" Christians who were presently remarried, with living spouses; but the two "guilty" spouses, who had remained unmarried, were in the choir too, and dating two other members of the choir. There was a constant subsurface anger that infected the whole choir, as the other members struggled to remain objective, not taking sides, in an attempt to defend the devil in their midst. Then they attempted to honor the Holy Spirit in the worship service resorting to loud, unholy music that engendered foot-stomping and hand clapping but no true presence of the Holy Spirit. Achan was in the choir! "Did not Achan the son of Zerah commit a trespass in the accursed thing, and wrath fell on *all* the congregation of Israel." Joshua 7:10-25; 22:20. The Holy Spirit can bless obedience, but never sin tolerated, covered up, and disguised as worship to the living God.

In that same local church body, where Adon was an ordained elder, there were six sequel marriages, besides the two in the choir, which he personally knew about. The children of those confused marriages were the primary ones who were routinely unruly and disrespectful to their parents, the pastor, and other church members; refusing to address adults with traditional, basic good manners saying "Yes, ma'am" and, "No, sir." These children unknowingly infected the other children, and church members wondered under their breath—"What's happening to the kids?"

The children from sequel marriages were predictably imitating the world which they observed daily, just as their parents were ignorantly following after the world buried in adultery. In their youthful innocence the children offered no respect to their parents since next week was daddy's court appointed turn for visitation from the kids—and after that shuffling they were back home with mom, and her new husband, and his church-hating kids to retire in their rooms with their TVs and computers to feast on a constant diet from Satan—often witnessing rampant, unrestrained adultery and not able to find solace from it in their own parents.

And the unsuspecting church leaders, believing that they are correct and fair by supporting the "innocent" one in remarriage, are sincerely attempting to administer the marrriage *concession* in the Mosaic law that was included *only* for the hard-hearted—those Israelites who, after forty years of daily instruction in the wilderness, had solidly rejected all obedience to the unchangeable commandment regarding adultery—no divorce.

Lamech, a descendant of the first murderer, Cain, was the first recorded adulterer, Genesis 4: 19, and he set the example for subsequent adulterers, who were atttempting to circumvent the law of no divorce, by taking on more than one wife. Four thousand years later Jesus warned the model offspring of those disobedient ones, saying, "Moses because of the hardness of your hearts suffered you to put away your wives: but from the beginning it was not so." Matthew 19:8.

The time has come to clear up all the ever-present confusion surrounding divorce. Therefore, the Holy Spirit is urgently persuading His church into the present age—the end-time age—to the very top of the spiritual mountain where Jesus is requiring, before his imminent return, full obedience to the unchangeable, pre-concession law, the pure law forbidding adultery—which demands no remarriage after divorce because the creation marriage, and any subsequent ones, can never be terminated except by death.

In God's eyes, the only eyes that matter, the creation marriage is the singly permanent, subsequent birth connection one can make with another. "And they two shall be *one* flesh. What therefore God hath joined together, let not man put asunder." Matthew 19: 5, 6. If church members clearly understood the true decisive role that death plays in marriage it would eliminate ninety-five percent of hasty, infatuation prone marriages, and God would be highly pleased to see another stronghold of Satan—sanctioned adultery in the Christian church—headed for defeat, slain by those who have made Jesus Christ first in their lives.

The apostle Paul supplies a practical illustration, in Romans 7:4, of the supreme role death plays in freeing the surviving spouse to remarry by comparing it to the new birth in Jesus Christ. He prefaced his instruction on the spirit of the seventh commandment by making it clear that, according to the Law, a woman is married to her husband as long as he is alive. Only his death allows her to remarry.

Then he says, "Wherefore, ye are also become dead to the law by the body of Christ," i.e. just as the Law requires that a woman is married to her husband until he dies, so also the death of Christ for the sins of mankind has freed believers from their previous marriage to death by the Law, not now having to die for their own sins. "That ye should be married to another," i.e. since the death of Christ has occurred to free believers from their first marriage to death for their own sins. "Even to Him who is raised from the dead, that we should bring forth fruit unto God," i.e. now believers can marry again, a new marriage, to the resurrected Christ wherein salvation is dependent upon His righteousness, and by His grace bring forth the fruits of a holy character, love, joy, peace, gentleness, goodness, faith, temperance, meekness, longsuffering, that are pleasing to God.

Romans 7:4 BOA Formula

Before the cross . . . married to death required by the Law.
On the cross . . . . . .freed from marriage to death.
After the cross . . . . free to remarry eternal life in resurrected Christ.

If the death of a spouse was not mandatory in Scripture to end a marriage, Paul could never, never have taught this lesson by this analogy. Indeed, he began his whole treatise on death and the Law, to clearly identify the source of his reasoning, saying, "Know ye not, brethren, *(for I speak to them that know the Law),"* Romans 7:1.

Truly, the modern Christian church suffers the consequences of sanctioned, emboldened adultery in their midst by believers practicing just as the world with respect to divorce and remarriage—resulting in a divorce rate that equals the world's.

Whereas, if the children could see Christ-centered obedience to the seventh commandment in their parents, foremost as not divorcing, and should a divorce occur definitely not remarrying after divorce—either one—it would bring about the deepest respect for their parents, seeing that they were willing to forgo a second attempt at marriage in order to remain faithful to God. Then, loving obedience to God because they have witnessed it in their parents—both of them—followed by highly esteemed respect for adults, and their Godly authority.

When the children reach the age where they begin to consider marriage for themselves, they perceive it in its true light as a lifelong, unbreakable commitment, which takes maturing time before entering into, and knowledgeable counseling, based on the church's truth based Biblical doctrine, by members who themselves are obedient to the spirit of the seventh commandment. "First cast out the beam out of thine own eye; and then shalt thou see clearly to cast out the mote out of thy brother's eye." Matthew 7:5.

Thus by discouraging sequel marriages, free will rebaptism of liable, repentant individuals, their living out chaste lives, and Christ-centered re-education of the unmarried youth, the rapid increase of divorce in the Christian church can be overcome—by Holy Spirit blessed obedience to "Thou shalt not commit adultery."

However, not everyone will obey!

6

From Eden to Concession

MEMBERS of the class of the hard-hearted in Scripture—who despised the requirements of God, and cherished the same spirit that crucified Christ, and violently murdered the apostles—when contrasted with those who were obedient to the commandments of God, are strikingly prominent. The earthly dividing line of the hard-hearted began with Cain, the first-born son of Adam and Eve who jealously murdered his brother, Abel, who brought the sacrificial offering that God had asked of them. Abel heads the column of the obedient.

From an early age Cain had internalized feelings of discontent and murmurings against God for cursing the earth because of Adam's sin. Whereas, Abel saw justice and mercy in God's dealing with man in allowing man, although he deserved to die, to be redeemed from sin and receive eternal life. In their youth they had learned the commandments of God from their father, Adam. They had learned that in order to be freed from the burden of sin that had engulfed the world—resulting from the sin of their parents—a Savior was to come, and shed his blood for the sins of the world.

Adam had patiently taught them the transgressions of the Ten Commandment law that he and their mother had committed, which had caused the downfall of the human race. Starting at the ninth commandment: "Thou shalt not bear false witness against thy neighbor," when Eve falsely stated what God had said as she talked to Satan, who was speaking through the serpent (the first evil spirit possession), respecting obedience to God. God had instructed Eve regarding the tree of the knowledge of good and evil, "thou shalt not eat of it." But Eve reported to the serpent that God had said, "Ye shall not eat of it, neither *shall ye touch it.*" God had not told Eve not to *touc*h the tree; that was her invention, and Satan knew from that point on that she was completely vulnerable to his subtle deceptions because she was willing to play around with, and misconstrue God's commandments. (Compare inserting "does not" in Matthew 19:9.)

Having beguiled Eve into entering into a dialogue with himself Satan relaxed some, and allowed her to naturally flow into the foundation for all sin which was breaking the tenth commandment, which says, "Thou shalt not covet thy neighbor's house, thou shalt not covet thy neighbor's wife [law of respect for another man's wife], . . . *nor anything that is thy neighbor's.*" Indeed, after Satan had aroused her interest in the forbidden tree, which belonged to God, Eve began to covet the tree, looking upon it with deep interest, forgetting the first rule of obedience to God, "For we walk by faith, not by sight," and as she continued to indulge her senses she acted upon her coveting. "And when the woman saw that the tree was good for food, and that it was pleasant to the eyes, and a tree to be *desired* to make one wise, she took of the fruit thereof and did eat," thus expanding upon her journey into disobedience to God's commandments.

From the tenth commandment, she entered into literal violation of the first, "Thou shalt have no other gods before me." Adam told his sons that this commandment was broken when Eve first encountered the serpent, and the serpent became her god, because she believed the serpent's words, "Ye shall not surely die!" instead of God's words, "But of the tree of the knowledge of good and evil, thou shalt not eat of it: for in the day that thou eatest thereof *thou shalt surely die.*" Gen. 2:17

Eve had heard the first spiritualism lie from Satan when he said man is immortal—after God had told Eve man is mortal. Eve believed Satan, who was then manifested as her god.

Eve went on from the first commandment to transgression of the second, "Thou shalt not make unto thee any graven image, or any likeness of any thing that is in heaven above, or that is in the earth beneath, or that is in the water under the earth: thou shalt not bow down thyself to them, *nor serve them.*" Since the serpent had become her god, although she hadn't made the serpent, *she served it* by her obedience to it. The serpent deceitfully said to her, "Yea, hath God said, Ye shall not eat of every tree of the garden?" Then Eve served the serpent when she swallowed the bait in his veiled assertion in the form of a question—that what God had asked her to do was unreasonable and selfish! And she went ahead and "took of the fruit thereof, and did eat, and gave also unto her husband with her; and he did eat." Gen. 2:17

From the second commandment Eve became a transgressor of the eighth commandment, "Thou shalt not steal," when she stole the fruit from the only tree in the garden that God had specifically said belonged to Him. "Of every tree of the garden thou mayest freely eat: but of the tree of the knowledge of good and evil, *thou shalt not eat of it.*" Then as Eve calamitously gazed upon the tree "she took of the fruit thereof, and did eat," and she became a thief of God's possession.

From the eighth commandment Eve plunged ahead to transgress the sixth commandment, "Thou shalt not kill," when she murdered her husband by feeding him deadly poison in the fruit, "and gave also unto her husband with her; and he did eat," after God had told her, "for in the day that thou eatest thereof *thou shalt surely die.*"

However, after all that Eve had done, by leaving the side of her husband and becoming involved with the serpent, Adam bears the burden for casting the new creation of God into sin. God had placed Adam in charge of all He had created, and Eve was to be an equal companion for him with identical needs for receiving affectionate love and sympathy. She was the perfect other half of himself, accepting guardianship from him, and giving encouragement and resourceful guidance to him as they went about their sinless occupation of populating the earth with beings like themselves, made in the image of God. "So God created man in His own image . . . male and female created He them."

But Adam made Eve his god! Fearing to lose her, he placed her above God, and chose to follow her into sin, and die, rather than remain obedient to the first commandment and trust God to provide him with another "help meet for him." So Adam, as the first son of God, and the protector of his wife, is foremost in being answerable to God for his transgression of God's commandments that caused the creation to sin.

The first brothers born subsequent to transgression differed in their obedience to the voice of God to bring an offering, and to spill the blood of that offering as a perpetual reminder, until the actual event, that, "without shedding of blood is no remission" of sin.

Abel was obedient to the voice of God, and brought an innocent lamb, typical of the innocent Lamb of God, and shed the blood of the lamb upon an altar. Cain and Abel knew that as long as they had faith in the spilt blood of the lamb, placing their sins upon the lamb, that God was "faithful and just to forgive us our sins, and to cleanse us from all unrighteousness."

However, Cain was disobedient to the voice of God and "brought of the fruit of the ground an offering unto the Lord," feeling that he didn't need a Savior, and that his own righteousness was sufficient to earn him eternal life. But Cain's offering of the works of his hands greatly displeased God because Cain's offering was incapable of shedding blood, and an affront to the Son of God who must shed His blood to save mankind. Cain was angry because God had rejected his elaborate offering of embellished products from his fields—that he had worked on for weeks to achieve excellence in preparation and surely to be gladly received of God—and accepted Abel's offering of a simple little lamb. God said to Cain, seeking to soften his hard heart, not seeing the merits in the shed blood of a Savior, "If thou doest well, shalt thou not be accepted? And if thou doest not well, sin lieth at the door." Genesis 4:7.

Cain's sinister anger and jealousy of Abel festered and seethed because Abel refused to join him in his rebellion against God, and, finally, "when they were in the field, that Cain rose up against Abel his brother, and slew him." Genesis 4:8. Because Cain had refused a Savior, and premeditatedly murdered his brother, Abel, God said to him, "And now art thou cursed from the earth . . . a fugitive and a vagabond shalt thou be in the earth." Then Cain left the immediate presence of Adam and Eve and "went out from the presence of the Lord and dwelt in the land of Nod, on the east of Eden." Gen. 4:16

Adam intimately made love with his wife Eve, and she conceived. Adam passionately loved Eve again, and she conceived. Adam knew Eve again and she conceived, and thus the earth became populated with the daughters of Adam and Eve. Cain married one of his sisters, "And Cain knew his wife; and she conceived, and bare Enoch." Gen. 4:17

The descendants of Cain rapidly multiplied and they made their home in the lush valleys tilling the ground and building grand cities. In the fifth generation from Cain, Lamech, the first recorded adulterer was born, and like his predecessor, Cain, he was a murderer too. "Hear my voice, ye wives of Lamech . . . for I have slain a man . . . a young man for striking me." Gen. 4:23 And the descendants of Cain, because they had followed in his footsteps in their rejection of God, were unconscionable sinners who engaged in the vilest acts against their bodies and nature, worshiping idols above the rolling hills and burning themselves with fire to appease their gods.

With few generations from Adam they were like high statues in height, ten and eleven feet tall not being uncommon for grown men and women, and they lived hundreds of years, possessing grand intellects that were not yet severely degenerated by millenniums of sin. Today, a man or a woman reaches intellectual maturity around the age of thirty, which is based on their few years of previous education. Comparatively, the antediluvian achieved intellectual maturity based on hundreds of years of experience and study, thereby, greatly surpassing the highest intellectual prowess of modern man, but in different areas of knowledge. They excelled in astronomical science (there was no rain, hence no hazy cloud cover to obscure their view of the heavens), and plant-based medicine, finding cures for their sin-induced illnesses in the multitude of plant life that God had created for man's enjoyment.

One may assume that their revered highest achievements were in biology, with inbreeding of the animals, a specialty of experimentation which produced disproportioned, lizard-like beasts with huge bodies, strong well-developed tails, long awkward necks and short forelegs, and hideous looking birds, in their search for excellence that overshadowed the excellence of God whom they hated. And their unrestrained proclivity to sin kept pace with their advanced knowledge.

Not all were disobedient, to the point of disclaiming God altogether, for the Garden of Eden was within traveling distance where the angels of God guarded the gates to protect the Tree of Life with flaming swords of fire. But those who claimed to worship the God of creation found excuse for their idolatry by demanding that their idols of wood and precious metals were merely reminders of the only heavenly God, meant to enhance their worship, as they reverently bowed down to them. But they were idolaters nonetheless, simply well-meaning idolaters, for the holy commandment says, "Thou shalt not make unto thee any graven image, or any likeness of anything that is in heaven above, or that is in the earth beneath, or that is in the water under the earth: thou shalt not bow down thyself to them, nor serve them: for I the Lord thy God am a jealous God, visiting the iniquity of the fathers upon the children unto the third and fourth generation of them that hate me; and showing mercy unto thousands of them that love me and keep my commandments." Exodus 20:4-6.

Adam and Eve lived one hundred and thirty years and Eve gave birth to another son, and called his name Seth. "For God," said Eve, "hath appointed me another seed instead of Abel, whom Cain slew." Like his brother, Abel, Seth was an obedient son who understood and accepted the symbolism in the sacrificial lamb, and he looked forward to the coming of the authentic Lamb of God. "And the days of Adam after he had begotten Seth were eight hundred years: and he begat sons and daughters." Gen. 5:4

Seth wore the mantle of worship, loving the commandments of God, in the obedient line of Abel. Seth lived one hundred and five years before his wife gave birth to first-born, Enoch. Enoch was a daily evangelist for righteousness in word and practice, proclaiming the coming of a Savior with the sacrificial lamb pointing forward to the grand event. His every deed to avoid sin was governed by the Ten Commandments taught to him early by his God-fearing parents. Then when Enoch had reached the age of three hundred and sixty-five, God saw fit to take him up to glory without seeing death. "And Enoch walked with God: and he was not; for God took him." Enoch was granted by God the distinction of being in the company of only two others named in Scripture, Moses and Elijah the prophet, who would reside in heaven before the second coming of Jesus and the grand resurrection of all the redeemed from the earth. "By faith Abel . . . Noah . . . Abraham . . . Isaac . . . Jacob . . . Sarah . . . Joseph . . . Rahab . . . Samson . . . David . . . Samuel . . . These all died in faith, not having received the promises, but having seen them afar off, and were persuaded of them, and embraced them . . . and these all, having obtained a good report through faith, received not the promise: God having provided some better thing for us, that they without us should not be made perfect." Hebrews 11:1-40.

However, the hard-hearted descendants of Cain had 205 years head start in their population growth, and their numbers exceeded the obedient descendants of Seth one hundred times over. The descendants of Cain dwelt primarily on the fertile plains, and the generations of Seth possessed the highest hills.

As long as the two distinct lines of the hard-hearted and the obedient remained geographically well-separated, the worship of the living God in the family line of Seth, headed up in the obedience column by Abel, continued unabated and the spread of the ugliest of sin was held at bay. But as the hard-hearted population continued to outpace the obedient, they demanded more territory in the region of the Garden of Eden, and forced the obedient to uproot and move to higher mountains to escape their warring against them and the contamination of their worship of the living God.

But the long separation of the hard-hearted and the obedient was obliged to dissolve as "the sons of God"—the obedient descendants of Seth, "saw the daughters of men"—the hard-hearted descendants of Cain, "that they were fair; and they took them wives of all which they chose." Genesis 6:2. The descendants of Seth began to quickly dissipate when "the sons of God came in unto the daughters of men, and they bare children to them, the same became mighty men which were of old, men of renown." Gen. 6:4

When the obedient and the hard-hearted merged, and rising sin completely dominated the earth, the debacle and violence accelerated exponentially and "God saw that the wickedness of man was great in the earth, and that every imagination of the thoughts of his heart was only evil continually," and God was very sorrowful that He had created man upon the earth, and it grieved Him deeply in His heart.

In order to stop the unbridled spread of sin God decided to destroy all humanity and every living creature from the face of the earth. But God loved mankind, and He then knew of one man who might obey all His commandments and, thereby, save the human race. As God considered this man, He saw that he was a disobedient sinner too, and would have gone ahead and banished mankind, "But Noah found grace in the eyes of the Lord," and God placed Noah in the column of the obedient, "and Noah walked with God." Gen. 6:8, 9

God instructed Noah in the building of an ark, strong enough to withstand the forces of a mighty flood, and large enough to hold two of every unclean beast and fowl of the air that God had created, and seven of every clean beast and fowl. Then, after 120 years, Noah and his sons had finished the ark, and because of Noah's faith and obedience God rescued Noah's wife, their three sons, and their three son's wives and instructed them to enter the ark when Noah did.

When the time for boarding had arrived, and Noah had stocked the ark with victuals, and the hard-hearted inhabitants of the earth had continually scoffed him, and "the earth was filled with violence . . . for all flesh had corrupted his way upon the earth," God had Noah and his family and all the natural, un-tampered with animals, creeping things, and fowls to occupy the ark. And "the Lord said unto Noah, come thou and all thy house into the ark; for thee have I seen righteous before Me in this generation." And the boarding plank was raised, and sealed shut.

Then God sent a flood upon the earth, "forty days and forty nights," with the waters cascading from the skies and gushing from the ground and the mighty rushing of the flood destroyed the gently rolling landscape of the earth, burying gigantic forests miles under the earth, and causing deep, rustic canyons and lofty, jagged mountains, and every living creature upon the earth, man and beast, were killed. But Noah and his family were spared inside the ark. After the flood waters had subsided, forming oceans, rivers, and seas, and dry land had appeared, Noah, his family, and all the clean and unclean animals and fowls, and creeping things, departed from the ark. "And God blessed Noah and his sons, and said unto them, Be fruitful, and multiply, and replenish the earth." Genesis 9:1.

However, the flame of disobedience that had engulfed the descendants of Cain was rekindled again in Ham, the youngest son of Noah. And Noah cursed Ham for his disobedience. The hard- hearted descendants of Ham became the violent and idolatrous nation of the Canaanites.

And from the descendants of Ham arose "Nimrod: he began to be a mighty one in the earth . . . And the beginning of his kingdom was Babel." On a plain, in the land of Shinar, the descendants of Nimrod declared, "Go to, let us build us a city and a tower, whose top may reach unto heaven; and let us make us a name," and they proceeded to build a city and a high tower "whose top may reach unto heaven." And God saw the wickedness in the people of Babylon, "And the Lord said, Behold, the people is one, and they have all one language, and this they begin to do: and now nothing will be restrained from them, which they have imagined to do." Genesis 11:6.

Then God went down in the midst of them and confused their language, so that they could not communicate, and they had to cease from building their tower. "Therefore is the name of it called Babel; because the Lord did there confound the language." And from Babel God scattered them everywhere upon the face of the earth, and they formed hard-hearted nations and peoples based upon their ability to communicate with a common language that set them apart from other nations. And because they could not communicate, except in paucity, God had slowed the rising tide of iniquity that was again saturating the earth.

The remaining sons of Noah, Shem, the middle son, and Japeth, the older, followed the obedient example of their father, and Noah blessed them. Four hundred and twenty-six years later, from the obedient descendants of Shem, rose up Abraham, the revered head of the patriarchal parenthood of the children of Israel (i.e. Jacob, whose name was changed to Israel). Abraham was faithful in his sacred worship of the living God, and God informed Abraham, "I will make of thee a great nation, and I will bless thee, and make thy name great; and thou shalt be a blessing." Genesis 12:2.

In the days of Abraham, and in the preceding antediluvian centuries, there was one commandment of the ten, that had been handed down from Adam, that received obedience, if only a partial obedience, but the rule was strict and adhered to not only by the God-fearing but by heathen nations as well. Even though polygamy was rampant in the land, the rule of conduct regarding respect for another man's wife was paramount. An upstanding man, who engaged in respectable polygamy, never had multiple wives who had ever been the wife of another man who was still alive. They took for themselves virgins, or widows. For instance Abraham, who did not engage in polygamy, had a confrontation regarding Sarah, in a heathen nation, which vividly illustrates the law of another man's wife.

Because there was a famine in the land of Abraham's travels, he and Sarah, and his company of relatives and servants, went into Egypt to wait out the famine. Sarah, Abraham's wife, was a beautiful woman and like all beautiful women she attracted the attention of men. "And it came to pass that, when Abraham was come into Egypt, the Egyptians beheld the woman that she was very fair." Gen. 12:16

Abraham knew that he was venturing into dangerous territory because of his beautiful wife, so he devised an elusive plan with Sarah to prevent himself from being murdered since, if a covetous man wanted his wife, Abraham would surely be killed before his wife was taken from him. (Only death ended a marriage, and then Sarah could become another man's wife!) So Abraham asked Sarah, if anyone inquired, to say that she was his sister, instead of his wife. (This was not a complete untruth; his wife was his half sister.) This way his own life would be spared if Sarah was taken by force.

The princes of Pharaoh, who beheld Sarah, told Pharaoh that

there was a beautiful woman in the land, in the traveling company of Abraham. "And the woman was taken into Pharaoh's house." Abraham was treated especially well because his "sister" was in Pharaoh's house. But Jehovah was *wroth!* "And the Lord plagued Pharaoh and his house with great plagues because of Sarai, Abram's wife." Gen. 12:17

When Pharaoh had learned that Sarah was truly married, he was very angry and "Pharaoh called Abram, and said, What is this that thou hast done unto me? Why didst thou not tell me that she was thy wife? . . . *So I might have taken her to me to wife* . . . take her, and go thy way!" And seeking to assuage the fierce anger of God, Pharaoh gave Abraham much of the wealth of Egypt to oust him out of his country—quickly—and as far away as possible!

Even the idolatrous, heathen nations respected the law of another man's wife, indeed—she was not to be claimed in marriage while her husband was living! There was no divorce, and the only lawful method by which a woman could remarry was the proven death of her husband. This was the worldwide commandment before the Mosaic law, permitting divorce, given forty years after Sinai.

God Himself enforced this rule since Abraham, dead or alive, posed no sort of threat to Pharaoh—it was Abraham's God, and His fierce wrath upon Pharaoh that pierced Pharaoh's heart with fear. This scenario involving Abraham, his wife, and Pharaoh is analogous to two other events in Scripture depicting heathen nations, the universally dreaded Philistines being one of them, with the same clear lesson—don't marry a *living* man's wife! (Genesis 20:1-18; and 26:6-11)

The inspired record of the Old Testament has not included a case (that the author has read) where a husband or wife became the true husband or wife of another, while a previous spouse was living. Granted, David married Michal, the daughter of King Saul, and later Saul gave Michal to be another man's wife. When David learned what Saul had done, he immediately sent for his wife, and she was taken from the man and delivered to her husband, David. Saul suffered the wrath of God for his evil deeds, this being one of them, since Michal was never eligible to be another man's wife. (2 Samuel 3:13-15)

Indeed, when King David lusted after Bath-sheba, the wife of Uriah, a member of David's army, and slept with her, and she became pregnant, the king had to order the death of Uriah before Bath-sheba could become his wife. (2 Samuel 12:9) As long as Uriah was alive Bath-sheba was off limits to marry, even to the king of Israel! If this was not the undisputed law, David, being the king, could have simply ordered Uriah out of Bath-sheba's life, sent him into exile, and married Bath-sheba. But David knew of Jehovah's past, righteous, vindictive dealings with affairs involving other men's wives, and he preferred the vile sin of murder rather than illicit marriage involving a living husband. He could surely confess and repent of murder, but not for unchangeable adultery, so long as he remained married to another living man's wife.

Likewise, when King David encountered Abigail, the wife of Nabal, he had met her on a dusty road, on his way to vanquish Abigail's husband for refusing to feed his men, after David had previously shown kindness to Nabal's servants, and protected them, while they labored in the field shearing their master's sheep. Abigail presented David with gifts and food for his men, and persuaded David not to carry out his plan to war with her husband. David was grateful to Abigail, and took special notice of her for "she was a woman of good understanding, and of a beautiful countenance." The next day, after Nabal had sobered up from a drunken party the night before, Abigail told her husband what she had done to prevent David from warring against him. Nabal took the news badly, and abruptly suffered a serious heart attack, and ten days later he died. After Nabal's unexpected death, David sent for Abigail, and married her, and she bore David three sons. (1 Samuel 25:39)

David, in the past, had taken wives upon his first encounter with them, but with Abigail, although he instantly desired her for himself, he was forced to wait until the certain death of her husband before he could marry her, which he immediately did. Truly, King David had multiple wives, but none who had a living husband. This was the honored law concerning remarriage.

Abraham had two sons while he was married to his first wife: Isaac, the youngest, born by his wife Sarah, and Ishmael, by Sarah's servant, Hagar. After the death of Sarah, Abraham married again, to Keturah, and she bore him six sons. Ishmael, his son by Hagar, married an Egyptian woman, and abandoned the worship of the God of his father Abraham, and began to worship the false gods of the Egyptians. But God said to Abraham, regarding Ishmael, "And also of the son of the bondwoman will I make a nation, because he is thy seed." Genesis 21:13.

Abraham was fearful for his son Isaac that he, also, would stray, into the idolatrous company of the Canaanites who were the hard-hearted descendants of Ham, and take for himself a heathen wife. Abraham found a wife for Isaac within his own line of the faithful worshippers of Jehovah, and her name was Rebecca, the niece of his brother, Nahor. "And the damsel was very fair to look upon, a virgin, neither had any man known her." When Isaac beheld Rebecca, she greatly pleased him, and Rebecca was enamored with Isaac, and after their engagement "she became his wife; and he loved her."

Isaac and Rebecca had two sons, Jacob the youngest, and Esau. The boys were twins, and Esau deserved the birthright of the oldest son because he came out ahead of Jacob. Isaac loved Esau because he was a roughed man, a skillful hunter, a man of the perilous field, and he loved to eat of the deer's meat that Esau brought home. But Rebecca loved Jacob the most, a much gentler person; however, he was cunning, and a deceiver.

Jacob and his mother, Rebecca, devised a plan to steal the sole blessing of Isaac away from Esau, which Esau had no real regard for, but it was due to him because he was the first-born son. They executed their plan and the blessing of Isaac, in his old age, along with the birthright, fell upon Jacob the unworthy one, and a minor, insignificant blessing went to Esau. Esau was very angry with Jacob, and vowed to kill him after Isaac their father had died.

Twenty years after obtaining the birthright by fraud, Jacob, his family and servants, were returning to his native land to re-establish his home there. As he came closer to the land of Seir, in the country of Edom, his foreboding thoughts of Esau tormented him, remembering that Esau had vowed to kill him for stealing the blessing from their father. Jacob sent messengers ahead to Esau, to ascertain his mood, and to forewarn Esau that he was returning home—not as lord over Esau, as the birthright granted, but as Esau's humble servant, seeking to make peace with him.

However, the messengers returned with no word from Esau, but with a frightful report that Esau was headed their way with four hundred savage men; and Esau's lack of reply sent Jacob's imagination into tailspins with scenes of bloody revenge upon himself and the slaughter of his wives and children. As a strategy against Esau's imminent attack, Jacob divided his family and servants into two companies, sending them off in different directions, so that when Esau rampaged upon one, the other might have an opportunity to escape.

After Jacob had sent his family and his servants with all of his possessions away, he was left alone around midnight by the river Jabbok. Rather than try to sleep, he decided to spend the rest of the night in prayer, pleading for the protection of God to spare the lives of himself and his family from the rapidly approaching stampede of his brother Esau.

As Jacob continued to petition Jehovah with strain after strain of deepest confession and repentance, he was attacked from behind by an assailant that he was sure was a robber, or one of Esau's evil spies seeking to kill him and return his limp, lifeless body to Esau. He fought back mightily against his attacker, summoning the strength to struggle to his feet, to turn against him, to fight him face to face. But his clung enemy forced him to the ground, a heavy weight around his midsection that tossed up the dirt as they landed on the ground, a unit of brawn and muscle, struggling for the advantage. Jacob felt the dewy dust clog his nostrils and burn his eyes as he rolled in the dirt, his assailant rolling with him, to this side and the other side, and Jacob was able to turn toward his attacker but in the blackness of night he could see no similitude of his countenance; only his strength, and the sweaty smell of his body identified him as a determined enemy bound to kill him, without fail.

An hour went by, and they closely fought; two hours went by and they wrested against one another, strength against strength, resisting, gaining the advantage, losing the advantage, biceps engaged in tight headlocks. Two hours went by, strong leg holds secured around a lean torso, a half nelson, broken, a full nelson regained, strength upon strength. Jacob bound him in a leg lock from the back with a mighty full nelson forcing his chin upon his chest. He held him there, resting some, attempting to break his neck against his chest. Jacob felt the strength of his attacker's neck raising his head from off his chest. He felt his sweaty, interlaced fingers giving way from the power in the rising neck of his enemy. He gratingly bared his teeth, recovering strength to his forearms and forced his attackers chin to his chest again.

The dawn began to break. As Jacob then prevailed against his attacker the sense of his guilt for the thing he had done to his brother, and every sin he had subtly executed swelled up in his mind, and burned within him, totally convincing him that "his righteousness was as filthy rags." But then, fiercely struggling to restrain his attacker, he remembered God's sure promises of cleansing, and his every being pleaded with God for forgiveness of all his sins.

Then the mighty Stranger "touched the hollow of his thigh; and the hollow of Jacob's thigh was out of joint, as he wrestled with him." Jacob felt his body abruptly weaken from the sharp pain encircling his right thigh, but he determined to hold on, for he knew then that he was wrestling with Christ Himself.

Then he heard the first words from the mighty Stranger, crying aloud, "Let me go, for the day breaketh!" Jacob felt total dependence upon the mercy of the Stranger, knowing that his very life was within the Stranger's grace, to provide him with complete forgiveness for his sins, and Jacob replied, "I will not let thee go, except thou bless me!" Then Jacob felt the nagging pressure, from twenty long years of guilt over his brother Esau, release its grip on his mind and body. His very soul felt free to praise God with shouts of joy and thanksgiving. He relaxed his tight hold on the Stranger, and He slipped out of Jacob's grasp, and stood to His feet. The Stranger kept his full back toward Jacob, and said, "What is thy name?" Jacob tried to stand up, but the gross pain of his injured thigh retired him to the ground again, at the bare feet of the Stranger. Then he answered, in utter peace of soul, "Jacob." The Stranger replied, "Thy name shall be called no more Jacob, but Israel: for as a prince hast thou power with God and with men, and hast prevailed." Then the Stranger placed His blessing upon Jacob, and departed. "And Jacob called the name of the place Peniel: for I have seen God face to face, and my life is preserved." Genesis 33:30.

Jacob and Esau had a peaceful reunion. "And Esau ran to meet him, and embraced him, and fell on his neck, and kissed him: and they wept." During the interceding twenty years from the time that Jacob had left Pdan-aram, to his night of wrestling with the Stranger, he had married two wives, Leah and Rachel, sisters, descendants in the obedient line of Shem, Noah's middle son. And Esau had received "his wives of the daughters of Canaan." The Canaanites were a warring, idolatrous nation, and the villainous descendants of Esau followed in their footsteps eventually becoming the hard-hearted, idolatrous nation of the Edomites in mount Seir.

Jacob (Israel) had twelve sons and a daughter, Dinah. Dinah was birthed by his wife Leah. Dinah was raped—"Shechem the son of Hamor the Hivite, prince of the country, saw her, he took her, and lay with her, and defiled her." Because of the foul deed that Shechem had done to their sister, "which thing ought not to be done," two sons of Jacob, Levi and Simeon, Dinah's brothers, murdered Shechem, and all the grown males of his family and "they took their sheep, and their oxen, and their asses, and that which was in the city, and that which was in the field, and all their wealth, and all their little ones, and their wives took they captive, and spoiled all that was in the house," to avenge Dinah, "because they had defiled their sister." Gen. 34:25-29 After her virginity was plundered Dinah was not fit for marriage to a respectable man, and she never married or bore children. (Neither did Shechem!)

The twelve sons of Israel, born to him in Pdan-aram, chronologically were: Reuben, Simeon, Levi, Judah, Dan, Naphtali, Gad, Asher, Issachar, Zebulun, Joseph, and Benjamin. These twelve became the heads of the families of all the nations of the children of Israel.

Joseph was a joy to his father, Israel: active, intelligent, and because Joseph was a child of his old age, Israel favored him even more. Joseph loved being taught of his father the stories of the fall of Adam and Eve, and the entrance of sin into the world, and that the God of Abraham and Isaac had provided a Savior that was to come. And all their sacrifices of a lamb was pointing forward to the time when the Savior would come and shed His own blood for their sins. Forever ridding them of their bondage to sin, preparing them for eternal life in a far better country, a heavenly home. Joseph learned obedient to the commandments of God, and Israel taught him the law of respect for another man's wife, as stated in the seventh and tenth commandments.

Because there was polygamy in Israel's household involving three women (Rachel died giving birth to Benjamin), who were the mothers of his ten sons, there was constant bitterness, jealousy, and loud arguments. The boys fought among themselves, internalizing the strife engulfing their mothers, and Israel was grieved by the feuding between his wives and sons. Though the boys were daily and continually at odds, there was one matter they all agreed on—they hated Joseph! To them he was a nasty little brat who took their father's attention away from them, and he was always, insultingly, intimidating everyone, telling them of his dreams of ruling over them. Oh, how they hated him!

Fed up, Joseph's brothers (all but Reuben and Benjamin), by evil connivance, sold him, at age seventeen, into abject slavery to the Midianites. "And the Midianites sold him into Egypt unto Potiphar, an officer of Pharaoh's, and captain of the guard." Genesis 37:36.

In Potiphar's house, over a period of ten years, Joseph rose to an enviable position of prominence, as guardian and operative of everything that Potiphar owned. Potiphar had no idea of the extent of his burgeoning wealth, but he knew that he was quite a rich man and he owed it all to Joseph, and Joseph was the director of investments for all that Potiphar owned.

For quite some time Potiphar's sportive wife had had her eye on Joseph, with thoughts of sleeping with him, because Joseph was a physically attractive man, with a six-pack abdomen, and well-developed shoulders and arms, quite the exact opposite of Potiphar's pot belly and flab. One evening, when everyone was out of the house, Potiphar's wife saw her chance, and made a serious play for Joseph "and she said, Lie with me!" Joseph knew it was coming since he had caught Potiphar's wife, many times, staring at him as he went about his duties in the house. But still he was caught off guard, and he told her on the spot, *"because thou art his wife:* how can I do this great wickedness, and sin against God," and Joseph immediately left the room.

Joseph's adamant refusal of her offer only made Potiphar's wife all the more insistent and "she spake to Joseph day by day" throwing herself at him, dressed in her most seductive apparel; but every time she had attempted to seduce him Joseph quickly refused her, and left her seething and upset. On one such occasion, later on, after she had calmed down, she thought to herself, I have no trouble tempting the other men in the house, behind Potiphar's back, but Joseph is different—he won't even talk dirty with me!

Once again, when all the men were out of the house, she saw her chance "and she caught him by his garment, saying, Lie with me!" Joseph tried to push her off, but she clung onto his shirt, attempting to smother him with kisses and thrust her arms inside of his shirt. In eager anticipation she ripped his shirt off, and tossed it around his neck, using it to draw Joseph toward her. Joseph slipped out of the noose of his shirt "and he left his garment in her hand, and fled, and got him out."

Potiphar's wife was very angry that she had been humiliated, again, by Joseph and in her own quarters she determined that if she couldn't have him, nobody would! She had kept the shirt that Joseph had left, and she called the men of the house and told them that Joseph had tried to force himself upon her, "and I cried with a loud voice," and Joseph left his shirt with her as he fled from the room.

When Potiphar heard his wife's accusations against Joseph, he had Joseph put into prison. Had Potiphar believed his wife's report he would have had Joseph hanged, for violating the law of respect for another man's wife, but he believed Joseph was innocent because Joseph had only displayed the highest level of integrity in managing his wealth and his household. He had to save face, and protect his wife's reputation, so he cast Joseph into prison.

Joseph spent two years in prison, and through a series of revelations that God had given him he was able to rightly interpret the dreams of Pharaoh that told of seven years of plenty in Egypt, followed by seven years of famine. Because Pharaoh now had a clear understanding of his dreams he let Joseph out of prison, and put him in charge of all the wealth of Egypt to prepare for the seven years of famine that was coming. "And Joseph was thirty years old when he stood before Pharaoh king of Egypt. And Joseph went out from the presence of Pharaoh, and went throughout all the land of Egypt." Genesis 41:46.

After the famine had commenced, and it was devastating—choking the life out of the nations around Egypt, and all of the land of Canaan—Joseph had his father, Israel, and all of his brothers and their wives and children to come down into Egypt, where there was plenty, so that they could survive the famine. Seventy members of Joseph's family journeyed into Egypt and Joseph had them established in the land of Goshen.

The children of Israel thrived in Egypt, and their population rapidly grew; and so long as the notoriety of Joseph was alive in the minds of the Pharaohs the children of Israel prospered and were treated with due respect. But soon, Israel died, "and Joseph died, and all his brethren, and all that generation," and after some time had passed, "there arose up a new king over Egypt, which knew not Joseph."

The Pharaoh took keen notice of the great size of the population of the children of Israel. "And he said unto his people, Behold, the people of the children of Israel are more and mightier than we." Then Pharaoh took severe action to curb the rapid population growth of the Hebrews, and to prevent them, in their great numbers, from siding with the enemy should Egypt find itself in a state of war he plunged them all into slavery, to build grand cities in Egypt.

But the more Pharaoh oppressed them, the more rapidly their numbers grew. Then Pharaoh ordered the midwives for the Hebrew women to kill all the male children that were born, but the females could remain alive. "But the midwives feared God, and did not as the king of Egypt commanded them, but saved the men children alive." God blessed the midwives for refusing to murder the male children, and the Hebrews "multiplied and waxed very mighty." Then Pharaoh ordered the Egyptians to take every son of the Hebrews that was born, and throw them into the river!

Pharaoh's daughter, and her servant women, went down to the Nile river to wash themselves, and Pharaoh's daughter saw a small ark made of bulrushes and slime floating along the river's edge "among the flags." Pharaoh's daughter ordered her servant to remove the ark out of the river—she obeyed, and they uncovered it, and saw a male baby crying inside of the ark. Pharaoh's daughter told the baby's sister (Miriam) to rush and find one of the Hebrew woman to nurse the baby. The baby's sister brought back the baby's mother, and Pharaoh's daughter told her to take the child away, and nurse it, and to return him when she was ordered to. "And the child grew, and she brought him unto Pharaoh's daughter, and he became her son. And she called his name Moses: and she said, Because I drew him out of the water." Exodus 2:10.

Further fulfilling His promise that He had made to Abraham, when He said "I will make thy seed to multiply as the stars of heaven," God raised up Moses. Moses, a descendant in the family line of Levi, was eighty years old when, by God's command, he led the children of Israel out of Egypt, out of slavery.

God had sent ten plagues upon the land of Egypt to compel Pharaoh to release the Hebrew slaves. Over two million persons, including the "mixed multitude" (those who were not Hebrews but left Egypt for fear of the plagues, or caught up in the excitement of the exodus, or were genuine worshippers of the God of Israel), set out on their journey to the Promise Land.

After the children of Israel and the mixed multitude had journeyed nearly one hundred miles from Egypt, Pharaoh sorely regretted that he had let Israel go. He convinced himself, then, that the plagues were just acts of nature, and not brought on by the God of Moses; and what would the other heathen kings think of Pharaoh—by his weakness—setting his slaves free. And his hard-hearted rebellion against God revived, and he sent his army after his slaves to bring them back to Egypt!

As the on-rushing clamor of Pharaoh's mighty army closed in behind them, the escaping multitude of Israel was trapped at the borders of the Red Sea. God miraculously parted the vast waters of the sea, and Israel crossed the Red Sea, all night, until everyone was safe on the other side. The waters remained parted as Pharaoh and his army pursued after Israel into the sea, and then Jehovah closed in the waters over them, and destroyed every soul of the Egyptians.

During their four hundred years of hard slavery in Egypt the sacred Ten Commandments that had been handed down from Adam to Noah, and from Noah's descendants to Jacob, whom God named Israel, was wholly forsaken and the Israelites had been caught up in the worship of heathen gods. Over time, and as their numbers increased, except for a small minority of the tribe of Levi, their lifestyle completely reflected the image of their captors, with widespread debauchery of every sort a day-to-day occurrence.

Because the Egyptians held certain animals (as gods) in high esteem, Israel had been forbidden to practice the sacrificial system of offering a lamb, shedding its blood, and confessing their sins over the lamb as a continual reminder of the Lamb of God to be slain for the sins of the world. Resting on the Sabbath day, a command God gave at creation, was also forced from their observance since the Pharaoh's ordered them to work, building luxurious cities, seven days a week.

Three days journey into the barren wilderness, after they had crossed the Red Sea, the exodus throng had run out of food. They bitterly complained to Moses that he had brought them out of Egypt to kill them in the wilderness, and then he would rob them of all their possessions, and make their children slaves to him. Moses earnestly appealed to God for what to do with this stiff-necked people; and how was their great number to be nourished in the hostile wilderness. God told Moses that on tomorrow morning, when the people arose that outside of their tents, in the open field, would be food from heaven. Sure enough, the following morning, as the people left their tents, they discovered little round cakes on the ground, like small coconut cakes that they called manna. ("What is it?!")

After the first morning, the manna that God had provided

was on the ground *every* weekday morning—for forty years—enough food for each person for one day without spoiling, except on Friday morning. On Friday morning they received a double portion that was to last each person for *two* days, without spoiling, so that they would not have to gather food on the seventh-day Sabbath. This was the method that God used to thoroughly teach the descendants of Abraham the forgotten day of worship that Egyptian bondage had forced them to abandon; which was to be continually observed, from that day forward, in honor of the living God.

When the Hebrews and the mixed multitude had arrived at Mount Sinai, at God's command, Moses halted the assembly and God called Moses to the top of Mount Sinai. Moses spent forty days on the mount in the presence of God, and God gave Moses the law of Ten Commandments that God had written in stone, with His own finger, to symbolize the permanence of the commandments that they were not just for Israel—but for all mankind, as long as their was life upon the earth.

As God gave the law the children of Israel, gathered at the foot of the mount, heard the awesome voice of God from the dark cloud that surrounded the mount, speaking the commandments as He simultaneously wrote them in stone. Then God gave private instructions for Moses to write down, which were the judgments—laws based on the Ten Commandments that were to be used by the magistrates to settle disputes that arose among the people. On another forty days and nights sojourn on top of Mount Sinai, God gave Moses the ceremonial laws that were to govern Israel's rites of worship, and these were to be performed until the day, on the cross of Calvary, the antitype Lamb gave His life for their sins.

When Moses came down from Mount Sinai, from the immediate presence of God, bearing the two tables of stone wherein was written the Ten Commandments, he discovered that the children of Israel, also instigated by the mixed multitude and involving Aaron, the older brother of Moses, had fashioned a molten image in the similitude of a golden calf, one of the gods of the Egyptians, and they were worshiping the image.

The people were in high revelry, some drunken with wine brought from Egypt, bowing down to the image and engaged in wild, ritualistic dancing around the image and blaspheming God's name. Moses was very angry and in his righteous indignation he threw the tables of stone at the people, and the stones were broken into pieces. Moses ordered the wild commotion to stop, and he had the image ground up into fine powder and he cast the powder into the stream flowing out of the mount that provided drinking water for the people, and Moses made the people drink water from the stream. At God's command, three thousand people who had taken part in the image worship, and were not repentant, were slain by the tribe of the Levites, who had not been a part of the idolatry.

Then God had Moses to return to the top of Mount Sinai, and He wrote out the Ten Commandments again in tables of stone with His own finger, symbolizing to Moses and all Israel that the law was eternal, and could not be gotten rid of by disobedience for the commandments are God's name, the written embodiment of His character that can never be done away with, just as God can never cease to exist.

To epitomize the lofty respect that Israel was to show for the law of Ten Commandments, when Moses built the tabernacle according to God's detailed instructions, and it signifying the authority of God over Israel and the center of their worship, the Ten Commandments were placed *inside* the golden ark that stood under the cherubim in the second apartment of the sanctuary called the holy of holies. The law inside of the ark, in the holy of holies, with the Shekinah glory above it, symbolized the presence of God in Israel. The authenticated Mosaic laws and the ceremonial laws were placed on the *outsid*e of the ark. The deliberate placement of the tables of stone containing the Ten Commandments inside the ark, like God, indicated their unchangeable permanence. And the ordinances, on the outside of the ark, their impermanence and room for interpretation.

At the conclusion of the first year of their encampment at Mount Sinai the building of the tabernacle was finished. The outer courtyard and the two apartments of the sanctuary were a replica of the sanctuary in heaven, and God gave Moses an inspired vision of the heavenly sanctuary to impress upon him the meaning of the sanctuary's furniture, the apartments, and the priesthood associated with the worship of God through the sanctuary. The sanctuary service was to be a lesson within itself of the plan of redemption for all mankind, exemplifying the role of Messiah on earth, and His work of judgment in heaven after His crucifixion.

The tabernacle was designed for ease of movement since it was to be disassembled and taken with Israel on their final journey to the Promise Land, on the other side of the Jordan River, and then it was to be erected again, in a designated location, for the nation of Israel to continue rendering specified, acceptable worship of God.

The children of Israel spent two years encamped at Mount Sinai and during that time, in addition to erecting the sacred tabernacle, God had given to Moses, for governing the people, additional statutes and judgments to arrest their state of moral degradation, brought with them from bondage in Egypt. The total book of laws were especially suited for Israel, and the circumstances surrounding the establishment of the new nation. The foundation of the judgments was the character of God, represented by the Ten Commandments, and the judgments were written to establish obedience to the Ten Commandments. God intended that Israel should be a model nation to the heathen nations around them, so that the plan of redemption could be visibly and indelibly taught to the whole world.

To this end it was imperative that Israel remove all sin from among them, sin made very plain by the Ten Commandments. Throughout their wanderings in the wilderness, rapid and harsh penalties were enacted for violation of the moral laws that in themselves were trampling upon the character of God. The seventh and the tenth commandments were strictly upheld, with the law of respect for another man's wife, given at creation, receiving equal attention with re-establishing the seventh-day Sabbath, to wipe out the violation of them lost in Egypt.

When Moses first came down from the mount with the law of judgments, the law addressed just two areas of rules relating to connubial relationships. One was if a man sold his Hebrew daughter, to be a maidservant, after six years she was not to be released as the menservants were.

If the girl (she *had* to be a virgin) was sold upon condition that she was engaged to her master, if he changed his mind, and didn't marry her after her contract had ended, he was to release her back to her father. He was forbidden to sell her to a foreign nation. If she was engaged to her master's son, she was to be treated with the privileges of a daughter-in-law. If her master married someone else, he was responsible for her total upkeep, including conjugal rights, if she so desired, for as long as she wanted to stay in his home. If *she* elected to enforce none of these three things, she was to return to her father without her master receiving any money for her. (Exodus 21:7-11)

The second judgment was if a man seduced a virgin who was not engaged, and had sex with her, he must marry her. If her father refused to give her in marriage, the man must pay a sum of money to the girl's father. (Exodus 22:16, 17)

These were all of the judgments regarding the tenth and the seventh commandments that were received by Moses upon his first law appearance in the presence of God. There was nothing about divorce, since God had not sanctioned divorce. There was nothing about remarriage—since divorce under God did not exist—there was no need to address remarriage!

However, within a year, Moses received another set of judgments from God regarding connubial relationships. Then God was more explicit, because the children of Israel were daily engaging in lewd practices that burnt the nostrils of God, and required detailed statutes to erase the disobedience from the people. (Leviticus.18:1-5)

Even as the sacred tabernacle was being built, among a rebellious and stiff-necked people, incest was running rampant. They had, shortly before the beginning of the building of the tabernacle, vowed to God that regarding His commandments, "All that the Lord hath spoken we will do." But the centuries old, ingrained, lifestyle of Egypt would not long remain subdued from overt practice among an idolatrous throng, and they wantonly pursued after the carnal intents of their hard hearts.

To address the unbridled acts of sexual indulgences with their near relatives God warned them: "After the doings of the land of Egypt, wherein ye dwelt, shall ye not do: and after the doings of the land of Canaan, whither I bring you, shall ye not do: neither shall ye walk in their ordinances." Lev. 18:3

Then Jehovah laid down over two dozen statutes relating to incest declaring, for instance, "The nakedness of thy father, or the nakedness of thy mother, shalt thou not uncover: she is thy mother; thou shalt not uncover her nakedness." Leviticus 18:7. And He said, regarding adultery, "Moreover thou shalt not lie carnally with thy neighbour's wife, to defile thyself with her." And on homosexuality, "Thou shalt not lie with mankind, as with womankind: it is abomination." Then He ended this occasion of speaking with Moses, saying, "Therefore shall ye keep mine ordinance, that ye commit not any one of these abominable customs, which were committed before you, and that ye defile not yourselves therein: I am the Lord your God."

On every occasion when God used the word "abomination" or "abominable" relating to sin, it was meant to indicate that it was a sin regardless of the age in which the abominable thing occurred. Sin is *always* sin, and can never be legislated into acceptability with God. Because governments very often legalize sin, homosexual marriage, for instance, does not change at all the fact that to God homosexual acts are an abomination, and will forever remain an abomination regardless of what governments may do. What God regards as sin—remains sin. This principle is applicable in ascertaining from the Mosaic law what is morally right and wrong in modern society. In the aforementioned discourse to Moses, every statute that God had given He said it was an "abominable custom," therefore, they were a sin when Moses received them, and they are a sin today. (Leviticus 18:1-30)

Again, in the speaking to Moses just mentioned, nothing is said by God about divorce or remarriage. In contrast, in this discourse, and in every other, God makes mention of stamping out idolatry and being consistent in observing the seventh day Sabbath. Idolatrous practices and violation of the Sabbath day were ongoing sins that needed constant vigilance by Moses to see that these sins were obliterated from Israel.

Instances of unlawful divorce must have occurred since God said to Moses that the priests were not to marry a divorced woman. "And he shall take a wife in her virginity. A widow, or a divorced woman, or profane, or an harlot, these shall he *not* take: but he shall take a virgin of his own people to wife." Leviticus 21:13, 14. And divorce is also mentioned in the case where the daughter of a priest may eat holy food (food left as an offering) the same as the priest if she was a widow, or divorced, with no children and she had returned home to her father's house. (Leviticus 22:13)

However, in neither case where divorce is mentioned does God indicate to Moses His position on divorce. It is implied in His instruction to all priests, not to marry a divorced woman that He does not regard a divorced female as equal in purity as a virgin; but neither is a widow, so in this instance He was not regarding divorce as any worse than being a widow. For the time being, the practice of divorce in Israel does not warrant a declaration from God, although unregulated divorce was occurring. Remarriage is not mentioned, at all!

As time went on, and the vilest of sexual offenses continued unabated (and burning up their children in idol worship), God revealed to Moses the certain punishment that was to be swiftly administered to all sinners who persisted in violating His holy commandments.

For sacrificing their children, God said, "Whosoever he be of the children of Israel, or of the strangers that sojourn in Israel, that giveth any of his seed unto Molech; he shall surely be put to death: the people of the land shall stone him with stones." Leviticus 20:2.

And the common sin of bestiality was likewise dealt with: "And if a man lie with a beast, he shall surely be put to death: and ye shall slay the beast." "And if a woman approach unto any beast, and lie down thereto, thou shalt kill the woman, and the beast: they shall surely be put to death." Leviticus 20:15, 16.

Adultery was regarded by God as a sin just as repulsive as burning up their children, and sex with animals, requiring the same punishment. "And the man that committeth adultery with *another man's wife,* even he that committeth adultery with his neighbor's wife, the adulterer and the adulteress shall surely be put to death." Leviticus 20:10.

Homosexuality continued to plague Israel, and God had to specify the swift penalty for that offense, telling Moses, "If a man also lie with mankind, as he lieth with a woman, both of them have committed an abomination: they shall surely be put to death." Leviticus 20:13. And, likewise, a man engaging in sexual intercourse with his daughter-in-law, "both of them shall surely be put to death."

But on divorce and remarriage, God withheld His judgments as Israel continued to run slipshod ahead in every imaginable vice, and corrupted themselves under the watch care of their Creator God.

Along with individual penalties for sin, God gave warnings that applied to Israel as a nation, both then and in the future, saying, in part, "If ye shall despise my statutes, or if your soul abhor my judgements, so that ye will not do all my commandments . . . I will do this unto you; I will even appoint over you terror, consumption, and the burning ague, that shall consume the eyes, and cause sorrow of heart . . . ye shall be slain before your enemies; they that hate you shall reign over you; and ye shall flee when none pursueth you. . . . I will bring seven times more plagues upon you according to your sins. . . . I will send wild beasts among you, which shall rob you if your children, and destroy your cattle, and make you few in number . . . I will send the pestilence among you; and ye shall be delivered into the hand of the enemy. . . . And if ye for all this will not hearken unto me, but walk contrary unto me; then I will walk contrary unto you . . . even I will chastise you seven times for your sins. . . . And yet for all this, when they be in the land of their enemies, I will not cast them away, neither will I abhor them, to destroy them utterly and to break my covenant with them. . . . But I will for their sakes remember the covenant of their ancestors, whom I brought forth out of the land of Egypt in the sight of the heathen, that I might be their God: I am the Lord." Leviticus 26:1-45.

After fourteen months of instruction in the vicinity of Mount Sinai, and the tabernacle was finished, the new nation of Israel began their journey to the Promise Land, Canaan, on the other side of the Jordan River. They took up the tabernacle, and in an organized regiment they set out on the eleven days journey. After a hazardous trip, full of murmuring and complaining, "it displeased the Lord," they reached the borders of Canaan, on the near side of the Jordan. While they rested, it was suggested that before they all cross over, to possess the land, that spies should be sent ahead of them to evaluate the country, and then bring back a report regarding what the people could expect to face once they had crossed the Jordan.

Moses selected twelve spies, one from each of the twelve tribes of Israel, and they went out from the camp. Forty days later, the spies returned from Canaan. They brought with them samples of the luscious fruits growing wild in the land. A good report of the land was given by Joshua and Caleb, and Joshua said, "surely it floweth with milk and honey; and this is the fruit of it." Then Joshua eagerly went on with his report, saying, "Nevertheless, the people be strong that dwell in the land, and the cities are walled, and very great: and moreover we saw the children of Anak there."

The children of Anak were fierce giants, and the rest of the inhabitants that Joshua told them about—the Amalekites, the Hittites, the Jebusites, the Amorites, and the Canaanites were just as fierce, and next to impossible for Israel to defeat in battle. But Joshua was excited about the goodness of the land and he wanted to break camp immediately, and face whatever difficulties that were ahead of them, knowing that God was their ever-present protector. The people began to lose some of their earlier enthusiasm after they had heard Joshua's report of their avowed enemies in the land; but Caleb was just as anxious to go forward as was Joshua, and he tried to calm the people. He stood up, so that everyone could hear him, and said, "Let us go up at once, and possess it; for we are well able to overcome it!"

However, the ten men who had journeyed with Joshua and Caleb, to search out the land, saw their opportunity to further discourage the people, and to cancel all plans to enter the land. The fears that they garnered within themselves—their mistrust of God—they spread among the assembly, saying, "We be not able to go up against the people; for they are stronger than we." Then they began to exaggerate the difficulties that lay ahead, making them sound insurmountable. "The land through which we have gone to search it, is a land that eateth up the inhabitants thereof; and *all the people* that we saw in it are men of a great stature. And there we saw the giants, the sons of Anak . . . and we were in our sight as grasshoppers, and so we were in their sight."

After hearing the ominous report from the ten cowards, the whole nation of Israel began to cry and murmur and complain against Aaron and Moses, and they charged Moses with their favorite accusation when they really wanted to get nasty, and enter under his skin, and they said, in one voice, "Would God that we had died in the land of Egypt! Or would God that we had died in this wilderness!" Then the leaders of the rebellion began rousing the Israelites to elect for themselves a leader, to return to Egypt.

That day they refused to enter Canaan and possess the land. Jehovah was highly displeased with Israel because their refusal to readily cross the Jordan, to the Promise Land, was an indication of their lack of trust in Him. He had provided them with miracle after miracle—not to mention the parting of the Red Sea two years earlier, a miracle He was ready to perform again with the Jordan River; and the pillar of cloud by day and the pillar of fire by night that continually guided them in all of their travels—to unreservedly prove that they had nothing to fear so long as they faithfully trusted Him. But the people, out of fright and faithlessness, steadfastly refused to possess the land.

As a punishment for their disobedience, God said that none of that generation—from twenty years old and upward—would ever see the fruitful Promise Land. Indeed, they would all be dead whenever Israel entered the land! Then the low cloud that guided them by day lifted up from over the tabernacle, and the people turned northward—back into the wilderness—to suffer the consequences of their hard-hearted disobedience.

The nation of Israel spent thirty-eight years dissenting and complaining in the hostile wilderness, daily indulging in their vices, warring with their enemies, and journeying from place to place until Jehovah, again, brought them to the borders of the Promise Land. This time they agreed to inhabit the land!

As God had said, all the men twenty years old and upward, who had agreed with the dastardly spies that the land was too treacherous for Israel to possess (which was all the men except Moses, Joshua, and Caleb), thirty-eight years earlier, were dead. God had told Moses, too, that because of an occasion of his disobedience (he spitefully struck the rock with his staff for water to come forth, when God had told him to speak to the rock), which was a bad example for the people, that even he was not to cross over to the Promise Land. In humility, as his manner was, Moses accepted his punishment, and the role of leadership over Israel was given to Joshua.

Before Moses had stepped aside, he presented Israel with the judgments that they were to live by, beginning that day, and after they had entered the Promise Land. The majority of the judgments and statutes were a restatement of ones previously given, since the people who made up that generation of Israel were children at Mount Sinai, and some of the older judgments they had never gleaned from the mouth of the lawgiver. Then because of their constant hard-hearted murmuring, disobedience, and complaining, more judgments than the ones given at Sinai, and later, were added to the book of laws to address their strongest grievances.

They had repeatedly petitioned Moses; they had recited the glory-days in Egypt, as once told to them by their deceased relatives; they had picketed; they held long sit-ins; they burnt the flag; they rioted; they engaged in long affirmation parades; they held rallies; they signed petitions; they knocked on tents; they protested in the valleys; they protested on the hills; they went on grueling hunger strikes; and then, finally, from Moses, after thirty-nine long years, on the banks of the Jordan River, at the borders of the Promise Land—they received the hard fought go-ahead to *divorce!* The words from Moses, loudly spoken from a high focal point, were like sweet celestial music to their ears—

"When a man hath taken a wife, and married her," Moses said, "and it come to pass that she find no favour in his eyes, because he hath found some uncleanness in her: then let him write her a bill of divorcement, and give it in her hand, and send her out of his house." Deuteronomy 24:1.

The cheers in the assembled throng went up heavenward, and they heartily tossed their turbans in the air. They danced, and applauded in sheer ecstasy for five minutes, then Moses held up his hand to quiet them, and he continued speaking—

"And when she is departed out of his house, she may go and be another man's wife." Deuteronomy 24:2.

The large crowd burst forth with cheering again, and presently Moses held up his hand to quiet them. Then he went on—

"And if the latter husband hate her, and write her a bill of divorcement, and giveth it in her hand, and sendeth her out of his house; or if the latter husband die, which took her to be his wife; her former husband, which sent her away, may not take her again to be his wife, after that she is defiled; for that is abomination before the Lord."

The men in the crowd peered at one another, with puzzled grimaces on their faces. They quietly began squabbling among themselves, trying to figure out what Moses was now getting at. Was he going to negate everything he had previously said with some ridiculous condition, or punishment, as he usually did? The uneasy, shifting movement among them gradually ceased, and they expectantly looked up at Moses again, surely hoping for some acceptable clarification. Moses went on—

"And thou shalt not cause the land to sin, which the Lord thy God giveth thee for an inheritance." Deuteronomy 24:3, 4.

The loud cheers went up again, and voices rang out, "We can live with that!" "We can live with that!" "Glory and honor to Moses!" "We can live with that!" (Author's quotes.)

The married women in the crowd were dumbfounded, for they had wholly depended on the law of no divorce to protect them from their promiscuous husbands, who then could only threaten them with putting away if they did not live up to his every expectation of a wife, as just a servant—with privileges.

Before that day's ruling, if the husband could prove adultery, she would be stoned to death, she and her illicit partner, then her husband was free to remarry because she was dead. But it would have been a very foolish married woman that allowed herself to be *caught* in adultery, so the stoning law was not a heavy threat to a woman's life, or marriage, since adultery was practically impossible to prove without being discovered in the act. But now, cruel abandonment by their husband was a sure possibility since simple hearsay, gossip, rumors of uncleanness was all-sufficient grounds for pursuing divorce. All the women quietly wept in their scarves!

The only solace they found, and the only sensible explanation for the altered Law in their favor, was that any allegations of uncleanness, as grounds for divorce, had to be regarded as trivial since she could remarry without a worse charge of adultery haunting her, and forcing her into social oblivion. Thank goodness—she could marry again! She could now become a permanent member of another man's household, and remain an acceptable part of Hebrew society. And not become relegated to the lowest fringes of society where previously married, non-virgin women, before the concession, were forced to subsist.

The young virgins in the crowd sorely wept on their mother's breast as their fathers went throughout the assembly consummating deals for marriage in payment for large sums of money. Men with many virgin daughters could become rich, now that the bull market for virgins was strong. Men with lesser monetary means, who could previously afford only one wife, now eagerly contracted for several with little resistance from likely women who were seeking to avoid forced entrance into base prostitution to support themselves. The rush to secure wily Israelites, who were eager to bear false witness against their neighbor, as paid expert testimony providing contrived evidence of meritless wives involved in "uncleanness" to validate their claims for divorce, skyrocketed too.

After Moses had finished with his dissertation on the laws to govern Israel in the Promise Land, God directed he and Joshua into the tabernacle of the congregation to entrust Joshua with the new position of leadership in Israel, and He said to Moses, also, "Behold, thou shalt sleep with thy fathers; and this people will rise up, and go a-whoring after the gods of the strangers of the land, whither they go to be among them, and will forsake me, and break my covenant which I have made with them. . . .

And I will surely hide my face in that day for all the evils which they shall have wrought, in that they are turned unto other gods . . . for I know their imagination which they go about, even now, before I have brought them into the land which I sware." Deuteronomy 31:16, 18, 21.

Then after Moses, the servant of God, had taught a sacred song of remembrance to Israel, and presented them with words of blessing, God took him to the very top of mount Pisgah, and as Moses took in the grand view from the high mountain, God said to him, "This is the land which I sware unto Abraham, unto Isaac, and unto Jacob, saying, I will give it unto thy seed: I have caused thee to see it with thine eyes, but thou shalt not go over thither." Deuteronomy 34:4.

After seeing the Promise Land, but without setting his feet on its fertile soil, Moses died in the land of Moab "over against Beth-peor."

As God's omniscient knowledge had said, the children of Israel mightily sinned against the Lord and wholly transgressed His commandments. Their history, after the death of Moses to the crucifixion of Jesus Christ, continued in the same ugly vein of rebellion as it was for forty years in the wilderness. They had calm periods of prosperity when they had repented, mainly from gross idolatry, and sought after God for His restoration of their existence as a nation. Then, this prosperity was again followed by a tragic downfall, sometimes taking the form of many years of hard bondage in captivity to heathen nations.

As the time drew nearer for the appearance of the promised Messiah, Israel was being harshly ruled over by the Romans. Their expectation, due to their hard hearts immersed in disobedience to God, of a triumphant military style ruler over Israel, to free them from the hated yoke of the Romans, left them totally unprepared for the virgin birth of a baby, born in a manger. Their lack of acceptance of the many prophecies of Scripture that pointed to the true coming of Christ placed them under the deceptive control of Satan; and Satan used their ignorance, and denial of the Savior, to cause the consanguineous Pharisees to seek a cause to murder Christ, during his entire adult ministry.

Rightly considering the essential cause for Israel incessantly petitioning a concession from Moses which would grant them authority to divorce their wives—their entire motivation being that their hard hearts desired freedom to commit *sin* without a penalty—it behooves modern Christians to shy away from an ancient law instituted solely to tolerate transgression, to pacify an intractable people who were in no wise agreeable to obedience to the eternal commandments of "Thou shalt not covet thy neighbor's wife," and "Thou shalt not commit adultery."

Modern parents who have recognized that their teenage children persist in engaging in premarital sex, insist that they wear a condom, or take birth control measures, to prevent STDs and pregnancy. Parents permitting the use of practices that mitigate adverse results from immoral sex does not condemn parents or their well-intended solutions; nor do parents and their solutions make premarital sex any less of a gross sin; they just lessen the immediate impact of willful sin on stubborn participants.

Likewise, when Moses tolerated divorce, there was no defect in Moses' character or the law; but divorce became no less of a transgression; his concession only quieted the protests of hard-hearted Israelites who desperately sought after legalized divorce. Their pseudo-victory did not change the eternal fact that marriage is permanent until death, and the Godly lived accordingly.

The leniency in the Ten Commandments law that Moses had approved may be compared with laws today that are legislated simply to appease a loud constituency, and usually permitting people to civilly separate themselves from God. In some states it is legal to gamble, but legalized gambling does not change gambling in God's commandments (Thou shalt not covet; Thou shalt not steal; Thou shalt have no other gods before me) from sin to non-sin. Likewise, because states legalize divorce does not, in any manner, alter the fact that couples who are divorced, with a living spouse, remain married to that spouse as long as one of them remains alive. ("One flesh." "What God hath joined together let not man put asunder.") If one remarries in stark violation of the Scriptures, one surely commits adultery—there's no getting around the Law simply because it disagrees with someone's beliefs, and strong desire for remarriage.

As can readily be seen, from His dealings with the children of Israel, God is not fickle about sin. Truly, He was justified in His final actions with Moses, too, by not allowing him to enter the Promise Land because he struck an inanimate object rather than speak to it. God expected of Moses only willful obedience, not presumption of pardon. Lowly human beings can't determine for God what is right. God is always right—human beings have been granted the exalted privilege of going along with His program. "One flesh"—until death—is God's program.

The question is often asked—Why do bad things happen to good people? Upon closer observation it is discovered that this is a misstatement of inquiry when in search of God's motives. The question should be—Why do *good* things happen to *bad* people? Indeed, all mankind are sinners, "For we have all sinned, and come short of the glory of God," Romans 3:23, and deserve to eternally die for our transgressions, "For the wages of sin is death," Romans 6:23.

So because we live in a world of sin, the daily norm should be for only bad things to happen. Bloody wars, destructive acts of nature and moral degeneracy are effects of transgression in the unfortunate lives of sinners. But since "God is Love" many good things happen to bad people. Good occurrences are the exception in a world of sin, and they only come about because God overcomes evil every day, to allow goodness to intrude upon a corrupted world—and God must be praised for His love.

When Jehovah's uplifted law requires that divorce is bad, and remarriage qualifies as outright sin, mankind must accept that these commandments are perfect for humanity, and worthy of obedience since they originated only with God—Who "became as one of us" and gave His own life for the *good* of mankind.

7

Mark 10:11, 12 (Context)

As Jesus had spoken to the Pharisees on the subject of divorce, and He had answered their insincere question that was intended to trap Him into denying Moses' law, Jesus left some unanswered questions in the minds of His disciples. The Gospel of Mark continues with Christ's explanation of divorce and remarriage, but with a concluding, clarifying remark that was intended only for His disciples. Mark records the same event in the same location as Matthew, but Mark's emphasis is on answering the question from the Pharisees, "Is it *lawful* for a man to put away his wife?" In contrast, the record of Matthew emphasizes Jesus' answer to the question from the Pharisees, "Is it lawful for a man to put away his wife *for every cause?"* Christ's answer to this question in Matthew's record is—No— it's not lawful for every cause. There is only one cause and that cause is fornication. Then He added to His answer that if they marry after they have divorced their wives for sexual immorality, they have committed adultery. And anyone who marries the wife they have divorced has committed adultery.

Mark begins his inspired recollection of this occasion in Mark 10:2 with the Pharisees testing Jesus with the question, "Is it lawful for a man to put away his wife." Then Jesus answered them with the question, "What did Moses command you?" In other words He's saying to them, since they were supposed to be experts in the law, expecting others to follow their teachings on the law, that they should know the answer to their own question. And He was not going to place Himself in their trap by saying something that they could misinterpret as blasphemy. So He had them to answer their own question. They replied, "Moses suffered to write a bill of divorcement, and to put her away." Then, from this point onward, Mark does not record any other words from the Pharisees (as Matthew does), but he provides all of Jesus' response intended to convict them of their wayward condition, and surely let them know that what God requires supersedes the concession that Moses permitted. "For the hardness of your heart," Jesus said, "he wrote you this precept. But from the beginning of the creation God made them male and female. For this cause shall a man leave his father and mother, and cleave to his wife; And they twain shall be one flesh: so then they are no more twain, but one flesh." From thoroughly qualifying His answer to their question, is divorce lawful, with indisputable evidence from the Lawgiver, Jesus then answers, "What therefore God hath joined together, let not man put asunder"—No! It's not possible for man to end a marriage.

This concludes Mark's record of this encounter that Jesus had with the Pharisees on the subject of divorce. But Mark continues Jesus' dialogue on divorce with His disciples after they have removed themselves from outside, to inside. In Jesus' previous outside conversation with the perverse Pharisees He had mainly centered his answers on addressing their selfish motive for divorce, which was their hard hearts. But "in the house" His reply to His disciples carries another emphasis.

Outside, all the disciples had just heard Jesus' answer to the Pharisees that Mark did not record, which was, "Whosoever shall put away his wife, except it be for fornication, and shall marry another, committeth adultery: and whoso marrieth her which is put away doth commit adultery." Matthew 19:9. But the disciples still needed further clarification, so inside of the house they brought up the subject again. They wanted to know, beyond a shadow of a doubt, what happens, after divorce, to the one who does the putting away? Is he innocent? Is he free to remarry? Does it make a difference if it's a man or a woman who does the putting away?

Inside, the disciples were not interested in cause for divorce, which was only fornication—they were clear on that—what they wanted to know was what happens to *them*, if they divorce their wives? Then Mark records all of Jesus' answer to their throbbing concern. Jesus replied to them directly, without mincing His words, saying, "Whosoever shall put away his wife, and *marry another*, committeth *adultery* against her"—That's the outcome of any man who divorces his wife and marries someone else. And this is the result of any woman who divorces her husband and marries someone else: "And if a woman shall put away her husband, and be *married to another*, she committeth *adultery.*"

"In the house" Jesus didn't repeat to His disciples His answer with respect to cause for divorce since the cause for divorce, whether it was fornication or dirty dishes, was irrelevant when compared to the fate of the person who remarries after divorce. Jesus was making it clear, in His reply to His disciples that they were not to be overly concerned with cause for divorce, as the hard-hearted Pharisees were—who were only seeking a legal reason to rid themselves of their wives—but the goal of His disciples was to attain obedience to the highest standard of the seventh commandment which was living absent of the sin of adultery. This, for His sincere disciples, because they were to exemplify obedience, meant adherence to the spirit of the law manifested by no remarriage after divorce.

Indeed, some of them may have been contemplating divorce because of their decision to follow Christ—hence their nagging interest in the subject inside the house. But should a divorce occur their obedience to the commandments would prevent them from marrying again. To be Christ's disciples they had to be aware of what constituted sin after divorce—and avoid it at all cost—else, His calling them to follow Him as teachers of the Word would be in vain.

In Scripture, Christ's teaching on divorce is progressive. He did not say everything necessary to have a full understanding of the subject in one session of discussion with either His disciples or the Pharisees. However, when all of His comments are taken together, and considered in relation one to the other, all sincere questions are answered and a clear view of truth is seen.

When considering the sequential arrangement of the lessons in the Gospels, Matthew thru John, it is helpful to observe that certain texts on divorce should be read as a unit. For instance, Matthew 19:9 and Matthew 5:32 should *not* be considered together (as is commonly done) because Christ is stressing a different point on each of these occasions. Also, He is teaching in two different locations.

In Matthew 19:9 and Luke 16:14-18, Christ is expounding on the same point in both instances. Therefore, it is helpful to consider these two teachings on divorce together. Likewise, Matthew 5:32 and Mark 10:1-12 should be studied together since they are compatible in point of doctrine, although, Christ is teaching on two separate occasions. (Matthew 19:1-12 and Mark 10:1-12 are the same occasion.)

With respect to divorce, Christ was in the company of the Pharisees on two separate occasions. Once He reprimanded them on cause for divorce ("except"), and one time He did not. Since Matthew 19:9 and Luke 16:18 are compatible, this is where the best comparison of what was said can be found. In Matthew 19:9 Jesus said to the Pharisees, "Whosoever shall put away his wife, except it be for fornication, and shall marry another, committeth adultery: and whoso marrieth her which is put away doth commit adultery."

By comparison, in Luke 16:18, where He was once again addressing the hard-hearted Pharisees, He wanted to bare open to them the un-compromised, unclouded truth on divorce and remarriage—with no misunderstanding—so He did not include non-pertinent "except" in His statement, but he went right to the heart of the matter, and said, "Whosoever putteth away his wife, and marrieth another, committeth adultery: and whosoever marrieth her that is put away from her husband committeth adultery."

Out of the mouth of Christ to the Pharisees, and to His own disciples who overheard His plain reply, and to every Christian whose desire is to be obedient to the seventh commandment this is the perspicuous truth on all divorce and remarriage, and time, laws, nor accepted custom can change Christ's commandments. Persons—believers in Christ and non-believers—who persist in violating His commandments He "will recompense them according to their deeds, and according to the works of their hands." Jeremiah 25:12-14

8

Matthew 5:32 (Context)

THE Sermon on the Mount was the first incident recorded in the Gospels where Jesus began to teach on the subject of divorce. As His method was, He had a point of emphasis in His specific words on divorce. In order to absorb the full impact of the lesson that Christ is teaching in Matthew 5:32, it is favorable to start back at verse 17. It will also be helpful to one's understanding if an analogy is presented making use of paraphrasing—taking what Matthew has recorded that Christ said and placing Christ in the modern day role of a professor in a classroom, addressing mature students, and administering a final semester exam.

Beginning at Matthew 5:17, Christ said to His disciples, and everyone else who could hear Him, including spies who had been dispatched by the Pharisees:

"Think not that I am come to destroy the law, or the prophets: I am not come to destroy, but to fulfill"—(Classroom in figure and paraphrased): Welcome to Sermon on the Mount 101. My name is Jesus Christ, and I'm here replacing your usual teacher to specifically administer your final semester exam. This two-hour class will run without a scheduled break today, so that you will have sufficient time to complete the exam. I have not come to change the rules that your professor has laid down, but I'm here to thoroughly administer those rules.

Matthew 5:32 (Context)

Verse 18. "For verily I say unto you, Till heaven and earth pass, one jot or one tittle shall in no wise pass from the law, till all be fulfilled"—So believe me, you can take this to the bank, 'till cows eat trees, not one letter of the rules will change 'till you have all received a grade for this exam.

Verse 19. "Whosoever therefore shall break one of these least commandments, and shall teach men so, he shall be called the least in the kingdom of heaven: but whosoever shall do and teach them, the same shall be called great in the kingdom of heaven"—Anyone in this classroom who is inclined to cheat on this exam, and attempts to asssist others in cheating, shall be called an ingrate by the three-member Faculty Committee. But those who do not cheat on this exam, and ultimately pass, and have assisted others to learn the material will be called great by the three-member Faculty Committee, and they shall receive a full scholarship to ELU.

Verse 20. "For I say unto you, That except your righteousness shall exceed the righteousness of the scribes and Pharisees, ye shall in no case enter into the kingdom of heaven"—Now listen to what I'm about to say: I'm going to grade the exam on a curve. The lowest score that anyone can receive has to surpass the scribes and Pharisees who have taken the exam already—and clearly flunked it! They've all received a failing grade for the whole semester. You have to score higher than they did or you will not, under any circumstances, enter the next school of higher learning.

Verse 21. "Ye have heard that it was said by them of old time, Thou shalt not kill; and whosoever shall kill shall be in danger of the judgment"—The old textbook from last year said, You shall not kill, and the person who kills someone, depending on the circumstances, shall be susceptible to the death penalty.

Verse 22. "But I say unto you, That whosoever is angry with his brother without a cause shall be in danger of the judgment: and whosoever shall say to his brother, Raca, shall be in danger of the council; but whosoever shall say, Thou fool, shall be in danger of hell fire"—The old textbook is not to be discarded—since it's the foundation for your present book. But to pass today's exam you need to remember the updated material. To wit, if you are angry with anyone without a reason that's the same as murder, and you could be prosecuted as a murderer. And if you angrily curse at your brother, you could be guilty of attempted murder. And if you angrily attack your brother, cursing at him, you can count on a charge of first-degree murder, and probably receive the death penalty.

Verses 23-26 (figuratively spoken by the Professor): To be on the safe side, if you know of someone who has a grudge against you, or you find yourself in an angry dispute with someone that could lead to murder—be smart! Agree with them before you lose your life, or cast into prison on an assault charge. Wherein, you may never get out of that mess you've gotten yourself into because of your anger, and your refusal to apologize.

Based on what I've just said, when the exam begins, I want at least a two-page, handwritten treatment on, Thou shalt not kill. Bad grammar and spelling will count against your score. Before you begin, listen to everything else I have to say.

Verse 27. "Ye have heard that it was said by them of old time, Thou shalt not commit adultery: But I say unto you, That whosoever looketh on a woman to lust after her hath committed adultery with her already in his heart"—The old textbook said that if you're married, you should not sleep around with other women. But to pass today's exam, you must remember that if a man looks at a woman, and wishes he could get in her pants, he has committed adultery with her already by his desire to lie carnally with her.

Verses 29, 30 (paraphrased by the Professor): And if you have trouble controlling what you look at, it would be better—as a constant reminder—to have one eye surgically removed, for it's better to be continually reminded with one eye, than to be eternally lost with two. The same principle applies to your hands, or any other part of your body that causes you not to overcome sin.

Verse 31. "It hath been said, Whosoever shall put away his wife, let him give her a writing of divorcement"—Last year's textbook said, if you want to get rid of the ole lady, just write out an immoral reason, and give it to her, and send her packing!

Verse 32. *"But I say unto you,* That whosoever shall put away his wife, saving for the cause of fornication, causeth her to commit adultery: and whosoever shall marry her that is divorced committeth adultery"—Now listen carefully, what I'm about to say is part of the examination. I want to make it very clear today that the old textbook includes the record of a concessionary law that was instituted solely to bring some peace to a nation of hard-hearted, primarily male Israelites who were determined to commit blatantly sinful acts.

Polygamy was practiced openly, but divorce was as an underground movement that eventually grew powerful enough to force Moses to institute a concession to appease the disobedient, and mitigate their lawlessness. It allowed the hard-hearted to divorce their wives, and their wives to remarry, so that Israel would not be a nation overrun with non-virgin, unmarried women at the mercy of scurrilous men. The Mosaic law gave them a legal right, even if polygamy was involved, to be in another man's home and part of an intact family. She was not subject to merited stoning to death for adultery since remarriage provided a means for her to have sexual intercourse with another man without being guilty of adultery. Under the Mosaic law, she could be forced out of one marriage, and enter another, and retain some respectability in Hebrew society.

Before the concession, men were falsely charging their wives with adultery, even collaborating with other men as witnesses, simply to legally stone them to death, thereby, allowing themselves to remarry under pretense of being outstanding, upright citizens obeying the law of no divorce. The thrust of permitting divorce was to protect women from unwarranted stoning death, and provide for their upkeep in another man's household. It was not to gratify the lusts of dominant men allowing them to often trade in their wives; therefore, after putting away their wives men were not permitted to remarry—not even to his previous wife perchance her subsequent husband(s) had divorced her, or died “for this is abomination before the Lord.” Deut. 24:4.

The reason that men were not allowed to remarry a former wife, who had since married someone else, was to prevent the widespread practice of wife-swapping.

The way it worked, before the Mosaic law, was that the lowest class of polygamists, who married living men’s wives, would select one of their own wives, whom another man desired, and sell her to the other man, who then married her so that he could have legal sex with her. Then after the second man tired of her, or at the end of his alloted time, he sold her back to her previous husband, who remarried her so that he could have legal sex with her again. This was collusion between two men, and a wife could not be sold to a third party. To stop this hideous practice, the new Mosaic law forbade all men from marrying anyone whom they had been previously married to; even if death occurred to terminate her marriage. If any subsequent husband had divorced her, or died, she could seek out another eligible man (willing to marry a living man’s ex-wife) but not anyone whom she had been previously married to. Her previous husband(s) she could not remarry “after that she is defiled.”

Now let me comment on what the new textbook requires: The Mosaic law demanded one area of cause for divorce, and that was sexual immorality, “uncleanness.” The specific offense could be incest or bestiality, and so on, but the offense had to involve some sexual uncleanness. Then the man who sought a divorce had to prove his allegations before a panel of judges, who then always awarded him a divorce, if he had a “creditable” witness. Again, he could not remarry, but the woman was permitted to, since nine times out of ten the servile woman was innocent of any wrongdoing and wholly deserved to be supported in another man’s household.

Matthew 5:32 (Context)

But the recalcitrant Hebrews did not like that law of proving uncleanness; it remained too restrictive, and expensive, for them to conveniently put away their wives. As centuries passed the acceptable custom became that they divorced their wives for any reason that seemed legitimate to them, and remarried at will. When the future generation had arrived where the disciples heard the Sermon on the Mount, the custom was practically an everyday occurrence. But some Jews adhered to one wife, and no divorce for any reason, and no remarriage until the death of a spouse, according to the seventh commandment, as Boaz and Ruth, Abraham, and other obedient ones in the Old Testament had done. But by and large divorce for any reason was the daily norm, with the Pharisees professing obedience to the Mosaic law of proving uncleanness but clandestinely divorcing for any reason—and engaging in the old ritual of wife-swapping.

When the disciples heard, for the first time, their bold Leader reaffirm the Mosaic law of a single cause for divorce, "saving for the cause of fornication," they were dismayed that as voluntary disciples they were included in that affirmation; but it was their Leader's next words that totally went beyond their understanding. Their Leader had said, "Whosoever shall put away his wife, saving for the cause of fornication . . ." They understood that: fornication or adultery, which was now the same thing according to His expanded definition, was valid grounds for divorce, as the Mosaic law stated.

Then He said, "*causeth her to commit adultery*." The disciples thought—What the heck does that mean? Causeth her to commit adultery?! He can't lay that awful sin of hers on me! If she committed adultery, she did it of her own self, and deserves to be stoned to death. I wouldn't have any trouble gettin' the fella's to testify against her—and she's outta my house!

Then the disciples heard their Leader say all that He had to say on divorce, that day. He concluded with, "And whosoever shall marry her that is divorced committeth adultery"—And He was done with divorce!

The disciples surely felt shortchanged since He hadn't talked enough about the husband, *them,* and the comment He had made seemed to only concentrate on the wife—especially if she was divorced, for any reason, as the Pharisees did. He had not provided them with a clear-cut understanding on divorce. As they heard Him going ahead on His next subject, which was oaths, their minds were still preoccupied with the guilt He had laid on them, by insinuating that they could *cause* their wives to commit adultery—as though they had any control over what their wives did behind their backs!

I want, at the very least, a four-page handwritten treatment on, Thou shalt not commit adultery. Don't neglect to include *"Causeth her to commit adultery,"* in your submission. Bad grammar, inept spelling, and writing with large letters to take up page space will count against your score. What I've asked you to write is the entire exam. After you pass in your papers, you may leave. For your information, fornication is the area of the exam where the scribes and Pharisees fouled up the most. It's not the amount of pages in the book, but the amount of Book in the pages—Good luck!

When everyone was finished with the exam, some laboring to the end of the extra 30-minutes they were given, and all of the papers were turned in, the Professor took the exams away to grade them. After five days had elapsed, the students who had successfully passed the exam found their grades posted on the Professor's website, using their student ID number and password to access their private page. The student, John L. Mark, received an "A" on his final semester exam for the class, Sermon on the Mount 101. The following is the response he submitted in writing on the exam topic, "Thou shalt not commit adultery."

Concurrent with the theme of faithful obedience, everything that Jesus Christ said in the Sermon on the Mount was a call to His disciples to rise above the humdrum of what is acceptable humanitarianism, to a much higher standard of interplay with their fellowman.

Matthew 5:32 (Context)

When Jesus spoke, "Blessed are they which do hunger and thirst after righteousness: for they shall be filled," Matthew 5:6, it was a clear message to me, too, to carefully investigate every motive that drives all of my actions, to determine whether or not I'm hungering and thirsting after righteousness.

I do not naturally hunger after righteousness. It is just as natural for me to sin without a second thought as it is to breath. So for me to become aware of sin in myself, I have to continually look to Jesus to supply me with an image of what is true righteousness. Then, after I have identified transgression in myself, I must sincerely want to change, to reflect the image of Jesus. He has promised me that He will supply all of the grace, which is also power, and the Holy Spirit that I need so that I may make conscious efforts to treat my fellowman as He would in every area of my life.

When Jesus spoke all of the Beatitudes in the Sermon on the Mount, I'm reminded of another one that I should aspire to, besides all of them, which says, "Blessed are the peacemakers: for they shall be called the children of God." Verse 9. This verse causes me to look especially at my home life, away from school. I question myself: Is Jesus living through me, so that I may be an instrument in His hands to foster harmony in my family, or do I bring about ferment and division? Again, unconscionable disruptive behavior is as natural to me, a sinner, as chewing food. Am I allowing Jesus Christ to be a good neighbor through me? A good citizen? Not just avoiding mishaps, but rising above the ordinary—actively seeking to be a peacemaker so that I, too, may be among those who "shall be called the children of God."

My intention is to follow Jesus Christ for as long as I live. One of my likelihoods, as I continue living, is to get married. Regarding marriage, I realize that the varied customs of the world today are contrary to lasting marriages. But the world is not seeking to please Jesus, as I am; therefore, when I see events in the world that are not in keeping with God's high calling for me, I stay away from those events, actions, or lifestyles. And, I'm aware that to the carnal world I may appear out of touch—for example, seeking to maintain my virginity, and to marry a virgin—even very odd, openly susceptible to derision, as the Pharisees derided Jesus; but I keep in mind that, "Blessed are ye, when men shall revile you and persecute you, and shall say all manner of evil against you falsely, for my sake. Rejoice, and be exceeding glad: for great is your reward in heaven: for so persecuted they the prophets which were before you." Verses 11, 12. These verses plainly say to me that what is pleasing in God's sight—worthy of an eternal reward—is foolishness to the world that is blinded by Satan's deceptions.

I receive a great deal of junk email, especially from dating services advertising mates. The women are usually very attractive, who, if I ever met them in my church, I would definitely be interested. But the fact that they have placed themselves on an Internet dating service to conveniently meet someone, with aspirations of marriage, lets me know that they regard marriage as a cattle-call, where they pick the best side of beef and hope that he tastes good, so that they might become interested in developing an ongoing relationship. So, if I get involved with this lifestyle—there departs my virginity, and likely she herself never met me as a virgin—so both of my higher aspirations that were pleasing to God are gone!

In Biblical periods, and not many years back in our modern day, virginity was the greatest personal asset that two loving people could bring to a marriage. Today, however, virginity is regarded as nothing of value to bring to a marriage, and worthy to be scoffed at, discouraged, and even prevented—what foolishness!

Persons who actively date around, attempting to find the best soul-mate, generally have no idea what successfully holds most marriages together. Sex with one person before marriage, or sleeping around with whomever seems attractive, for men and women, is a sign of total disregard or ignorance of what God demands of marriage.

Persons who sleep together prior to marriage have already, before it has begun, cut in half the chances for their union to be a lifelong relationship. Any marriage that follows premarital sex is prematurely headed for ruin. This is a rule embodied in the human makeup wherein the impact of sin has fostered conflict between God and man. Jehovah demands purity of body, which is part of His image in mankind. When sin is willfully indulged in, such as premarital sex, it further separates woeful man from Jehovah, and reduces the possibility of Jehovah manifesting Himself through the individuals. Hence the nature of sin guides the resulting marriage toward ruin and, ultimately, another broken relationship follows. Persons have no self-control over this rule, except to surely avoid sinful activity both before and after marriage.

At the creation, in the Garden of Eden, when God declared, "Therefore shall a man leave his father and his mother, and shall cleave unto his wife: and they shall be one flesh," Genesis 2:24, He meant that a man should enter his first marriage relationship as a virgin. A man should go from a birth to maturity environment with his parents, directly into a lifelong marriage relationship with his wife. There should be no sowing of wild oats between his parental upbringing and his first marriage. Any oats that are sown, God demands, must be with his wife. This is a high calling for a *man* to maintain his virginity until he finds a wife—it matters not the amount of time that elapses between him leaving "his father and his mother" and getting married.

What God requires, virginity in men before marriage, is the exact opposite of what is imposed upon men by worldly custom (such is the ferment of sin). From their childhood, boys are encouraged to investigate sexual activity and "score" on a girl as soon as the opportunity arises. The more conquests they achieve in the sexual arena the more boys are admired in modern society. By the time they are men, and married, it is next to impossible to defeat the ingrained urge to cheat on their wife—because all of their life, before marriage, this is what they have been well-trained to do! The act of marriage cannot rip out a trait that, before marriage, a man was admired and idolized for.

Indeed, women sought to date him because he was desired by other women. Many times the woman who married him did so because she beat out the other women who wanted him. Then when his uncontrollable urge to have other women is manifested, divorce follows, the family is shattered, and another nail is driven into the coffin of the breakdown of society. Women who marry sexually active men are marrying a cheating time bomb, since his mind is geared from youth to desire more than one woman. Practically everything he absorbs from modern media is aggressively guiding him to cheat.

Whereas, if a man enters a marriage as Jehovah intended him to—a virgin—his sensual experience takes place with his wife, which becomes his expectation for sexual fulfillment, and he naturally stays home to receive it. His chances for remaining faithful to his wife are greatly enhanced because now love for his wife is working in conjunction with the self-discipline that helped him to marry as a virgin, and the two harmonious forces working together are a powerful incentive to remain faithful to his wife. Combine this with his trust in Jesus Christ, to receive eternal life if he is a dutiful husband, and this is a man who possesses the integrity to survive in a lifelong marriage.

The conscious attitude that women project toward men produces a deliberate response in women that is conducive to a man becoming attracted to her. For instance, if a young woman sees a young man and she feels that she would like to meet him, possibly date him on a regular basis, her attitude toward him is interest in becoming aquainted with him. Her next thought is what does this young man like in women? Does she herself fall into the category of women he may desire? She then begins to evaluate herself—if she has what it takes to capture his positive attention. To make this final decision she has to closely observe him, to see if she can determine what he approves of in women. If she subsequently becomes aware that he esteems women who wear short skirts, tight belly-button pants and low-cut tops, she begins to dress that way too, because she perceives that this is what he looks for in women. Her attitude toward him has determined how she may make herself attractive to him.

Expand this scenario to a national level, and it can be seen that most women who dress provocatively do so because modern society has relegated men to a very sexually active lifestyle. And women who desire to be attractive to men, and ultimately marry, must appeal to this premarital expectation of sex in men. So women dress accordingly—in a highly seductive manner—to appeal to sexually active men.

On the contrary, if a woman's attitude toward a man is that he values celibacy, and wants to remain chaste until he is married, her whole method of becoming attractive to him changes. Instead of overly concentrating on her outward appearance, she begins to evaluate ways that she may appeal to him that rises above just sex. First, if she's like-minded, she wants to agree with his goal to remain a virgin, therefore, she dresses attractively, but not overly providing him with sexual stimulus. If he is a healthy man, she will know if he is sexually attracted to her. From this type of beginning—a meeting where virginity and celibacy are important to both individuals—a lasting marriage has a valid chance to prosper because self-control, an important ingredient in marriage, has been a part of their maturing lifestyle and premarital dating.

Today, all the emphasis (what little there is that still remains) is heaped on women to maintain a higher degree of sexual respectability before marriage. However, while this is good and right behavior by women—to be virgins along with men—it is the man in Scripture who bears the weight of responsibility to be an example for his wife, and society.

Truly, God directed the man, in the Garden of Eden, to go and "cleave unto his wife."

Indeed, it was Adam’s sin, not the woman’s, which plunged the earth into chaos.

Customarily it’s men who bear the responsibility of being a protector of women.

It’s men who ordinarily ask for women in marriage.

It’s men who are primarily heads of households.

It’s men who, also, bear the responsibility of entering into marriage as virgins.

Men have no more natural privilege of sleeping around than do women. When men alter their lifestyle, to include virginity and celibacy, most thoughtful women will change their methods of becoming attractive to men, thereby advancing society to a better model of conduct than is common today.

Nowadays, all of the impetus for staying in a marriage union is based on happiness. Happiness has become the standard that people strive for when they consider whom to marry. Will he or she be happy with their combined incomes? Will they be happy with the appearance of the kids? Will they be happy with where their incomes determine that they will live? Will they be happy with their class of friends? Will they be happy after they are old? Happiness is an important factor in marriage, and should not be discounted, but it’s not happiness that holds marriages together. Obedience to all of Jehovah’s commandments is the cement that permanently holds marriages together. Happiness is a variable, which may be present for a time, and not present for long periods of time. Obedience to God is constant, and can be counted on to carry one through any periods of emotional variations that may arise in marriage, and in life.

God did not create several women for Adam, He created one woman and she was to be his lifelong partner. Even after they had increased the human family in number she was to remain his only “help.” One woman for one man was the way that God set up the one-flesh union between a man and a woman, and His method of maintaining that union today, marriage, is still the *only* means by which persons may have sexual intimacy without committing sin. Happiness in marriage is great, and should be present; but far and above happiness is obedience to God's commandments—this is what keeps marriages together. And God will bless a couple in many ways they can't imagine, including happiness, when their motive for marriage, and staying married, is to please Him.

Without casting aside all the textbook niceties of marriage: propagation of the human race, family units, emotional growth, and the like—the absolute essence of marriage is to avoid the sin of adultery! In Scripture, before Adam and Eve had sinned, marriage was the essential requirement to avoid the sin of adultery in their sexual relations. Since there was no sin, so long as they maintained a faithful "one flesh" relationship marriage was the method whereby their sensual enjoyment in increasing the human family continued sinless. Indeed, after sin had entered, marriage remained paramount to circumvent the sin of adultery.

Outside of holy matrimony, sex, for any reason, or by any method, is transgression. God would surely rather eternally save persons unhappily married, celibate, or virgin, than lose them happily living in sin. Jesus gave a lasting clue regarding how essential it is to resist sin when He said, "If thy right eye offend thee, pluck it out . . . If thy right hand offend thee, cut it off . . . It is profitable for thee that one of thy members should perish, and not that thy whole body should be cast into hell."

As Jesus taught His disciples in the Sermon on the Mount, he spoke briefly on divorce. But, all things considered, He didn't speak briefly! Taking into acount their later questions to Him, centered on themselves, in other parts of the Gospels, they only heard Him briefly, not at all comprehending His limited words. They didn't recall all He had said, before speaking on divorce, about rising to a *higher* standard of obedience to God's way of doing things. If they had heard, "Blessed are they which are persecuted for righteousness' sake: for theirs is the kingdom of heaven," they would have perceived that to be persecuted for righteousness implies a calling out by Jesus to be righteous. Especially regarding divorcing their wives.

"Except"

When Jesus said, "Whosoever shall put away his wife, saving for the cause of fornication, causeth her to commit adultery," verse 32, they should have heard—Whosoever shall put away his wife, and the reason has *not* been for fornication, this *causeth* her to commit adultery.

This was an open call to not seize on grounds to divorce their wives, lawful and unlawful, as the Pharisees did, but to seize on Godly meekness, and look for reasons to stay in the marriage. The right motive for all the disciples of Jesus, that's in keeping with all the Beatitudes, was to seek out the highest standard of marital conduct, for, "except your righteousness shall exceed the righteousness of the scribes and Pharisees, ye shall in no case enter into the kingdom of heaven." Verse 20.

What Jesus was teaching His disciples was that divorcing their wives according to the custom of the day, for any reason, placed her on the doorstep of hellfire, and their hearts were no less hardened than the Pharisees. And even though their wives may have committed adultery, already, and they themselves hadn't caused this valid grounds for divorce to occur that they should look far beyond what they have a legal right to do—to an action that was well-pleasing to God, and harmonious with their high calling as disciples.

When Jesus said "*causeth* her to commit adultery," causeth is the word that should have engendered humility in His disciples, which would have provided them with a desire to assist their wives toward righteousness, rather than being the stumbling-block to their destruction. Jesus was encouraging them to lay aside their traditional advantage over their wives, even, by the concession, having lawful cause for divorce and consider for a moment what they were doing to her, virtually forcing her to commit. And because they were "one flesh,"—that even adultery couldn't separate—at what they were doing to themselves.

As Jesus spoke about what divorce would cause their wives to commit—adultery—He was appealing to a higher sense of forgiveness in them, and He was referring directly to the day in which they were living. For instance, today, when women are more overtly independent, divorce would not necessarily cause a woman to commit adultery. Adultery would occur, of course, if she remarried, or fornicated. But a sincere Christian woman can live quite independent of a man, and many chaste Christian women do, and live the balance of their natural lives without committing the sin of adultery.

But in the Biblical epoch, that the Sermon on the Mount took place, citizenship for single, non-virgin women was an entirely different matter. Under the Mosaic law, if a woman's husband divorced her, and she was not then stoned for adultery, her first objective to support herself was to become a married member of another household—thus committing spiritual adultery (fulfilling "causeth" as Jesus had said). Her choice after that was base prostitution—thus committing public adultery. And if her looks were not conducive to selling her body, her next choice was beggar-woman. So for a man to put away his wife, as the Pharisees were doing, was an indication that she was a sexually corrupt woman, or her husband was devoid of any regard for the well-being of his wife, children, or society—a hard-hearted trait that was wholly unacceptable for a disciple of Jesus.

So Jesus was saying to His disciples, appealing to their high calling as His gospel emissaries, that even though they may have perfect grounds for divorce—and definitely if not, and they were following the example of the Pharisees—to take a closer look at the horrible outcome of their actions. Jesus was asking them, could they follow Him, and proclaim a gospel of pure love to the world; and could they reveal Him through themselves when they had been, and continually were, such a willful stumbling-block in someone else's life. Better for His disciples to never forget, "Blessed are the merciful: for they shall obtain mercy," verse 7, than to exercise their license to divorce, or divorce for selfish reasons. Jesus could not instruct any lesser mind set in His disciples with respect to the compassionate treatment of their wives, for He Himself was the greatest Mercy that heaven could bestow on sinful, unworthy, mankind's behalf.

And then after all the societal and spiritual damage they had engendered in their wives by putting them away, really contemplate what she does to the person who may unwarily marry her: "And whosoever shall marry her that is divorced committeth adultery." This Biblical fact spoken by Jesus is for every epoch of time, and summarily applies to all human beings—and all the desperate maneuvering by the disobedient, from Adam through today, by way of religions, traditions, compromises, fault-finding, customs, mis-education and well-meant but erroneous counsel has not altered in the slightest way the Godly demands of, Thou shalt not commit adultery. Only death, not divorce law, ends a marriage. Those who divorce and remarry, contrary to the plain teachings of Jesus, are living in a state of adultery, both spouses; and if one of them should die in adultery, "the wages of sin is death." Judgment, and then permanent death.

Whenever I marry, I earnestly pray that I will marry a woman who wants to follow Jesus as steadfastly as I do. And we will stay married happy, or usually seeking help, because we intend to be obedient to the loftiest standards of God's unchangeable commandment of "Thou shalt not commit adultery," and God will not fail to eternally reward us for our fidelity to Him.

Faithfulness to the highest standards of Christian love, and loyalty to wives and mankind are the lessons in Jesus' Sermon on the Mount when He spoke these words: "Whosoever shall put away his wife, saving for the cause of fornication, *causeth* her to commit adultery: and whosoever shall marry her that is divorced committeth adultery."

I solemnly pledge to remain dedicated to my marriage and never divorce, though it may be permissible and expedient, and certainly not perform any act that causes my wife to fall into sexual immorality, nor anyone she may encounter; but I shall endeavor to perform—always— that which is righteous and compassionate in the mind of God.

John L. Mark #787632908

9

Luke 16:18 (Context)

THE parable of the Rich Man and Lazarus, starting at Luke 16:19, was told by Jesus to the hard-hearted Pharisees as a direct result of His previous conversation with them, verses 14-18, regarding divorcing their wives. The story was intended to firmly convict the Pharisees of sin: that no matter what Jesus Himself said, not even after His Messiah-ship was confirmed by his subsequent resurrection ("neither will they be persuaded, though one rose from the dead"), if they were not going to obey Moses and the Prophets nothing was going to convince them that they were base sinners in need of repentance.

As He began His final attempt, before the Lazarus parable, to convince them of the utter sinfulness of their outward piety His perspicacious acuity—"But God knoweth your hearts"—had determined that the best route to pierce their stubbornness was to address their most secret sin, that of lasciviousness, in the matter of divorce.

The Pharisees had a habit of passing themselves off to others as the most learned and obedient to the Mosaic law. They had taught the masses that the epitome of earthly success was to live rich and act proud, as they did, with the favor of God being the justification for their lifestyle. But their private lives, away from the temple, abounded with adultery and sensual pleasure of every variety. From the beginning of His conversation on divorce Jesus wanted them to know that He was not fooled by their outward show, and His first words to them were, "Ye are they which justify yourselves before men; but God knoweth your hearts." Luke 16:15. Then He let them know the true extent of their favor in God's site—since they were convinced of the self-righteousness of their conduct—that nothing they thought or performed rose beyond their own foreheads, for, "that which is highly esteemed among men is abomination in the sight of God." The Pharisees knew that the implication of their conduct, which Jesus described as an *"abomination,"* was a reference to the Mosaic law, in which Moses had sought to halt their ancestor's wife-swapping by preventing them from twice marrying the same woman. The Pharisees knew then that Jesus was privy to all of their insider trading.

Then Jesus said, in verse 16, "The law and the prophets were until John: since that time the kingdom of God is preached, and every man presseth into it." Jesus was informing the Pharisees that the Mosaic law, up until John the Baptist, was a sufficient goal for their attainment but after John, what Jesus preached was to take precedence over anything in the Mosaic commandments. And He knew that everyone already felt qualified, by their own works, to receive all that Jesus taught.

After Jesus had stated His preeminence in the realm of Godly obedience, He led the Pharisees to a knowledge of which law He expected them to continually aspire to by referring to the eternal law of Ten Commandments. He said, "And it is easier for heaven and earth to pass, than one tittle of the law to fail." (This was not an exaggeration, but a fact.)

Now they were sufficiently reproved to hear His specific grievance with them—their coveted sins of adultery, which they thought were hidden from everyone but their inner-circle of self-righteous, hard-hearted scribes and other Pharisees. And what they were doing was violating the unchangeable law of God, and they could not escape the penalty of their transgression except by repentance. He plainly stated the pure law, with no reference to cause, since they were disregarding the Mosaic law anyway, and divorcing for any reason. Cause was irrelevant since there was no innocent party. He said to them, straight out—"Whosoever putteth away his wife, and marrieth another, committeth adultery: and whosoever marrieth her that is put away from her husband committeth adultery." Luke 16:18.

Then, after He had provided them with the unadulterated Ten Commandments law respecting divorce and remarriage He progressed directly into the parable of Lazarus, to unequivocally let them know that because their hearts were hardened to the point of only seeking cause to kill him—that nothing was going to dissuade them from their course.

In the story the rich man, speaking from hell, asked Abraham to send Lazarus, "that he may dip the tip of his finger in water," (seems there was some water in *this* hell!) and slightly cool the rich man's tongue. Abraham replied, from "afar off"—No! He couldn't send Lazarus to hell. (Afar off could not have been literal heaven, since when Abraham died he "received not the promise." Hebrews 11:39, 40.) Then the rich man pleaded that if Lazarus couldn't come to hell, to send him to the five brothers of the rich man (who were adulterers) to warn them, so that they wouldn't die in sin and "also come into this place of torment." Then Abraham told the rich man that his living brothers had "Moses and the prophets," and if they truly obeyed what they instructed, that would keep them out of hell's torment. The rich man cried from hell, "Nay, father Abraham." By his urgent, negative response, the rich man was informing Abraham that Moses and the Prophets, evidently, were not sufficient motivation for his brothers to give up wife-swapping, but if someone came to them from the dead—that would definitely *scare* them into repentance.

The scribes and the Pharisees claim to respectability in Israel was their proclamation of the Mosaic law, saying that God had judiciously replaced Moses with them. And they loved to dress ostentatiously, pray in public, and be called rabbi. But Jesus knew their true religion of disobedience, and He pierced their dark veil to the depth of their hard heartedness by the final verse in the parable, the moral of the story directed at their adulterous behavior, saying, "If they hear not Moses and the prophets, neither will they be persuaded, though one (Himself) rose from the dead." Luke 16:31.

Some will thoughtfully study what Jesus said in Luke 16:18, "Whosoever putteth away his wife, and marrieth another, committeth adultery: and whosoever marrieth her that is put away from her husband committeth adultery," and simply conclude that there is an innocent party in this law on divorce—the one that is put away. They are right! The one put away is not guilty of adultery *so long as they do not remarry.* In keeping with the Mosaic law, which Jesus upheld, civil divorce does not constitute adultery. Remarriage subsequent to divorce, "and marrieth another," is the sin of adultery—for both parties to the divorce. Divorce does not end, "what God hath joined together." Cause for civil divorce has no affect on determining spiritual adultery. Remarriage does!

If it were possible for the one put away, the innocent one, to slip under the sin of adultery should they remarry, they are then certainly, potentially guilty of premeditated murder—since they have allowed someone to commit adultery, by becoming their husband or wife. And perchance their spouse should die while in the marriage, their spouse has died in sin and the innocent one murdered them into eternal death by permitting their illicit marriage to take place. And if the innocent one should slip under murder, idolatry certainly looms ahead—since the other person whom they wished to marry, and married, was valued higher than keeping all the commandments of God—which is idolatry. "Thou shalt have no other gods before me." Exodus 20:3. There are no innocent ones for couples who divorce and *remarry* while a spouse is living. Cause for divorce is not a mitigating factor.

Luke 16:18 (Context)

Note: All that Jesus spoke on divorce agrees. Just the emphasis varies to include both principals and any third party.

Jesus On Divorce Emphasis Texts

Principals: Doer, and Done To.

Cause and Doer . . . . Matt. 19:9
Doer and Foolish (who marries Doer) . . . . Luke 16:18
Done To and Foolish (who marries Done To). . .Matt. 5:32
Doer Man or Woman . . . . .Mark 10:11, 12

Jesus On Divorce Texts:
<u>Matthew 19:9.</u>
And I say unto you, Whosoever shall put away his wife, except it be for fornication, and shall marry another, committeth adultery: and whoso marrieth her which is put away doth commit adultery.

<u>Luke 16:18.</u>
Whosoever putteth away his wife, and marrieth another, committeth adultery: and whosoever marrieth her that is put away from her husband committeth adultery.

<u>Matthew 5:32.</u>
But I say unto you, That whosoever shall put away his wife, saving for the cause of fornication, causeth her to commit adultery: and whosoever shall marry her that is divorced committeth adultery.

<u>Mark 10:11, 12.</u>
And He saith unto them, Whosoever shall put away his wife, and marry another, committeth adultery against her. And if a woman shall put away her husband, and be married to another, she committeth adultery.

Matthew 19:6.
Wherefore they are no more twain, but one flesh. What therefore God hath joined together, let not man put asunder.

God On Divorce Texts:
Genesis 2:24.
Therefore shall a man leave his father and his mother, and shall cleave unto his wife: and they shall be one flesh.

Exodus 20:14.
Thou shalt not commit adultery (by fornication or remarriage after divorce).

Malachi 2:16.
For the Lord, the God of Israel, saith that He hateth putting away (divorce): for one covereth violence with his garment, saith the Lord of hosts: therefore take heed to your spirit, that ye deal not treacherously.

Moses On Divorce Texts (Mosaic law):
Deuteronomy 24:1-4.
When a man hath taken a wife and married her, and it come to pass that she find no favour in his eyes, because he hath found some uncleanness in her: then let him write her a bill of divorcement, and give it in her hand, and send her out of his house. And when she is departed out of his house, she may go and be another man's wife. And if the latter husband hate her, and write her a bill of divorcement, and giveth it in her hand, and sendeth her out of his house; or if the latter husband die, which took her to be his wife, her former husband, which sent her away, may not take her again to be his wife, after that she is defiled; for this is abomination before the Lord: and thou shalt not cause the land to sin, which the Lord thy God giveth thee for an inheritance.

Luke 16:18 (Context)

Paul On Divorce Texts:

<u>Romans 7:2, 3.</u>

For the woman which hath an husband is bound by the law to her husband so long as he liveth; but if the husband be dead, she is loosed from the law of her husband. So then if, while her husband liveth, she be married to another man, she shall be called an adulteress: but if her husband be dead, she is set free from that law; so that she is no adulteress, though she be married to another man.

<u>1 Corinthians 7:10, 11.</u>

And unto the married I command you, yet not I, but the Lord, Let not the wife depart from her husband. But and if she depart, let her remain unmarried, or be reconciled to her husband: and let not the husband put away his wife.

<u>1 Corinthians 7:13-15.</u>

And the woman which hath an husband that believeth not, and if he be pleased to dwell with her, let her not leave him. For the unbelieving husband is sanctified by the wife, and the unbelieving wife is sanctified by the husband: else were your children unclean; but now they are holy. But if the unbelieving depart, let him depart. A brother or a sister is not under bondage in such cases: but God hath called us to peace.

<u>1 Corinthians 7:27.</u>

Art thou bound unto a wife? Seek not to be loosed. Art thou loosed from a wife? Seek not a wife.

<u>1 Corinthians 7:39, 40.</u>

The wife is bound by the law as long as her husband liveth; but if her husband be dead, she is at liberty to be married to whom she will; only in the Lord. But she is happier if she so abide, after my judgment: and I think also that I have the Spirit of God.

10

Divorce: Episode Two

ADON sat staring at his computer screen, reading over and over the short email message from Jewel.

"Hi, Adonis. If you can spare the time, I would love to see you. I have something special that I want to discuss with you. Let me know. Jewel."

He read it over again. Attempting to read between the lines, to venture a guess at what was behind the message. He had not seen Jewel in over three years, and during that time he had only spoken to her over the telephone, briefly, regarding Princess' medicine and graduation from high school.

When their separation had first occurred his troubled mind was constantly overflowing with words he desired to say to her—words he should have said the last time that they talked—words he would say the next time. He had even made notes. But three years had passed without being in her presence, and he felt that he was finally able to reclaim his thoughts, and keep her out of his mind.

He read it again.

She never uses the word love, he thought; her emails are always dry, short, and to the point. Not even caring to sign her name. But, there they are—love, *and* her name! What must she want?

On various occasions, when Princess was sick, she would

simply write, "Princess = medicine. Call me!" And leave her work number. But this time there was *nothing* about Princess.

She asked me if I had the time, he mused. That, coming from Jewel, a kind consideration of my feelings, outside of her own demands upon me, is unusual, too.

He decided right then to email her back, and not try anymore to figure out her motive for writing him. He clicked on Reply, and the message box appeared. He typed: "Hi, Jewel: I was surprised, as usual, to hear from you. Hope everything is okay. Tell me what's on your mind. Adon." He clicked on Send, and the screen reverted back to her message.

The time and return address on her email indicated that she had sent it from work, so he didn't expect to receive a response to his reply until the next day, and he would see it when he himself arrived home from work, around 5:30 P.M. He exited his email, and turned off the computer.

While Adon and Jewel were married, she had very seldom cooked, unless it was a dish to take to someone, or a requirement from her job for a festivity dish. He was fortunate to have church friends who regularly brought food to eat together on various Sabbath afternoons. He and Jewel had a large home, so space to accommodate many people was not a problem. He and Jewel's friends routinely left desserts, crunchy casseroles and spicy vegetables at his home, so there was usually food in the refrigerator. Then, after he had started the business, he was not home much around dinner time so weekdays' food at home became even more of a rarity. Jewel was a good cook, and had she not worked full-time everyday, he suspected she would have enjoyed exercising more of her culinary talents.

However, he himself coming from a large family, his mother had always been at home, and she cooked, and between meal snacks were strictly forbidden because they took away food that could be used for the family meal. If he missed dinner prepared for the whole family, it was too bad, until breakfast, which, by that time, it was imperative that he was first at the table. His mother made sure that a hearty breakfast made up for the dinner he had missed. He knew, from gut-growling experience, why the first meal of the day was called, break-fast.

Growing up, his time spent in the kitchen was to drink water. He had never learned to cook—he had no interest in learning to cook. He didn't like the feel of heavy juices, flour and cooking oil on his hands. Car grease, and outside grime were fine, but not cooking stuff.

When he was hungry, now that he was single again, it was just as satisfying to throw a peanut butter and jelly sandwich together, and eat that, rather than go through the misfortunes of trying to prepare a meal. He could boil spaghetti, and cook a pot of beans, but that was about the extent of his cooking.

However, spaghetti was still somewhat of a challenge. He hadn't figured out, yet, how to cook enough for just himself. It seemed that no matter how little he broke in thirds, and put into the pot, when it was done cooking it was always enough for ten people. He had even bought a smaller pot, one half the size of the one he had replaced; but then, instead of serving ten, he had cooked enough for five—and he was already using the smallest pot sold for home use.

His refrigerator was consistently stocked with plenty of cold water, orange juice, and sandwich bread. Those items took up all the shelf space. Then the door was crammed with mustard, ketchup, barbeque sauce, pickles, mayonnaise—and half empty bottles of salad dressing. He had a weakness for buying salad dressing. In his kitchen cabinets he had a collection of every flavor. All that Kraft sold. All that Newman's Own sold. He was actively resisting the urge to lower himself to buying the cheaper supermarket brands. He had his pride to consider! He was not a collector, since he planned to eat every dressing that he bought; he just, as he stood in the supermarket aisle savoring the flavors, thought that he wouldn't have to worry about ever running out, if he went ahead and bought it then. When he opened his cabinets, he admitted that there was probably not enough years left in his life to run out.

Because of his dread of cooking, he seldom had more than one food item at a time on his plate, and he ate that every day until he was tired of it. He ate spaghetti with mushroom sauce for a solid week, then switched to black-eyed peas. He ate black-eyed peas until they were all gone; then he switched to collard greens. He ate out everyday until his conscience bothered him, wasting all that money, then he ate at home again, and so on.

The next day, after he had arrived home from work, he turned on his computer. Jewel had been on his mind all day, again. He didn't relish the idea of being in another relationship with her, and her parents—"Divorce me once, shame on you; divorce me twice, shame on me!" But he still had deep feelings for Jewel.

Early in their marriage, Adon had tenderly accepted Jewel's annoying faults as part of her personality makeup, and he loved her much more than her faults annoyed him. In bed, sleeping, she snored like loud thunder, and he had been awakened many times, but he never mentioned it because he realized it was something she was not aware of, and he put his pillow over his head, and went back to sleep.

Outside of sex itself, she was not affectionate, and this was something that he really missed in her, but, again, to him they were married for life, and he loved her more than he missed the moments where he wanted her spur of the moment tenderness. She had a lot of admirable qualities, too, that, if she could have ever broken away from her parents, she might have been more inclined to freely share with him.

Seventeen years with Jewel had engraved her on his mind, and even though he didn't like her, he still loved her, and regretted they had forfeited the chance they had to weather the storm of their difficulties, which is what brings married couples closer together. He missed that kind of growth in love for himself and Jewel. He felt that, long before their divorce, she had given up on him too quickly. He could have eventually been everything she wanted in a husband, if she had put God's holy commandments and her sacred marriage vows first, and stayed in the marriage.

He was practicing celibacy, and although he had frequent sexual desires he knew that it would not only be a sin to sleep with women, but it would also become another hindrance for a reunion between himself and Jewel. Turning off the TV for long periods of time (until football season) he found, greatly assisted him in not being overly burdened with thoughts of sex.

From his keyboard, he went to the Internet, and left clicked on the envelope icon that brought up his email page. He typed in his password, then watched the email messages flow into his Inbox. He wondered how they selected who to send the Viagra junk mail to. Did women receive as much as he did? The last thing he needed, he thought, was Viagra. There it was, Jewel's message! The last one to pop in. He hesitated, before clicking on it.

In the past he had tried to communicate with her by email, but he found that it was too nerve-racking for him—knowing that she could respond, within several minutes, but usually it would take weeks for her to write him back. And when she did, she had neglected to follow up on their last conversation, when he had thought of practically nothing else but hearing from her. Rushing home everyday to turn on his computer, and finding nothing there, from her—it was just too nerve-racking—so he gave up trying to communicate with her through email. But this time, she had written him right back—What must she want?

He clicked on her message line. He read:

"Hi, Adonis: Thanks for writing me back. . . ." Why was she addressing him by his full name, he thought; she never did that unless she was in a mood for lovemaking. He read on: "I can't tell you by email what I want to say, because it's personal, and I don't want a record of it on my computer. And a phone call, well, I know how you hate to talk on the phone. Believe me, in this case, seeing you is better. Love, Jewel."

He leaned back in his chair, his cold fingers interlaced behind his head. Could he dare to think that she could be considering making up with him. She still had not apologized for the nasty way she had divorced him. But, maybe, she had finally come to her senses, and realized that what they had together was worth attempting to save. Right then, when buried hope seemed possible, he was really glad that he had not slept with anyone since he and Jewel were intimate, three weeks before she left him.

After being married for so long, being a single man was hard work. He wondered if Jewel was finding it just as unpleasant being single as he was. He had loved being married. He especially liked the idea of having someone close by that was meant just for him. He liked not attending social functions alone. He liked not having to be constantly concerned with chance meeting someone, evaluating every woman that he saw, wondering if they were married, and, if not, going through the maze of getting to know them. Then, finding that she was just another one he didn't like enough to call back.

But, he had found Jewel, and she was his, and he loved her. He was proud of her quiet beauty, and he loved being in public places with her. She had excellent taste in clothes, her own and his, and he could trust her to purchase clothes for him as gifts, even neck-ties. She was always clean and freshly scented every day, and tenaciously kept her personal appearance up. She made him feel that he was necessary to someone's happiness, and he loved being there during those moments when she (seemingly) wanted to confide only in him.

But he was single now, and he had recently noticed that he was not as particular about the way he dressed. While he was married, he had never gone over two weeks without a haircut—but now he was whacking it himself, with scissors, and it had been over six months since he had seen a professional barber; and his white shirts were not going to the laundry as often. The starched collars had gotten wrinkled, and a little too brown. But he wore them anyway, thinking that nobody really cared what he looked like.

“Except”

To him, women seemed to have a sixth sense, and they could somehow tell when a man doesn’t have a wife at home.

One of his female co-workers had told him, one morning in the parking lot after he had arrived at work, that his sport coat collar looked better if he turned it down—before he left home. And she knew it was quite easy to forget, going out the door, *alone*, every morning. Then she motherly turned him around, and turned down his coat collar. That simple act by her stayed with him all day. The slight attention she had given him, just in that brief moment of turning down his coat collar, felt so good to him. Her small hands were affectionate against his body; her tender voice was soft, and reassuring; she smelled clean and fresh, with a tantalizing scent of White Linen perfume. The scent of her stayed in his nostrils all day, too, along with the memory of her touch. The next morning, with his coat collar down, and a clean shirt, he looked for her in the parking lot.

She drove up, after he had backed his car into an empty space, and parked four spaces away. He left his car, and walked over to her car, on the near driver’s side, before she had turned off the engine. She rolled down her window, and warmly smiled up at him.

“Good morning,” she said, first.

The previous day he had hardly gotten a good look at her, he was so surprised at what she had done, and she had turned and walked off without holding a conversation with him. However, all day he had kind of remembered what she looked like, but he wasn’t sure. He had never seen her at work before.

“Good morning,” he replied, “mind if I wait for you to get out?” Without answering, her window went up, she shut off the engine, turned her body toward the door, and got out. He added, “I saw you drive up. And I didn’t get a chance, yesterday, to thank you for keeping me looking respectable.”

“Oh, you don’t have to thank me for that. It was my pleasure. I see you’re looking in top shape, this morning.”

He saw that her figure was streamline. Her above-the-knee

skirt was fitting close, to complement her appealing shape. She was wearing black high heel shoes and sheer nylon stockings that gave her well-sculptured legs a sensual but unsolicitous look, the way that high heels with expensive panty hose will do for an attractive woman. She had a naturally pretty face, white, even teeth, and light makeup. She placed her black hip-hanging purse over her shoulder.

"I'm not always as careful about the way I look, as I should be," he said. "Do you have far to walk?"

"No, my office is not far. In fact, it's right over there," she said, pointing towards a row of tall, dark tinted office windows on the ground floor of their ten story suburban office building. Between the parking lot and her office was an expanse of low-cut, landscaped shrubbery and green lawn. "I usually come to work an hour before now. But, we're having eight-o'clock meetings all week, so I'm here a little later than usual."

"My cubicle is that way, too, on the fifth floor. May I walk with you?"

"If you'd like. I have a few extra minutes. You can have them, if you don't mind talking, here?"

"I don't mind. I'm early, anyway."

The morning air drifted the fragrance of her pleasant, unforgettable perfume pass his nose. He saw her walk a few steps away from her car, point her keys toward the door, and lock it with an audible snap from the door. Then she put her keys in her purse and folded her arms under her breasts, facing him.

"I was hoping that I didn't miss you this morning," she said. "I usually see you from my office, when you come to work. For a while, you didn't park on this end of the lot. But, lately, you have been."

"When I leave work in the afternoon, my car's not as hot inside, because of the trees."

"That was smart. I never thought of that."

"What's your name?" he asked.

"Corliss. I would ask you yours, but I already know it. It's

Adonis Johnson."

He set his briefcase on the asphalt next to his feet. "How did you know that?"

She smiled pleasantly, as if she knew his thoughts. "Don't worry, I'm not a cop. I work in accounting. Payroll. I looked up your name, yesterday, from your badge number."

He laughed. "You are a spy! You know everything about me, already."

She was glad he hadn't felt offended, and said, "That's the advantage of working in payroll. I get to know anybody in the company that I want. You seemed interesting, so I looked you up."

"Well, I guess if I'm in the same boat as everyone else, I forgive you. But call me Adon, with a long A."

"I like your real name, with a short A. It's different."

"All of my brothers and sisters have different names, so I'm used to nicknames."

"I like Adon, too."

"Yours is pretty, Corliss. Can't very well make a nickname out of it, though. Wouldn't go over in my family."

"I have a shady uncle that calls me Lissy. But, fortunately, I don't see him that often." She looked pass him toward his immaculately restored '84 Monte Carlo. "Why do you drive that old car? It doesn't look that bad, but it's *old.* You certainly make enough here to afford a new one, if you wanted it. Do you have bad credit?"

"It's not the best, but it's not that bad. I had a business once, and toward the end, I let some bills go unpaid. I don't use credit, anyway. I mean, not to buy things. I've learned, if I can't pay for it, I don't buy it!"

"Well, you don't have to buy a *new* car, but a newer one might be in order."

"You're all in my business, aren't you?" he said jokingly. She was easy to talk to, and he didn't mind her intuitiveness. He was enjoying her fearless spirit.

Divorce: Episode Two

"I told you, payroll has its advantages," she said, sensing his willingness to be friendly.

"If something goes wrong, I can fix it," he replied, "You can't say that for what you're driving. You *have* to take it to the dealer."

"I couldn't fix it, if I had an old one, like yours. So I'd have to take it someplace, anyway."

"You've got a good point, there. I'm pass the days of buying things, to make people think that I'm something, that I'm not."

"I know a couple of people like that. They always drive new cars. But they wouldn't think of sending their kids to a private school. I guess, you can't see an education—right away."

"What I really like are trucks—big ones! Like the tractors that haul cross-country. When I get my finances back in order, I'm going to buy a bus—a big one—a good, used Greyhound, or Trailways. Fix it up inside, so that I can live in it, and travel."

"I see you're not wearing a wedding band," she said. "Does that mean anything?"

"It means I'm not married; well, sort of—not. I never wore one, anyway."

"What does that mean, sort of, not? You're just separated, so far?"

"No. I'm divorced. But there are extenuating circumstances that impact on how I regard divorce, that requires explaining."

"Either you are—or you're not."

"It would seem that way, depending on what your religion is—Are you married?"

"Would it make a difference to you, if I were?"

"Not, really. But that, too, requires some explanation."

She pleasantly smiled, and touched his forearm. "I'd better look at the rest of your file. You've got a lot of explaining to do."

"You didn't answer my question."

She turned from him, and went between her car and the one next to it, to the paved pathway bordering the parking lot. He hesitated. She turned back toward him from the pathway. "You can walk with me now," she said. He picked up his briefcase and met her on the pathway. Then they walked together toward the walkway that led to the building. Presently, she added, "I guess I have some explaining to do, too. I want to be honest with you. Yes. I'm married. But I took my band off, because I wanted to talk to you."

"Is that all it takes to get unmarried, is take your ring off?"

"I hear some disapproval in your voice. And, you've got a right to feel that way. But, at least I know if I'm married—or not!"

"Are you a Christian?" he asked.

"Sure. I go to church, whenever I feel a need."

"Then I can talk to you about the Bible?"

"I believe in the Bible."

"I've recently learned, from the Bible, that your creation marriage, which is your first marriage, doesn't end until one spouse dies. That's why I said I'm divorced, but I'm sort of, married."

"That's rough! But if that's what you believe—that's what you believe!" She walked on several steps, and then stopped. He stopped when he realized she wasn't walking, and turned back to her. Then she asked curiously, "Does that mean you can have a girlfriend, but you can't get married?"

"I can have a friend, who is a woman. No. I can't get married."

She walked up to where he was waiting, saying, as she walked, "You'll have to show me that in the Bible. Then I *still* may not believe it!"

They continued walking together. He replied, "It takes a total surrender of mind to follow Jesus—so long as the Bible, in every way, supports your decision."

"That's too hard to even think about!"

"Change has always taken place in the church. Consider all the changes the Reformers made, when they learned that the truth had been distorted. For instance, some changed back to underwater baptism, according to the Bible. And when they discovered in the Bible that salvation came by faith in Jesus, not by works, they began to teach that, too."

"Isn't that what you're trying to do, be saved, by being good? Isn't that the same as works?"

"Obeying God's commandments is not works. That's just common sense! Why would He have a law, if we didn't have to obey it? Do you have kids?"

"Two."

"Do you have household rules, and post them, that they don't have to obey?"

"Of course not! I don't give them rules they don't have to obey. That would be a waste of time, and stupid, too."

"You have to admit that God is a lot smarter than you are. Do you think He would have a law, that He wrote in stone, and didn't care if anyone obeyed it?"

"Well, since you put it that way. But never getting married again—is a bit much!"

They arrived at the walkway, and turned toward the entrance to the building.

"As long as you follow the Bible," he said, "no matter how hard it may seem, you're perfectly safe, and not off base. Folks may think you're strange, but people can't do for you, what God can."

"You don't seem all that strange, as a matter of fact, I'd like to get to know you better."

"I'd like that. But since you're with your husband, I'd like to get to know him, too."

"So what are you saying, now? That there's no future for us?"

"You're a very beautiful woman. I'm sure your husband is a jealous man. I would be, if you were mine; and he wouldn't approve of us becoming too friendly, without his knowledge."

"He wouldn't *have* to know."

"Sure, he would, since I would be sure to tell him, that I

respect him too much, to flirt with his wife behind his back.”

They arrived at the entrance to the building. He opened the door for her, and they walked into a large foyer where the elevators waited. Inside, she stopped and turned to him. “You’re the first man I’ve ever met, without a wife, that wasn’t *looking* for sex. I don’t know how to tell the other two women in my office, who’ve also been noticing you from our window. You’re not gay, are you?”

“Far from it!”

“Well, I think I’d like for you to meet my husband. Maybe we would like to find out what you’ve learned from the Bible. And, where you go to church.”

“Call me when you get to your office,” he replied, “ and let’s make arrangements to get together. I’d love to share the Bible with you. Seeing that you work in payroll, getting my extension, there, would be faster than getting it from me, now.”

"Touché!" she said, and smiled. They shook hands, and she hastily walked towards a connected corridor while he headed for an open elevator.

Adon positioned his chair closer to his computer screen. He clicked on Reply, and the message box appeared. He typed:

“Hi, Jewel. How do you figure that we could see each other? I don’t have any vacation time. I just returned from vacation, so I couldn’t come there. You’d have to come here. Save yourself some inconvenience, write a letter, and send it by snail mail. Adon.” He clicked on Send. He rose from his chair, took his coat off, and removed his tie.

He went to his refrigerator, and casually looked in. He chose the orange juice, and poured himself a full glass. After he had drank it down to less than half full he filled it again, and put the carton back into the refrigerator. He took the glass with him, and returned to his computer. The Inbox icon was rapidly pulsating. He wondered if Jewel could have written him back so quickly. Her time zone was an hour ahead of his, so he thought that she should be home, and not at work, where his emails had been going. Out of curiosity, he sat down and typed in his password again, and clicked OK. One message flowed into his Inbox—from Jewel! He clicked on her message line. He read:

"Hi. I hoped you would write me right back. As you can see, I'm still at work. I didn't want to wait until tomorrow morning to see your email. I can purchase an e-ticket for the 18th. There's a special promotion, a round trip there, and back, on the same day. We wouldn't have to leave the airport, and we could have two whole hours to talk. Let me know if the 18th (two weeks from Thursday) is okay with you. If so, I can purchase the ticket before I leave work, and write you back with the airline and time of arrival. I know it's an evening flight, so you wouldn't have to miss any work. Love, Jewel."

He took a long drink of orange juice. He clicked on Reply. He typed:

"Sure. Let me know your ETA, and I'll be there. Adon."

It was early Fall of the year, and the multicolored foliage of trees was a daily reminder of the reasons that the Southeastern part of the country had some advantages over the inland West Coast. The far-west ocean was a beauty to behold; its strawberry swirl sunsets, and broad vanilla beaches—if one could just afford to live close enough, or high enough, to see it. But the luscious, billowy trees of an eastern autumn were everywhere a plenty—and free to anyone who cared to look.

Adon left the un-congested highway and took the circular off-ramp that wound underneath the highway to the boulevard that led to the entrance to the international airport. Two miles from the off-ramp, he drove onto a side road where a green sign had read, Long Term Parking. He waited in a short line of cars until he had reached the ticket meter. He removed the ticket from the slot, and the yellow barrier arm raised for him to enter. Inside, he stopped at the hand signal of a uniformed security officer. The officer directed him to turn left. Then he stopped his car in front of a National Guardsman who came to the car and asked for his driver's license and registration. Another

National Guardsman went around his car with a mirror attached to the bottom of a long pole, checking underneath the car as he gazed into the mirror. The Guardsman at the window asked Adon to unlatch his hood, and get out of his car, and open the trunk. He followed the orders of the Guardsman, and then stood outside while the two Guardsmen thoroughly went through his car, inside and out. Within five minutes, the Guardsman who had taken his I.D. and registration gave them back, and Adon got into his car, and drove toward the far end of the parking lot.

Jewel's flight was due in at 7:47 P.M., and he had arrived at the airport to meet her one and one half hours ahead of time.

Earlier in the day, he had had lunch with Corliss and her husband at his job, outside, in the patio area. That was his third time in their company, but their first time meeting at work.

The other two occasions were at their home, where he had shared with them the Holy Bible's teaching on divorce. His first meeting with them at home had confirmed the initial encounter he had had with Corliss—that they were having very serious marriage problems. Her husband was cordial, and thought that Adon had just procedurally stopped at the house from witnessing in their community, and Corliss had mistakenly let him in. Why else would he be in their home, her husband later told Adon.

That evening, before Adon left, Corliss had told her husband that she knew Adon from work, and she had invited him to stop by, when she knew her husband would be home. Her husband was a salesman for a drug manufacturing company, and he was forced to spend a lot of time out of town. Corliss had told Adon ahead of time, at work, that they were planning to divorce but, as yet, they had not contacted their respective attorneys. During their first meeting, Adon tactfully made sure that he gave them his Bible study on divorce, fully stressing that divorce, in God's commandments, doesn't end a marriage. On his second meeting with them, he had shared some other widely misunderstood conceptions about the state of the dead (to expose Satan, so that

Corliss would not continue to believe that her deceased twin was advising her to divorce her husband), the second coming of Jesus, and salvation is only in Jesus Christ as their personal Savior.

The day that Adon had had lunch with Corliss and her husband, which was the same day he was to meet Jewel, they had informed him that they had laid aside their plans to divorce. Their problems were not severe enough to face life apart, and remain married anyway, and not able to marry anyone else. Her husband had given up his out of town girlfriend, and Corliss was not seeking affection away from home. They said that they had not realized it, before Adon had shown them, that the Bible has answers to all of their hard questions about how to live their lives now and look forward, with hope, to eternal salvation too. As enlightened Christians, they were not so foolish as to let divorce cause them to live in adultery, and miss out on everything worth living for in the life to come.

The primary reason they had previously agreed to divorce was, surely, there must be someone else out there, in the world, that they could be happy with. Indeed, her husband already had someone in mind. Corliss had begun looking. They had to keep their affairs secret from one another before the divorce, so that their attorneys could not rob the other of what they thought was rightfully theirs, including custody of the kids. Now that they had decided against divorce, and remain together, happy or unhappy, it was a worrisome burden that they had freed themselves from, and that alone had reduced their conflict level so that they could begin to enjoy one another's company again.

Inside the airport terminal, Adon checked the flight arrivals' monitors. He saw that Jewel's flight was scheduled for an on time touchdown. Since he didn't have an airline ticket, he was not allowed to pass the security check, and enter the departure gate to meet Jewel as she left the airplane. He had forty-five minutes left before she was scheduled to arrive. He thought he would use his remaining time to peruse the terminal, to seek out a place for them to talk, once she was there. He felt himself becoming apprehensive, and a slight dread of seeing Jewel was overtaking all his efforts to resist it—What must she want?

He had gotten a professional haircut, and he had worn a pair of nice slacks that Jewel had purchased for him as a gift, and he knew that she liked, so that she would see that he was not gaining any loose weight after she had dumped him. And, he had begun to do one hundred or more pushups a day so that his muscle tone would be up, and a hint of his bodily attraction would show through his snugly fitting shirt. He didn't want her to leave that airport thinking that nobody else wanted him—just because she didn't. Yet, he hated himself, for caring *what* she thought! He should have gone to meet her unshaven for a week, and looking like a washed-out bum, he wily thought, so unkempt that she would be embarrassed to talk to him, and be forced to spend the whole two hours in abject misery from having to endure his foul odor from the damp, sweaty, mildewed clothes he had put on—the clothes he had let his cat pee on for a month!

He shook those retributive thoughts from his mind, and asked God to help him to show kindness to Jewel, which would heap more coals on her head than anything he could think of. He recalled the exact words from the Bible: "Therefore if thine enemy hunger, feed him; if he thirst, give him drink: for in so doing thou shalt heap coals of fire on his head." Romans 12:20. Besides, he then considered, he didn't want to unnecessarily discourage her, if she seemed as though she was repentant for the low-down way she had divorced him. Even Corliss and her husband had discussed their pending divorce, and they were aware of what their near-future state would be. And they hadn't made a pretense of being obedient Christians! Right then, in his righteous skulduggery, he thought about simply leaving the airport, and let Jewel sit there by herself for two hours. That would heap more hot coals on her head than kindness—and a lot more *immediate!* If she would just apologize to him—he could rid himself of those evil thoughts!

Adon left the area of the flight monitors, and strolled away, back toward the public entrance to the terminal. When he first came in, he had noticed that there were many more people inside the terminal than was indicated from the outside—but no more traffic than usual, outside—and he remembered seeing a fast food court inside with several national fast food restaurants busily serving customers. He maneuvered his way forward, without actually running, pretending he was a swift-of-foot running back, through the onrushing defensive throng coming toward him pulling rolling luggage, and fast-striders weighted with back packs, and motorized carts driven by a smiling skycap sitting next to passengers with canes; all effortlessly plowing a path of no resistance to the small security gate where everyone stopped to be coldly evaluated by an eye with no vision, except into the private lives of everyone's luggage. He made it to the end zone, and turned the corner to his left, and entered a table clustered enclosure where a tall clown with big, loose britches and long yellow shoes stood happily bolted to the floor, greeting the burger-expectant multitudes with silent red lips.

He spent several seconds under the shadow of the clown, and decided that this was not the mood that was right for him and Jewel's important meeting, too much light, and noise; so he left, and walked pass two other similar atmospheres, and came to a video game arcade. He stepped over the threshold into the action-packed clang of bells, buzzers, ascending and descending whistles, and stood for a moment letting the high decibels drive out the dread of seeing Jewel from his mind. He determined that the lighting was better than the last three places, but there was no place to sit, and they would have to hear each other, first, before they could talk. He stepped back over the threshold, and continued on.

He passed a sports bar filled with bright TVs, and men sitting around a circular bar smoking big cigars and cigarettes. They couldn't very well talk if they couldn't breathe, and this was not the place for a woman—not even Jewel.

The adjacent establishment was a busy newsstand, and after that he saw a small, horizontal electric neon sign above his head protruding out from the wall that read, Cocktails. The outside decor of the business was a replica of a city street, and the lounge itself had a fake plate glass window and a real door. He never frequented places where alcohol was served, since he didn't drink, and he thought about the impression that he could leave on a church member who might see him and a woman in a cocktail lounge. But then he thought that they couldn't see him—if they weren't there!

He opened the door, and went inside. His first impression was—it's perfect! The lighting was bluish, and mellow; people sat closely around small tables and in booths along the walls, not involved in anything else but their own occasional sips and secretive reasons for being there. Soft, unidentifiable music tenderly caressed their dim privacy; the whole atmosphere was inviting, cozy, and conversational. Then he thought that neither of them drank, so what would they order for two hours? And even if no church member saw them, God sees everything, and He would know that they were not there spreading the gospel. His conscience warned him that even though the place, to him, seemed ideal, that when it came to a question of right or wrong, not to rely on his own understanding, but to adhere to the Word of God, and do what was pleasing to God. He remembered the words of Scripture: "Wherefore be ye not unwise, but understanding what the will of the Lord is," Ephesians 5:17, and, "In all thy ways acknowledge Him, and He shall direct thy paths." Proverbs 3:6.

He left the cocktail lounge, although faintly discouraged, and headed back in the direction from which he had come. He arrived at the corner sideline of the playing field that led to the departure gate. He crossed the field to opposite sideline, and recognized the names of several national car rental firms that had walk-up counters for convenient service to the public.

Then a bright revelation came to him. He had rented enough cars in his old business, and in his present job, to know that the larger firms have comfortable waiting rooms for clients waiting to have their rental cars brought to the terminal. He hadn't rented a car, he thought, but it was worth a try!

He walked up to the counter that was awash in vivid green, including the plastic backs of the computer monitors. A green uniformed customer service person, standing behind the green counter immediately said, with a broad smile, "Thank you, for choosing *me!* We have rentals for every need. How can I assist you this evening?"

"Good evening," Adon replied. "I've used your firm many times, and you've always provided me with excellent service. I'm planning to rent from you again, on my next business trip. However, right now, I'm in need of another service that you could provide for me."

Twenty minutes later, Jewel's flight had arrived, and he stood outside of the departure gate, tall enough to peer over the heads of most of the small crowd that had gathered to one side of the checkpoint to await the arrival of family and friends. His previous, slightly agitated, state at seeing Jewel had increased to plain fear! She hadn't given him a clue as to why she wanted to see him. It had to be something frightful, he thought, for her to have to see him in person—or something so good that she was sure it was worth his time and effort to meet her. It could be either very good, or very bad, and the two worrisome choices were the long spikes in his hands as he hung on the cross of bloody expectation.

He saw the first wave of people off the plane, disheveled, but eager, headed toward the gate. Jewel was not among them. He had a liberating, welcome moment of relief as he thought—hoped—that maybe she was not aboard the flight! He had gone directly to the airport without going home first, to check his email. However, there was nothing on his work email. Maybe she had just missed her flight, and hadn't had time to inform him. Please, Lord!

Then he saw her, coming toward him, readily appearing and disappearing in the second wave of people off the plane. She was still too far away for him to clearly see her face, or what she had on. She appeared again, closer, for a brief moment, and then he saw that she only had her purse hung on one shoulder. Like Jewel, he noticed that most of the other passengers did not have carry-on luggage, either. Then it brightly dawned on him—this was the reason inside the terminal was so busy. Like Jewel, people were arriving and not planning to stay overnight. They were meeting significant others right there in the terminal: eating, standing, drinking, sitting everywhere talking. Instead of people going out for overnight or longer accommodations, the terminal establishments were getting all of their business before they departed on their quick return flight. Smart! He mused.

The first wave of passengers came through the arrivals exit and the small crowd who were waving and calling out names shattered into human pieces—tightly embracing, facial smacks, and some dutifully grabbing carry-on luggage to demonstrate their happiness in greeting their loved ones. He saw Jewel hurriedly step from behind a broad man into his view, and she was close enough for him to see her face. She hadn't seen him, yet, and he was appreciative of a vital moment to look at her without having to provide her with a clue to how he was feeling.

Her head was sort of down as she put forth effort treading up the long incline before reaching the arrivals gate. Her dark hair was longer than he remembered, and it fell forward alongside her cheeks as she mastered the incline. He could have tried much longer to see her face, but he was running out of time, and his eyes dropped down to her body. She was wearing blue jeans, of all things, he thought, but she was casting out every discouraging misconception that a mature-figured woman in her forties couldn't wear blue jeans. She was filling them out with the sole intention of every tense thread focused on holding those bad-boys together. His eyes quickly dropped to her shoes—tan and red colored fabric with wedged heels and her red dotted toes shown below her ankle-high blue jeans. Going up again, she was wearing a sheer fabric, splash painted blouse that he could almost see her bra through were it not for the daze of colors hindering his view, but he could see the traces of her bra through the fabric and he thought about her bent for cleanliness that had always pleased him so well.

Her blouse was tucked in her pants, and he could see that she was not wearing a belt through her belt loops, of all things, he thought. Maybe she was trying to tell *him* that she was still able to dress up to par with any woman half her age, and she had the firm hips and high smokestack to not require a belt—and come out a winner! And to him, looking at her, she was just that—a winner!

Seventeen feet from the gate, behind a group of people who were edging their way through, she stopped to await her turn. He couldn't take his eyes off of her, and his meddlesome stare must have mysteriously caused her to look toward him. Their eyes met. She smiled, and he felt as though her eyes were penetrating his mind, observing his thoughts. He smiled back at her, and at that moment over three years of mean thoughts about her left him. Whatever it was about her—that she herself was not aware of when it happened—that made him desire to provide her with every earthly treasure, was happening again. In that instance, he knew that he still loved her, as he had when he had married her, over twenty-one years ago.

He moved from his observation position over to the edge of the flow of people coming through the arrivals gate. Then she was out of his view, but he knew that, momentarily, she would emerge from the crowded entry. He didn't know what he would say, or how he would greet her when she was actually in front of him, he couldn't think that far ahead. Then he didn't have to consider it anymore—There she was, stepping away from the bustling people, coming toward him. She had a broad cheerful smile on her pretty face, and that made him feel much more at ease. Instinctively, he reached for her, to embrace her, and she returned his motion with her arms outstretched to receive his tender greeting. They hugged closely, and he was sure that she could feel his heart pounding. They held each other for the time it took for the memory of a familiar touch to pass, and then he was able to speak, as they released one another, and dropped their arms to their sides, back to a resignation of the moment.

"I'm glad to see you, Jewel. For a minute, I thought you weren't coming. How are you?

"I'm fine. I fell asleep on the plane. I left right after work. How are you? Have you been waiting here long?"

"I've been in the terminal, well, pretty close to an hour. But it didn't seem that long. I looked around some, for a place for us to talk."

"Did you find anyplace?

"Yes. It's near the entrance to the terminal. About a five-minute walk from here."

"Well, we'd better get started. I don't have long."

They turned together, and began walking in the same direction as the greater number of people were doing. He was close beside her, and he felt the repeated jolts of her purse against his arm. He moved to her opposite side, away from her purse, and then he could feel her soft arm next to his. He wanted to hold her hand. It seemed like the natural thing to do. As he was about to give in to the temptation, she put her hand into her purse, and then handed him a small, sealed envelope.

"Princess said, Hi. And to give you this," she said.

"Thanks. I'll open it later." He put the envelope into his shirt pocket. "How is Princess?"

"She's fine. She has a boyfriend, that I'm not so sure about."

"What do you mean?"

"Well, I think they're too serious."

"She's not pregnant, is she?" he asked, in a semi-lowered, expectant tone.

Jewel caught the inclination in his voice that sounded rather suspicious of Princess. "No. She's not pregnant! Why would you go there?"

"Well, it happens."

"Princess is a very responsible girl. You'd know that if you had spent more time with her. Like coming to her graduation."

"I couldn't come, after they had changed the date. How was I to know that Washington would be under a terrorist alert?"

"You could've come—if you had really wanted to."

He heard the old pang of unforgivable accusation in her voice, and he knew that the honeymoon of their greeting was over—just that quickly. He tried to think of something nice to say, but it just didn't seem appropriate to let her get away with her old habit of having to be right about everything. "You never give me even a slight break, do you? I said I *couldn't* come after they changed the date. I had to be on the other side of the country on that day. There was nothing I could do about it!"

"What about all the other affairs of hers that you've missed, while she was growing up. They pile up, you know. You were so busy with your business!"

"It was *our* business. I was working for us!"

"If you had given your family as much attention as you gave *that* business . . . well."

They arrived at the area of the long corridor where the men's and women's restrooms were located. Men on one side of the corridor, and women on the other. Jewel crossed the bustling corridor to the women's side, and halted at the entrance to the restroom.

"I have to take a minute to freshen up. I won't be long," she said, and went inside.

Adon waited outside of the women's restroom, staying close to the wall, out of the path of the passengers going pass him. Presently, Jewel came out, and they resumed walking towards the entrance to the terminal. After they had regained the quick pace of their walking, stride for stride with the hurried public, Jewel changed the subject of their light conversation back to—

"What about the loan my daddy made to you, for the back payments on your business equipment?"

"Why do you always refer to the business, as *your* business, in that nasty tone of voice?"

"Because it was *your* business; it took all of *your* time."

"It wouldn't have taken all of my time if I could've gotten some help from you, as you promised me, over and over!"

"All of your other attempts at business had failed, I knew, eventually, that one would fail, too."

Adon felt his heart ache from Jewel's scathing remark about the business he had worked so hard at—for her; like a doctor who has done all he could for his open heart surgery patient, and his patient was expected to make a full recovery, but his patient caught a common cold, and died. "The business failed because I didn't have any help from you! You were the key, Jewel! You could've provided that ounce of prevention that I needed to make a go of it. I think you wanted it to fail, that's why you refused to help me!" So you could be right, again—You always have to be right!"

"And I was right. It failed, didn't it? And you can't blame that on me!"

"I'm not blaming it all on you. I'm just trying to make you aware of how close I was to taking it nationwide—if I had had someone with me that I could trust, and I didn't have to pay just to open their mouth. You already had all the training. You could've stepped right in, and ran the marketing."

"I had a job I could count on. I wasn't about to give it up to risk my future in your hands."

"You didn't quit that lousy job because you're a coward, and your parents told you not to quit!"

"Yes, my parents advised me not to quit. But you were the reason I didn't quit—not them. I wanted Princess and I to keep on eating, even if you didn't care. With your high-risk taking, all the time."

Adon felt himself becoming too involved in her indulging in

his faults, and she could get the upper hand if he didn't back off, calm down, and not respond to her emotion trap. He forced himself to remain silent, as she was, until they had arrived at the wide open space of the terminal entrances and business establishments. Then, after they had stopped walking, and she was looking about the terminal, he sincerely asked:

"Have you had dinner? Are you hungry?"

"No. I'm not hungry," she sweetly replied. "I had a snack on the plane that I had brought in my purse."

"Well, that car rental place, over there, has a nice waiting area, where I thought we could talk—whatever it is you want to talk about."

"Why don't we just sit out here in the open. . . . There's a couple of empty chairs, right over there," she said, showing him where she was referring to by walking away in that direction. "Behind that old couple."

Adon followed after her. "I thought you'd like someplace more private. I spent a lot of time finding the waiting room!"

"Right here, is just fine," she said, standing in front of two empty black chairs in a long line of occupied terminal chairs, directly behind two senior citizens who were napping, with their heads leaning against one another.

Adon and Jewel sat down, facing the exterior of the terminal. The loading and unloading zone was within their view through the windows. The green car rental company with the comfortable waiting room was behind them. Seated next to Jewel was an eight-year-old boy, roughly jerking at the controls on his remote controlled, red pickup truck that he had careening back and forth on the floor in front of him. His mother, with a small baby in her arms, sat next to her son, the trucker. Seated next to Adon was a teenage girl dressed in all black, including her lips and fingernails, with an overstuffed black backpack on the floor between her legs. She was reading a black paperback book.

"If I had known you wanted to sit out here, I wouldn't have wasted my time, looking."

"This will do," she replied. "So, what have you been doing with yourself, lately?"

"Just working everyday. I finally found a church that doesn't mind having me." Adon was aware that his reply was intended to be scornful, and he didn't mean to allow his soreness to arise again, after his resolution not to fall into her emotion trap. But it seemed that his thoughts were aggressively manipulating his tongue, since she had arrived, and he couldn't resist the repeated impulses to make her aware of how he felt. He knew that she would pretend she didn't know what he was talking about. That was her tactic for avoiding any blame for her own actions. "I haven't changed my membership yet. But I'm planning to. You didn't advance my reputation any. I mean, the way you divorced me."

"I divorced you like everybody else gets divorced. There's not a *lot* of ways to divorce."

"We had made an agreement, before you moved out, that we were not going to divorce. I was counting on you, to keep your word!"

"I didn't say we would *never* divorce. That's just what you heard."

"I know exactly what I heard, and you do too. You're a liar, and can't admit it."

"I didn't come all the way here for you to keep insulting my character!"

"What do you think you've being doing to me, all these years?"

"I didn't know anything about that. Anyway, that's what *you* say. Nobody's ever said anything bad to me, about you."

"How could you not know? I told you myself, in a letter, before I left the house!"

"I said I never heard it from anybody, *else*."

"They were bad enough, but I didn't mind the church members too much. But your dad knows every senior pastor in the denomination, you being a preacher's kid, they know you, too.

Since you divorced me, as soon as they learn who I am, they've been looking down their noses at me, thinking they know the truth, because you're a preacher's kid. And you didn't try to deny it! You know I've never laid a hand on you."

"You did when we first got married."

"I pushed you against the wall. You attacked me! I was just protecting myself, from you! And why did you go way back there, to the *first* year of our marriage?"

"Well, I didn't think you had hit me. But, when I told Mama, she said you did. A push is just as bad as a hit! And I believed her."

"Ooh! That's how it got started! Even though nothing like that ever happened again—and I apologized to you, over and over. And you accepted my apology."

"You know how Mama is. She never forgets anything."

"So what are you going to do about it, now? Since it's out there, today—affecting me!"

"What can I do about it? You seem to be handling it okay."

"That's what I thought you'd say!"

The lady senior citizen, sitting directly behind Adon and Jewel, looked back over her shoulder, from leaning her head against her husband, and slyly said to Jewel, "I'm on your side, honey!" The constantly whining red pickup truck on the floor made a sharp U-turn and slammed into Adon's feet. He picked it up from its tipped over crash, and handed it across Jewel to the boy.

"Thanks. But I'm not suppose to let anybody touch it. When my dad gets here—I'm gonna tell him you touched it!"

After being reprimanded by the kid, Adon said to Jewel, "Are you sure you want to sit here!"

"Yes. I'm fine."

"We could still go to the waiting room."

"Here's fine—What are you going to do about Princess? She's pretty angry at you. And I think you need to address it."

"Is that the reason you're here, to discuss Princess?

"No. I'm getting to why I'm here. When are you going to talk to her—in person?"

"Do you know what her letter is about?"

"I didn't read it, but she pretty much told me what it says."

"Well, after I read it, I'll call her tomorrow. I don't want to hear anything second hand, from you."

"If I had known you were going to be in such a bad mood, I would've stayed home."

"It was your idea to come here, not mine. You insisted on it! . . . So, why did you divorce me, behind my back? You had to know what you were going to do when I was at Rudy's house. You must've talked to your attorney, right after I left. Why didn't you let me know about it, first?"

"After you left Rudy's, I didn't know where you were. I didn't know if you were in, or out of town. I couldn't notify you."

"That's not what I mean—notify me of what you had *already* done! I mean discuss with me what you were *planning* to do. So that I could agree, disagree, protest, scream, hide, holler, do *something* to have some say-so about my life. Not having it shoved down my throat, without me so much as coughing."

"Well, before you left Maryland, I told you it wasn't going to work out. I thought you knew what that meant."

Adon stood to his feet, and walked off a few paces down the aisle. Jewel called after him—"You're not leaving, are you?"

He turned back to her, "No. I'm not leaving. Just—just, let me alone a minute!" Presently, he came back. The girl in black, seated next to him, had put her backpack on his seat. He said to the girl, "I'm not leaving," and took her backpack from the seat and set it on the floor in front of her. Then he sat down again.

"Why didn't you tell her the seat was still taken?" he said to Jewel.

"I knew you'd move it when you got back."

"You wouldn't lift up a finger, to consider my feelings—would you?"

Divorce: Episode Two

"Have you cared about how I've felt about anything?"

"That's all I think about, is how you feel. You know how much I loved you, when we were together. That's why you took advantage of me the way you did. You played on my love for you, to get me to sign your legal separation. Then you rolled it into a sharp point, put an ice-pick inside, and stabbed me in the back with it."

"I did what I had to do, Adon."

"And you didn't care how I felt. I begged you not to leave. Do you remember standing in the kitchen, and I got down on my hands and knees, and kissed your feet to show you how much I loved you, and I wanted you to stay? You remember that?"

"Yes. I remember it."

"But, you—you," Adon's voice choked up, and his misty eyes brimmed over with tears as he sat looking at Jewel. "You hurt me bad, Jewel, and I can't help it." He put his head down on his knees, and quietly cried. Presently, he raised his head. The lady senior citizen turned half way around in her seat and handed him a dangling white napkin. "Thanks," he said, and dabbed his eyes dry.

Jewel had silently observed him as he softly wept, and after he had received the napkin she removed her hairbrush from her purse, and brushed her hair back off of her face, two strokes, one on each side, while he dried his eyes, then she put her brush back in her purse. She turned her face toward Adon.

"At one time," she said, "we had a lot of money in the bank. But I have no idea where it all went. You didn't gamble, at least not at a casino, so that's not where it went. Do you remember, when I had the accident in my car?"

"The brand new BMW, I bought for you?" he accusingly asked.

"Yes. That one. Well, when the insurance check came from the accident, I don't know where all that money went. I didn't spend it! Do you know where all that money went? If you do, you never told me!"

"Now, you'll say you don't remember—but I did tell you, that I needed that money to cover my payroll."

"Was that *after* you had spent all of it—or before—I don't remember!" she said mockingly.

"If you needed to check up on everything that I spent, why did you let me handle our finances?"

"You *took* that responsibility! I never gave it to you!"

"You never complained, as long as the money was rolling in. I gave you $3000.00 a month, over what you were making on your job—for you to spend however you saw fit. I didn't check up on what you did with it. You knew where all of my time and money was going—into the business—for a decent future for all of us."

"Now, what do you have to show for it? All of that time, and money? You're a lot worse off today, than when you started. No money, to speak of, in the bank—bad credit, and debts you may never pay off!"

The man senior citizen turned his head back to Adon, and said, "She's a cold one, ain't she son?"

Adon resolutely stood to his feet, facing Jewel, "Either we go to the waiting room—or I'm leaving!"

Jewel stood up, too. "Alright, whatever you say. But it'll just take up more time if we leave."

"It'll be worth it!"

"I think I'd like something to drink. Something cold."

He relaxed some. "Is orange juice still your favorite?"

"Yeah! That sounds great," she said, in a lighter frame of mind. "Have you seen a juice bar around anyplace?"

"There's one down that way, pass the cocktail lounge."

"That'll take up way too much time, to go that far. How about that fast food place, I think they have orange juice. But I don't want concentrate, I want the real thing."

After Adon had nimbly skipped over the red pickup truck that was whining and speeding between his legs, they started walking towards the clown with the big feet. The little boy remotely driving the truck noticed that they were leaving. He yelled after Adon—"I'm still gonna tell my dad!"

At the fast food counter they asked for two medium-sized, squeezed orange juices with no ice. Adon paid for their order, and from the restaurant they crossed the playing field corridor that led to the flights departure gate, and then on to the second car rental company, with the green decor, on the same side as they were walking. At the counter, Adon spoke to the same customer service person as he previously had.

"Hi. I'm back!"

"Sure, Mr. Johnson. Our client waiting room is right this way, through that door." The customer service person walked over to a side door facing the end of the counter, and opened it. Adon let Jewel go through first, he followed, and the service person closed the door behind him.

Inside of the spacious, well furnished, waiting room they were the fourth and fifth persons there. They looked around for a moment, and then sat down on a green, fabric upholstered sofa, with a polished antique coffee-table in front of it. They set their half full cups on coasters on the coffee-table. They were a friendly distance away, and out of quiet voice range of the other three people in the room. Across from them was a wall mounted television with the image turned off. The remote control lay on the coffee-table.

"This is much better, isn't it?" Adon said.

"It's nicer in here. But I don't have much time left," she replied, looking at her watch. "About forty-five minutes. My departure gate is farther than where I came in, so I'll have to figure on more time than it took to get here."

"You're looking great, Jewel. You're smaller than the last time I saw you. Divorce has been good to you"

"A good tomato ripens just as well off the vine!"

"You're lucky there's other people in this room, or I'd be trying to sample your salad."

"So, that's why you were so anxious to change places.

Thought you could get me in here, alone, uh?" she said, with a seductive tease in her voice.

He touched her just below her armpit, and moved his hand up and down, where three years ago he had felt three rolls of excess calories.

"They're not there anymore, and they won't be back," she said, removing his hand from being too close, and staying too long in one place. Then she smiled, appreciative of his noticing her feminine attractiveness. "That's one thing I could almost always count on from you. You thought, for awhile, that I was more than any other woman in the world."

"It was easy. You were, and still are."

"Then, let me ask you something, Adon," she said, getting back to business, and discouraging any further progress of an amorous moment. "When the doctors thought I had cancer, and I might have to have one of my breasts removed, why did you act so disgusted, like I wasn't going to be a person you wanted to be around anymore, let alone sleep with, if I had to have that operation. Fortunately, I didn't, but you made me feel real bad during that time. I don't think I'm over it, yet."

"That was a long, long time ago."

"Remember what I said about Mama, she never forgets anything? Well, I'm just like her! You always try to make me out to be the bad guy, *I divorced you for no reason*, and all that crapola. You were full of yourself—and nobody could tell you nothing, about anything. You wouldn't listen to anything I had to say, about *anything*. You were your own man. I don't need any advice—you always said! You put me out of your life, and I couldn't get back in. *Love is more than just words*. You have to back up those words, with action. You wouldn't go to counseling—They don't know anything about *me*, so why should I listen to them—you always said. So, I gave up trying to get through to you. Period!"

"I never intentionally did anything in my life to hurt you, Jewel. I had my faults, I admit it, but you didn't have to give up on me. We were married. I thought for life. I thought we had time to work things out."

"See! *You* had time. I wanted to be really happy during the marriage, not when I was old, gray, and ready to die! I loved feeling appreciated, and sought after, sexually appealing to my husband. But you drove all of that out of me, when you thought I had to have that operation." She took a small napkin box out of her purse, ripped out a white napkin, and placed it over her eyes under her hand. Adon moved nearer to her and placed his arm around her shoulder, drawing her closer to him, in a tender consoling way. For a moment she didn't resist, but then she abruptly drew back—"Stop! Stop! It's too late for that now!"

She quickly moved farther away from him on the sofa than she was before. Adon put his forehead in the palm of his hands with his elbows firmly resting on his knees, feeling that he had thoughtlessly violated her just cause to be angry with him—He had blown it! Presently, he raised his head, and looked at Jewel.

"Why did you come here?" he asked resignedly.

"Do you think this is easy for me?" she replied, looking away from him toward the floor. "Do you think I don't ever think about us getting back together?"

"I think you're a cold-blooded person, for some of the stuff you did to me."

"Attack! Attack! Attack! That's all you know to do is attack!"

"I didn't attack you just now, when you jumped back, like I was poison!"

"I haven't seen you in over three years, you think I can just fall into your arms on a moments notice?"

"You fell into some man's arms, behind my back! Um . . . uh! What about that love letter I found in the mail?"

A flash of hot anger erupted from her face, and she turned to Adon—"You had no business going through my mail! That was my private mail!"

Adon shot back, pierced by her raw nerve to be defensive—"Since when is adultery private!?"

She flared louder than she should have with other people present—*"I did not commit adultery!"*

His voice rang out to match hers—"Oh! I guess you don't remember that, either! You thought I hadn't read the letter, didn't you? You thought I was stupid enough not to read it, and just believe what you told me it said. You little liar! It wasn't from some old school mate, playing a practical joke. It was from your lover! And I read every word he said to you!"

Her angry emotions brought her to her feet—"I'm glad I divorced you! And I'd do it a million times over. Cause you're nothing but a piece of nosy trash. What Brian said in that letter, was just lies . . . "

"Oh! He's Brian now! You told me his name was Bruce! But since you thought I didn't know, you could tell me anything, couldn't you?"

"Yes. His name is Brian! It was Brian then, and it's Brian now! I loved him then, and I love him now!"

Adon stood up, close in her face, dismayed and angry at her words—"You're still seeing that guy! That's why you divorced me, so that you could be with him? And you call yourself a Christian. When you're nothing but a whore!"

"Yes, I've been seeing him! But I've never had sex with him! *I am not a whore,* and you have no right to call me that, after what you've done!" She took control of herself, and Adon too, by turning, with her back to him, and talking through clinched teeth. "Sit down, please! I've got to get this out. I can't hold it in any longer. I'm about to scream, I have to get it out so bad!"

Adon sat down again, responsive to her knowing from experience how to quickly calm him down. She sat down, too, and faced him, wringing her hands. The patrons in the waiting room lowered their heads, and went back to their reading. Then she spoke to him in a calm tone—after Adon had said, "I never have, but right now I sure feel like smacking you."

"Adon, shut up! If you don't let me talk, *I'm* leaving."

"That's the big reason we're here, your *talking!"* She took her purse off the coffee-table, and stood up, looking down defiantly at Adon, with one hand paused on her hip. "Alright, say what you've got to say," he said, looking up at her, giving in to her threat of leaving. "But I can't promise I won't say anything. I've held a lot inside, for a long time, and you haven't helped one bit by coming here. But I can tell, this meeting is just about you. To Hades with my feelings. Sit down—and talk!"

Jewel sat down again. She placed one hand on her forehead with her head bowed. "I need to pray a minute."

"You should have thought of that before you got here."

She looked at Adon. "For your information, on the plane, when I wasn't sleep I was praying! Evidently, that's something you haven't done for awhile."

"I had the silly idea, before you got here, that we were going to pray together, and put our marriage in order. But since you're in love with another man . . ."

"Adon, shut up!" She bowed her head under her hand again. Adon took her free hand, and bowed his head, too. They both prayed silently. Adon raised his head first, and released her hand. Then she raised her head. "Are you going to let me talk," she calmly asked.

"Sure. Go ahead," he replied in like manner. "But I'm not promising."

"If you have to say anything, be kind about it."

"I'm not promising I won't say anything you don't deserve to hear!"

Seeing that she was not going to dampen his resolve, she began—

"Yes. I admit it. Brian is not an old friend from school. We've known each other for quite some time. . . ."

"How long?"

"Does that matter?"

"How long, Jewel?"

"Eight years."

"Five years before our divorce!"

"Something like that. Anyway, he was married when I met him. His wife died . . ." She quickly raised her palm toward his face—"Don't ask me when, or how!" Adon hadn't attempted to speak. Then she continued, her hand withdrawn. "He has two lovely children. They've both just become teenagers. They're darling kids, and I like them a lot."

"We could have had more kids."

She haltingly raised her palm close toward his face again—"I'm not going to go there, right now!" She left her hand up, and then emphasized her objection to his interrupting her with two short thrusts of her hand toward his face. She lowered her hand. "When I met Brian, I didn't know that he was married, or that he had children. He's like you, he doesn't carry pictures in his wallet."

"He's not like me! I don't mess with other men's wives!"

". . . We were working together—not dating—on the same committee at a medical conference on diabetes. He's a doctor. At the conference, we got to be friends. . . ."

"Just that quickly, uh?"

"He didn't live in the same city that we did . . . but he began to call my office . . . it was just by phone, business conversation!" She was experiencing difficulty choosing her words, but she dragged herself on, speaking: "I knew that I had liked his personality, and . . . he did kiss me at the conference." She thought about it, and then forced it out—"Alright—I *let* him kiss me!" Adon turned his head from her with painful imagery in his mind, but he kept silent. She saw that she had passed that difficult milestone without a testy inquiry for more information from him, and she bravely went on—before he changed his mind. "Then I found out by accident—I wasn't asking around or anything—that he was married. The next time he called me, I told him not to talk to me about anything but business. I told him that I was happily married, and I intended to stay married. And what had happened at the conference was a disgrace for both of us—and it would never happen again! After that was when he wrote me the letter that you found. Why he mailed it to our house—to this day, he can't explain it to me. . . ."

Adon sat upright again, recovered from his journey into pity, and said, "Because he's a constipated rectum—and needs his butt kicked!"

Jewel lost her moment of humility. "He's a very nice person! And you shouldn't be threatening him!"

"If I ever see him, I'm going to do more than threaten him. I'll righteously give him the best fist-whipping he ever had! And you've got the rotten gall to sit there, and defend him! You were *my* wife, and he was too far out of line, intruding himself into my home. And you deserve the same retribution that he does—for letting him!"

"I tried to stop him! But he wouldn't stop! He called me at my job. He sent letters to my job. And, yes—if you have to know—after awhile I *wanted* the attention! I wasn't getting any from you, at home! And when I told him about the operation I once thought I had to have—he said he didn't cherish me for just the outside, but he loved me for what I was on the inside! That's more than you ever said to me about that operation—and you were my husband!"

"And you fell for that come-on like a cast-iron dummy!"

"See! Fool! You still don't get it! You pushed me to him!"

"You can't blame your illicit affair behind my back on me! You made all those decisions to get involved with him, yourself. That's your *big* problem, Jewel. You never want to bear the blame for anything! It's always somebody else's fault—but yours!"

"It was your fault, too! And I did break it off with him! I didn't see him anymore after the conference until our divorce was final. And I did not commit adultery—And I haven't yet committed adultery!" She was on the edge of the sofa and facing Adon, with one knee almost touching the floor from being highly agitated. She turned her body fully back onto the sofa again. She took a minute to calm herself down, as Adon was turned to one side, glaring at her.

"You're full of it, Jewel. You know that? Full of it!"

She spoke with her back against the sofa, but looking straight at Adon. "I want you to listen to me," she said confidently and calmly, "and I want you to listen better than good! I've been seeing Brian since our divorce. His wife had died, and we were divorced, so there was no reason that we couldn't find out if we might have a future together. Well, we've decided, we do, and we're planning to get married. His children and Princess want us to get married. We make a happy family. I want more children: his two and Princess. I want to be a mother again. I'm not ready for the old folk's home!"

"Jewel, you can't get married!"

Her emotions began to get the best of her again as she moved forward on the sofa. "I want to get married! I want to stay home with his kids! I've been working since high school, all through college I worked, I worked everyday of our marriage. Brian can afford for me to remain at home—and that's what I want to do, before I'm too old to be a young mother again!"

"Jewel, you're not hearing me—you can't get married!"

She courageously turned on the sofa, fully facing Adon. She had the reached apex of her purpose for seeing him, and she was desperate to put it behind her—"I can if you've committed adultery, first! That's what I had to come and see you about. I want to know—I have to know—for sure, if Brian and I can get married in the church. He wasn't saved when I first met him, but now he's been baptized, by immersion, and everything he's done is in the past, and we want to get married in the church. But, Adon, *I have to know from you,* first, if you committed adultery while we were still married, or even since we've been divorced? My whole future with Brian depends on you telling me the truth! Please, tell me the truth! Please, say you have, so that I can be with Brian!"

Adon was sympathetic, but firm—"Jewel, it doesn't matter what I've done—you can't get married!"

Divorce: Episode Two

"Why can't I get married? I know you committed adultery, first, while we were married. I'm sure of it! I just need you to admit it to my face, so that I can tell Brian it's absolutely true, and you've admitted to it. Then he won't have any doubts about getting married!"

Adon rose from the sofa, took his plain orange juice with him from off the coffee-table, and drifted away to the magazine rack across the room against the opposite wall. He selected a travel magazine, and thumbed through it, sipping on his orange juice. Jewel remained on the sofa for a moment, and then met him at the display case. She gently lifted the magazine from his hands, and replaced it on the rack.

"Adon, I don't have time, now, for you to sulk, and clam up on me. I'm going to have to leave soon, and I need to tell Brian the good news when I get back."

Adon straightened up, from leaning against the wall. "I'm not sulking!" he replied, and began walking back toward the sofa. Jewel followed him. "I'm just thinking about what you're asking me to do." Adon set his juice on the table, and they sat down again.

"What's there to think about?" Jewel pressed him. "Just tell the truth, that's all! You know what you did while we were married. I know, Mama knows, everybody knows but Brian! I need to tell him when I get back." She moved closer to him, facing him. "You understand what I'm saying, don't you?"

"Jewel, you're not going to like what I'm going to say, considering how much you love Brian, but the Bible says we're still married!"

She flared up in righteous indignation—"The Bible doesn't say that! The Bible says the innocent one can remarry! I'm the innocent one, and I can remarry! I just need to tell Brian that you admitted it to my face—that will solve everything!"

Jewel, listen, I know you want to be saved, or you wouldn't be so concerned about what I've done, but the Bible teaches, plainly, that your first marriage stays intact until somebody dies. Somebody, in our case, would be you or I. Can you understand you what *I'm* saying?"

"I understand that you're not making any kind of sense. What church are you going to? Are you involved in some kind of satanic cult, that teaches that? That's not in *my* Bible!"

"It's in *everybody's* Holy Bible! If I had a Bible, I'd show it to you."

"Adon, my daddy's been a preacher for forty years. Don't you think if that was in the Bible, he would have told me. I've seriously talked to him about me and Brian. Don't you think that if I couldn't marry Brian, he would have told me? If you don't want to tell the truth about what you've done, that's a decision you'll have to live with, but don't start calling my daddy a liar."

"I'm not calling your daddy a liar, but I am saying that maybe he doesn't know. I didn't know, until someone showed it to me."

"And you believed it? People say the Bible says a lot of things it doesn't say. But you can't go running after everything people say is in the Bible. Some people take one verse, and say this is what the Bible says. But you know we don't study the Bible that way. So why are you changing your study habits now. Don't you believe the *whole* Bible, anymore?"

"That's the problem, Jewel! What you're relying on, to get married again, is not in the whole Bible. Not even a small portion of it. What I'm telling you, is—It's in the *whole* Bible, beyond a doubt!"

"Adon—are you looking for money, to tell me what I want to know? I'll pay you to tell me the truth, if that's what you want! If I don't have enough for you, I'm sure that Brian can come up with it. You just name it, and I'll get it for you—somehow!"

"Jewel, I've said some things since you got off the plane, that you provoked me into saying, calling you a liar, and a whore. I apologize for saying it. But what you just said to me—you need to apologize to me, for. Calling me a criminal extortionist—when all I'm trying to do is keep you out of hell—was a total defamation of my motives, and you need to apologize to me!"

"I'm *not* going to apologize—I meant what I said! If you need money, tell me, and I'll get it!"

"Okay, Jewel," he said, for him a final confirmation of the lowest morals class she placed him in, "I'm going to show you in the Bible about our divorce. I don't want your blood on my hands, for not showing it to you. Then I want you to get back on an airplane, and I *never* want to see you again!" He calmly stood up, and turned to face the other people in the room, and then spoke loud enough for everyone to hear. Two of the three people had moved one seating arrangement closer to him and Jewel. "I'm sorry, for interrupting your usually quiet wait with this drama that's going on. But my wife and I are discussing some serious issues. Does anybody have a Bible, that I can borrow for a minute?"

The people had responded with friendly understanding smiles when he spoke about his involvement with Jewel, but then they negatively wagged their heads regarding a Bible. Then Adon stepped around the coffee-table toward the door—he abruptly stopped, came back to the sofa and sat down, facing Jewel.

"Wait a minute!" he said, with a gleam of past recollection in his eye.

Jewel interrupted his thought—"I am not your wife!" she emphatically stated.

Adon ignored her comment. "Why didn't I bring my Bible out of my car?" he asked rhetorically. "I didn't bring it because *you* have a Bible! You always carry a Bible with you. The little red one, that snaps close, that your mother gave to you in college. You never go anywhere without it!" He looked at Jewel suspiciously, wringing the truth out of her with his eyes. "That Bible is in your purse, isn't it?" He glanced at her purse, lying on its side on the coffee-table. He knowingly looked back at her. They both determined at once to get the purse—The contest erupted. She grabbed for it first, a beat ahead of him, and he barely missed it, leaving his fingernail marks on it from being so close, while she dragged it off the coffee-table into a two-arm clutch in front of her, knocking over Adon's orange juice cup as she snatched it into her grasp. The lid flew off the orange juice container, and its pulpy contents spilled out onto the coffee-table. The thick liquid quickly spread toward the far edge of the coffee-table, then slowed down to a sluggish crawl at the point of going over, onto the floor.

"Give me that Bible out of your purse, Jewel!" he steadfastly demanded.

"No! I'm not giving it to you! I don't want to see anything you want to show me from the Bible! I already know what the Bible says!"

"You're not willing to even think about what I'm telling you?"

"I've already thought about it! A lot of people before you have thought about it, and they agree with me—not you!"

"You need to see it, Jewel! And at least, once, consider it. Everything you've lived for is at stake! Give me your Bible!"

"No, Adon! I'm not going to look at it! Just tell me what you've done with another woman, and I'll leave!"

Adon lowered his level of urgent concern for her Bible. "That orange juice is about to spill on the floor, and ruin this people's table, *and* carpet," he said, not moving his body, but indicating the crawling orange juice with a tilting of his head toward the coffee-table, keenly keeping his eyes on Jewel. She glanced at the slowly advancing liquid, and back at Adon. He added, "In another second or two, that stuffs going to drip on the floor. Take a napkin, and stop it. You've got napkins in your purse."

Jewel looked at the spill, and then down at her purse firmly clutched under her arms. She momentarily wrestled with the decision to clean up the spill, or hold on to her purse with both arms. Her bent for preventing household messes won, and she removed one arm from over her purse. She unzipped the top zipper, keeping her eyes on Adon—*"Don't you touch me!"*

She put her free hand inside her purse, and fumbled with the contents, then began to withdraw her hand. She looked down for an instant, to see what she had in her hand, shifting her eyes away from Adon. He reacted in a super-flash, and ripped her purse from her one arm grasp as she held the napkin box in her other hand.

"Give me that back, Adon!"

She lunged for her purse before he could get inside, and forcefully jerked on it by its leather strap. He held on to the body of the purse, attempting to get her Bible out.

"I'm going to show you, whether you like it or not! Your blood's not gonna be on my hands!"

She vigorously jerked on the strap, restricting the opening, preventing him from getting inside—"Stay out of there, Adon! And give it back!" Then, suddenly, she stopped jerking on the strap, and released it to him. "Alright. You can take my Bible out, but give me my purse back."

"That's better," he said. "It's about time you showed some sense."

"I'm not reading anything you show me. I just want my purse back."

He looked, and then reached inside of her purse and removed a small, red, KJV Bible. After he had it out, she snatched her purse from him, and brought it under the close protection of her bosom again with the small outside pocket on the purse facing out, toward Adon. Adon, feeling victorious at having the Bible, thumbed through it, seeking out his texts.

The entrance door to the waiting room opened slightly, and the counter customer service representative poked their head in and spoke to the persons who had moved one seating arrangement closer to Adon and Jewel. "Ms. Wade, and Mr. Kimball, your cars are here."

The alerted people rose, and went to the door. Mr. Kimball, middle-aged and dressed in a business suit, stopped, and turned back to Adon and Jewel before going out the door. "I'd love to stay, and hear the end of this. But I have to go," he said, and went on out the door behind the customer service person.

Ms. Heidi V. Wade, a younger woman, smartly attired in a light-blue airline stewardess' uniform, stopped at the door, too. "I hope you can work things out. Bye!" she said, and went out the door, closing it behind her.

"See what you're doing?" Jewel said. "Making a public spectacle out of me. You're just ignorant, Adon!"

"You didn't mind it out there," Adon replied, returning to his Bible search, "so don't complain about nothing in here. Why don't you wipe up that mess on the table, while I find all I'm looking for?"

"I don't care if you find it now, or next week. I'm not listening to you. I just need you to tell me what you've done, and I'll leave. I should've been at the security gate by now. You're just wasting valuable time with that."

Jewel placed her purse against the back of the sofa, with the outside pocket facing out, and began wiping the coffee-table with several napkins from her box. Presently, an audible single beep was heard. Jewel, without thinking, looked back at her purse. Adon noticed her reaction to the sound. He had heard it too.

"What was that?" he asked.

Jewel realized her mistake—drawing renewed attention to her purse, and continued wiping the table, as though she hadn't heard Adon's question.

"Jewel, what was that?" he asked again, with more emphasis on *"that."*

She knew she had to quickly respond to his question with a reasonable answer, or he might look in her purse, to see where the beep came from.

"Oh, you heard it, too?" she innocently replied, still cleaning up the orange juice. "That was my cell phone. I set it to beep once, so that we wouldn't be disturbed while we talked." She finished wiping the table dry, and deposited the wet napkins in the empty drink cup. She thoroughly dried her hands with more napkins, put them in the cup too, and replaced the plastic lid. She leaned back, and turned all her attention to Adon. He had stopped looking through her Bible. "Are you ready to admit to your adultery?" she asked coldly.

"I didn't see a cell phone in your purse when I took your Bible out," he said, sensing that he had her against the ropes. "Where is it? That sound came from your purse!"

Then Jewel fidgeted for an answer, thinking by his previous silence that she had wriggled out of his hot pursuit. Her top lip quivered. "I . . . I don't keep my phone in my purse, I have a special place for it."

Adon went in for the quick kill—"Jewel, I use miniature tape recorders, too. I know the distinct sound they make—when the tape runs out!"

Jewel completely lost her composure, and screamed at Adon, facing him squarely—"Why are you doing this to me?! Can't you see I'm a nervous wreck?! I'm about to lose my mind, and you're driving me crazy, Adon! Stop it! Stop it right now! Tell me what you did, Adon! You know what you did! So tell me right now, and stop driving me crazy! Tell me! Tell me! Tell me!"

Jewel stopped screaming out her words, and held her angry, frustrated emotions in tow, glaring at Adon, waiting for him to confirm what she was sure she already knew.

Adon closed Jewel's Bible with a punctuating snap of the latch that held it closed. He placed the Bible back in her purse, holding her purse open with one hand, and dropping it in from six inches above. He zipped her purse shut. Then he took his little finger and poked it between the interlaced leather of the small pocket on the outside of Jewel's purse, all the time watching Jewel, savoring every spiteful expression on her face from his methodology of revealing her plot to tape him. His finger was prevented from going no deeper in between the laces than half the depth of his fingernail, stopped by a hard surface. He moved his little finger up and down, letting Jewel know, as she watched him, that his fingernail had struck a hard object. Then, he removed his finger, and opened the top of the little pocket by unzipping it. He stuck his thumb and forefinger inside, and slowly pulled out a small silver tape recorder. He held it up in front of Jewel. "Is this where the beep came from—your cell phone?"

Jewel grabbed for it once, but he quickly pulled it back, and she missed. "No! No!" he said. "Not yet." He opened the face of the recorder and removed the cassette tape. He replaced the recorder in her purse the same as he had done with her Bible, six inches above, and dropped it in. Then he held the tape up between his thumb and forefinger, in front of Jewel's frowning face. "This is mine; it's of no value to you, since I haven't said what you want me to say."

He looked at the tape, speaking as he observed it. "Sixty minutes. That's not very long—now is it?" He deposited the tape into his shirt pocket, behind Princess' letter, the same as he had purposely done with her red Bible and tape recorder, six inches above, and dropped it in.

"So when did you turn it on?" he interrogatingly asked. "You turned it on too soon, didn't you? They sell 2-hour tapes, you know. A longer tape, and I would've never known I was sharing my private business with whoever you wanted to play it for. Let's see, an hour ago? When you went to the bathroom, after you got off the plane, to freshen up, you said. No! That's too far back. Let's see, an hour ago? I've been with you all the time, so . . . Ah! When I was out there bawling! That's when you turned it on, wasn't it? In my weakest moment, you thought I was going to break down, and confess, and you wouldn't be sitting there right now—now would you? You would've left me an emotional wreck—but you would've had what you came for, and you wouldn't be sitting there right now, caught like the fox you are—now would you? That's why you didn't want to be alone, so you could handle it, if you had to—or, there would be too much noise for me to hear it, if it went off. But you forgot it, didn't you?

"You slandered my name, as a wife beater and adulterer, so that you could divorce me with no questions from anybody in the church. But you didn't expect Brian to question you, and want more than your foul-mouth say-so. So, to here you came, with your hidden tape, to get the evidence—now didn't you?"

"Are you done with your little charade—I don't need the tape. Brian will believe what I say. Soon as you tell me, I'll be away from you, for good!"

"You've been away from me—for good, for a long time."

"I hate you, Adon!"

"Just like your mother hated me, after she had finished praying, to who knows what, and then told me she didn't care if I was eternally lost. And you sat there hating me, right along with her, and didn't say one word to lessen my pain. Yes, you hate me! That's why you took me off your health insurance—and didn't tell me—so that I might get badly injured, and die, without proper medical treatment. Yes, you hate me! That's why you probably crawled into bed with another man while I was out killing myself working, to give you a decent life—up to *your* standards of high-class living!"

Adon was about to say something else to Jewel that he hadn't contemplated saying. He was positioned on the edge of the sword, and the blade was cutting him in two. He could jump off, and save himself the pain, but on one side of the blade was the pleasure pit of sin, that would give him the worthy satisfaction of hurting Jewel the way she had hurt him. On the other side of the honed blade was the requirements of his faith, that squeezed selfish motives to do evil out of his heart; that placed his love for Jesus, and His way of doing things, above his own carnal inclination to commit sin. He was in the boiling cauldron of war with himself that Paul wrote about when he said: "Know ye not, that to whom ye yield yourselves servants to obey, his servants ye are to whom ye obey; whether of sin unto death, or of obedience unto righteousness?" and, "For the good that I would I do not: but the evil which I would not, that I do." Rom. 6:16; 7:19

Adon was no less different than Adam, driven by the same consuming desire to commit sin. Adam wanted to transgress God's commandments because, at that moment, he loved Eve more than God, and couldn't bear the thought of being without her. Adon wanted to transgress God's commandments because, at that moment, he despised Jewel, and he didn't want to hinder her rapid plunge toward hell with her home wrecking lover. For love or hate, Satan doesn't care about the reason for sin—just do it!

"Jewel, I'm going to make a confession to you, and you can do with it whatever you want. I didn't commit adultery while we were married . . ."

"Your lying, Adon! Why don't you tell the truth. For once in your life, *tell the truth!*

"No, I didn't commit adultery while we were married—but I have since we divorced. I guess, as you say, I've committed adultery, first!"

Jewel quickly rose from her seat, threw her purse over her shoulder, and headed for the door. She stopped at the closed door, and turned back to Adon, still seated on the sofa—"That's all I wanted to hear! What's her name? So that I can give Brian a name."

Adon hadn't thought about a name, so he said the name of a person who first came to his mind. He wanted to give Jewel everything she needed to take back to Brian—"Corliss! That's her name, Corliss."

"Ummh . . . Corliss!" Jewel spitefully replied, "that's an ugly name," and she went out the door, slamming it behind her.

Right after Jewel had slammed the door, the customer service representative opened the door, and poked their head in. "Mr. Henry, your car is here," she said.

Mr. Henry rose from his seat and walked toward the door. He stopped at the sofa where Adon was seated, slouched back with one hand upon his forehead half way over his closed eyes, and said to Adon, "Don't sweat it, my good friend. You're better off without her." Then he went out the door behind the customer service representative.

Adon had willfully lied, to get even with Jewel, to heap his own coals upon her head, believing that if one or both of them died, Jewel or Brian, before he did, that that would send one or both of them into hellfire, and eternal death—where they both belonged—for hurting him, and living in the sin of adultery.

His plan for their death at the hand of God was long-term, and may take a lifetime to be fulfilled, and in the meantime the happy couple would be living as though heaven awaited them, not the slightest bit aware that he had lied about his adultery—to cause them to commit subtle suicide.

They deserved it, was his rational, for not believing the Bible on divorce, and going ahead with their presumptive style of obedience. He had witnessed to similar people, like Jewel, who purposely avoid knowing further truth; refusing to understand their Bible in areas where they don't want to change; assuming that God does not require any more from them than that which they're already doing. Anyway, God will not punish me, if I don't know! King David repented of presumption, and prayed: "Keep back thy servant also from presumptuous sins; let them not have dominion over me: then shall I be upright, and I shall be innocent from the great transgression." Psalm 19:13.

Presumptive religion—"the great transgression," assuming a belief to be true based on old tradition, declarations of clergy, habits of involvement, careless interpretation of Scripture, supposing that God does not relentlessly hate all sin, and He will let some "little" ones go by, unrepented of. He is too loving to punish those willing abusers with death since they, themselves, didn't think that their sins were so bad—no worse than anyone else's. Indeed, a long, successful marriage cannot be bad. Even if it happens to transgress God's holy law, it's only a minor, victimless, infraction since marriage is honorable, and people deserve to be happy in another marriage.

Lest they forget, what they *deserve* is death, as a justifiable result of sin, and they will not receive eternal life because they presumed on God's goodness to overlook sin, nor by amicable deception, denial of plain truth, or their own merit, but by Jesus Christ pleading their case with His shed blood, confession, and repentance of their sin of adultery. "The sacrifices of God are a broken spirit: a broken and a contrite heart. O God, thou wilt not despise." Psalm 51:17.

At that moment of transgression, "Thou shalt not bear false witness against thy neighbor," Adon had entered into the same tranquil arena of long-term deception as practiced by Satan. Causing people to live in the mild clutches of sin—unaware that they are engulfed in sin—until that final day of judgment when unrepentant sinners cannot enter into that bliss of eternal life. Satan gloats over such as these, because they have no desire to change. Truly, without knowledge and conviction of their sin—they will never change.

Satan knows that blindness to sin is the fine art of deception. Persons who are deceived are so deceived that they do not know they are deceived. They will not know they've been deceived until they've become undeceived. Likewise, one does not know he's been sound asleep, until he wakes up! Satan's avowed purpose is to keep Christians asleep, with respect to divorce and remarriage, until they wake up in the *second* resurrection, then, that final death, that no one awakens from.

11

1 Corinthians 7:15 (Context)

IN the apostle Paul's discourse to the neo-Christian church at Corinth, as stated in 1 Corinthians Chapter 7, there is an application of "Thou shalt not commit adultery" that provides the underpinning for everything that Paul teaches on divorce and remarriage. Therefore, it is helpful in arriving at a clear understanding of the verse that is most commonly quoted in 1 Corinthians to apply this commandment, and some of its various wording, to all pertinent verses previous to the commonly quoted verse which is: "But if the unbelieving depart, let him depart. A brother or a sister is not under bondage in such cases: but God hath called us to peace." 1 Corinthians 7:15.

This text is usually interpreted to mean: that if a Christian is married to a person who does not hold in high regard the same Bible doctrines as the Christian does, and the Christian is abandoned by the unbeliever, the believing Christian is now free to divorce the one who willingly departs from the marriage, and marry again, with the blessings of God; so long as they marry a Christian who holds in high regard the same doctrines as the one who was abandoned.

This interpretation is correct, and in keeping with the tenor of the whole Bible on the subject of divorce and remarriage, except in one vital aspect—the one who was abandoned, under the law, is *not free to remarry* without committing adultery!

"Except"

In Paul's letter to the Corinthians, he stays within the strict guidelines of the holy Law (and does not contradict himself, nor places the Bible in conflict) and his own personal decision to remain without a wife. To reveal the law of remarriage in Paul's discourse the following commandment, and decision of Paul to remain unmarried, will be applied to the texts in 1 Corinthians 7:2-15, which includes the commonly quoted verse.

Exodus 20:14 . . . Primary Decalogue Commandment: Thou shalt not commit adultery.

Tenets of Primary Commandment

Genesis 2:24 . . . . And they shall be one flesh.

Matthew 19:6 . . . . What therefore God hath joined together, let not man put asunder.

Luke 16:18 . . . . . . .Whosoever putteth away his wife, and marrieth another, committeth adultery: and whosoever marrieth her that is put away from her husband committeth adultery.

1 Corinthians 7:7 . . I say therefore to the unmarried and widows, It is good for them if they abide even as I.

Paul begins his instructions to the church in Corinth, in verse 1 of chapter 7, by restating what he had previously said with respect to the importance of abstaining from fornication. He wrote: "It is good for a man not to touch a woman." (Applied law Exodus 20:14)

Then in verse 2, he provides the only way that fornication can be avoided, and that is for men and women to get married. (Applied law Exodus 20:14)

He goes on to say in verses 3-6 that since a vital function of marriage is to avoid the sin of fornication, that the husband or the wife should not withhold themselves from sexual involvement if one of them is desirous of having intercourse. And that the body of each spouse regarding sex, because of marriage, belongs to the other, and if they abstain from sex it should be by mutual consent. (Applied law Genesis 2:24)

In verse 6, he makes it clear that what he has previously said regarding fornication and the obligation of intercourse in marriage is gleaned from the Law, but what he is about to say is from his own personal knowledge and experience; and because he has been called by God as an apostle, his teachings are trustworthy and in keeping with God's commandments.

Then he advises the Corinthian Christians in verses 7-9 that if they can remain single, without ever having married, as he has done, he highly recommends this lifestyle. (Note: Paul was never married, therefore, he is using the word unmarried to mean never been married, as the case is with him.) But he is aware that every man or woman is not suited to an unmarried lifestyle, because some are able to control their sexual desires, and some are not. However, if they can exercise self-control, he recommends that since they have never been married, not to get married. And if they are a widow, not to remarry. (Applied law Exodus 20:14 and 1 Corinthians 7:7)

He concedes in verse 9, that if they are eligible for marriage by never having been married, or they are eligible because their spouse is dead, it is better for Christians under these circumstances to go ahead and marry, rather than to continually desire sex, and, therefore, be in constant danger of committing the sin of fornication. (Applied law Exodus 20:14)

Paul moves from his personal, trustworthy recommendations on marriage, for those who have never been married, and widows, to the requirements of God's law as it pertains to those Christians who are married, and both spouses have the same Christian faith, and they agree on obedience to God's commandments with respect to marriage.

He writes in verse 10: "Let not the wife depart from her

husband." (Applied law Matthew 19:6) But he recognizes, in verse 11, that extenuating circumstances involving some troubled marriages may force a spouse to seek a divorce on Biblical grounds (sexual immorality), and in severe cases such as these a divorce may be unavoidable, and even necessary. If a divorce occurs, neither person can marry again, unless they remarry their previous spouse. But, if at all possible, a divorce is not to be initiated by either spouse. (Applied law Luke 16:18)

Then in verses 12-15, Paul returns to his role of an ordained and trustworthy spokesperson for Jehovah and provides his own counsel to those married couples who find themselves unequally yoked to an unbeliever. He begins verse 12 with, "But to the rest speak I, not the Lord." He has already addressed situations involving Christians who have never been married, widows, and married with the same religious faith, so now his personal admonitions are aimed at married couples where one spouse is a believer and one is not, "the rest." (Applied law Genesis 2:24 and Matthew 19:6)

He outlines a scenario wherein a Christian believer is married to a person who is not a believer, but the unbeliever wants to remain in the marriage. And, although they are unequally yoked, the believer is forbidden to divorce the unbeliever. Paul stresses the point that even though they are unequally yoked, but because they are one flesh, the Christian believer provides the unbeliever with God's grace, to achieve growth in sanctification, which could ultimately lead to their total conversion to Christ. And, because they are one flesh, God places much more emphasis upon their married state than the fact that they are unequally yoked, therefore, God looks upon their children as holy, and not bastards.

However, in the unfortunate circumstance that an unbeliever wants out of the marriage, and decides to go his or her separate ways, a loyal Christian believer is not wholly obligated to continue their efforts to obtain a one-faith home, and that bond of sanctification that the believer provided for the unbeliever has been broken (the unbeliever rejected it), and the believer is free to seek legal release from the unbeliever (divorce), so that peace and harmony from a volatile situation can be restored in the Christian's home. Jehovah will continue to bless the spouse who has sincerely attempted to be a Christian example for their mate, where the unbeliever willfully quit the marriage. (Applied law Luke 16:18)

It is important to note that the situation in verse 15, where a spouse has left the marriage, and the situation in verse 11, are the same. In both cases the marriage has been damaged because one spouse decided to leave. The causes for the breakup of the marriage may differ, although verse 11 does not give a definite cause (verse 15 does, an unbeliever) the scenario is the same—one spouse was dissatisfied with the marriage and abandoned it. Since the scenario is the same, the applied law is the same in both verses. (Paul's defector is not specifically an adulterer, but an unbeliever.)

Indeed, the spirit of the seventh commandment states: "But and if she depart, let her remain unmarried." If the spirit of the commandment is consistent (which it is) when a spouse departs in verse 11, and cannot remarry, it is logical to assume that if a spouse who is an unbeliever also deserts a marriage the applied law of Luke 16:18, "and whosoever marrieth her that is put away from her husband committeth adultery," is forced into action, and the believing spouse cannot remarry. The common interpretation of verse 15 becomes highly suspect, to assume that because the believer was unfortunately abandoned by the unbeliever, that the believer now has grounds to remarry. This is not the case anywhere in the Bible, save the concession made by Moses for the hard-hearted in Israel, else the teachings of Jesus and Paul are of no effect respecting a return to the highest practice of obedience to the seventh commandment.

If Paul is providing grounds for remarriage in verse 15, "A brother or a sister is not under bondage in such cases," how could he then do a complete about face and say, in verse 39,

"The wife is bound by the law as long as her husband liveth; but if her husband be dead, she is at liberty to be married to whom she will; only in the Lord," and remain creditable as a keeper of the commandments and a spokesperson for God. Paul cannot contradict himself. The truth is that Paul is consistent (See also Romans 7:2, 3), Jesus is consistent, and the Bible is consistent, since in both cases, verses 15 and 39 (verse 15, the disputed text, is sandwiched between verses 11 and 39 which both dictate the outcome of the one no longer under bondage in verse 15), a spouse must surely be dead before any remarriage is possible without committing the sin of adultery. Divorce, for whatever the cause, does not unreservedly end a marriage—death does.

12

Tell It Like It Is

In most instances, there are three broad classes of divorce: two of which involve parties to a divorce who are presumed innocent of adultery, and parties who are presumed guilty.

A divorce in marriage where no adultery has been committed by either person is said by God to be a marriage that is still spiritually binding, and neither person is permitted to remarry. What a person does after this kind of divorce, in the way of sin in an attempt to nullify the spiritual marriage, cannot change the circumstances in effect before the divorce. If there was no adultery before the divorce, adultery after the divorce still does not end the marriage.

A divorce in marriage where one party is guilty of adultery, and the *guilty divorces the innocent,* is said by God to annul the marriage, and the one who did not commit adultery may *choose* to remarry. The person who committed adultery is not at liberty to remarry while their former spouse remains alive. This rule, appearing to adversely affect the guilty spouse, seems unfair to human understanding and, therefore, is frequently violated in ignorance of the lasting consequence of willful sin.

A divorce where both spouses have committed adultery is said by God to render both persons ineligible to remarry until one spouse has died.

Although, in each of the above cases, differing circumstances surround the causes for a divorce all the cases have one thing in common—each person involved in their unique divorce, if they have subsequently remarried, has broken the seventh commandment: Thou shalt not commit adultery.

Even the innocent who accepted their divorce initiated by their adulterous spouse, and the innocent has remarried, falls under the spirit of the law of adultery. Such a person, provided they have married someone who was eligible, has not committed public adultery but the spirit of God's law has been violated, wherein, they have remarried while their spouse is living. (God upholds the Mosaic law instituted solely for the hard-hearted; and under strict conditions remarriage for them is not accounted as *public* sin. This in no way alters God's law, since God is unchangeable.) "For I am the Lord, I change not." Malachi 3:6.

While the innocent spouse (guilty divorced the innocent) has been permitted to legally remarry, the sacred vows of their first marriage, and any subsequent marriages, have remained on firm record in heaven; the spiritual bond intact in complete accordance with God's law. And the innocent spouse faces a matter of true repentance in the judgment, when all similitude of sin is either blotted out, or left on record. Confession and repentance on the part of the accused sinner is the deciding factor.

The Bible clearly teaches that there is earthbound warfare in progress between mighty satanic influences that undertake to cast human beings into eternal damnation, and the power in the love of Jehovah Who gave His life to redeem mankind from a future of separation from Himself. There are just two divisions in the controversy: the side of God, and the side of Satan. Satan has already lost the big war, and he knows that the time before his total destruction is frightfully limited. But being totally evil, and unredeemable, he continues to fight his kind of war, which is unmitigated deception targeted at all individuals who have demonstrated a willingness to reject the saving power in the Word of God.

Satan's deceptions are centered in the law of God containing

God's Ten Commandments. Satan's supernatural knowledge has calculated that if he can destroy in mankind the respect of, and obedience to, God's Ten Commandments he can successfully obliterate all vestiges of the character of God in mankind.

Part of Jehovah's plan to redeem mankind is to recreate in the fallen race His own name, which is His character that is manifested by obedience to the Ten Commandments. As God was preparing Moses to return to Mount Sinai, Moses made a heartfelt request of God. "And he said, I beseech thee, shew me thy glory." By his petition Moses wanted to know who God was; what was His infinite belief system—show him His *character!* God answered Moses. "And He said, I will make all my goodness pass before thee, and I will proclaim the *name* of the Lord before thee." Exodus 33:18, 19.

Then Moses did as God had commanded, and he took two tables of stone upon Mount Sinai. "And the Lord descended in the cloud, and stood with him there, and proclaimed the name of the Lord." Exodus 34:5. God showed Moses His glory, His character, His *name* by writing the Ten Commandments in the two tables of stone.

Likewise, "And I looked, and, lo, a Lamb stood on the mount Sion, and with Him an hundred forty and four thousand, having His Father's name written in their foreheads." Revelation 14:1. The Father's *name* written on the mind of the 144,000 was put there by obedience to the Ten Commandments—which are the name of God. "These are they which follow the Lamb whithersoever He goeth." Revelation 14:4. The 144,000 do whatever Jesus Christ did; they reveal His character by obedience to all of His Ten Commandments. They have "His Father's *name* written in their foreheads."

If Satan can slyly disguise God's Ten Commandments, he can keep individuals in sin and, therefore, hinder the plan of God to return mankind to the image of Himself through obedience to His law.

Satan, the devil, is a practiced masterful deceiver, and he has a fine-tuned deception for everyone who is willing to deviate to the slightest degree from the Ten Commandments law of God. All religions, whether Christianity, Judaism, Islam, and others, which have succumbed to the subtle sophistries of Satan are in some aspect violating precepts of God's law.

A large body of Christians readily thinks to ignore the law of God by teaching that the law was only for the Old Testament Jews, and no longer binding upon New Testament Christians.

Some Christians declare that the Ten Commandments law is still holy, and should be observed by all serious Christians; but the fourth commandment, which states that the seventh day of the week (Saturday) is the true Sabbath, can be substituted with Sunday, the first day, and this traditional substitution, initiated by the Roman Catholic Church, is okay with God because Jesus was resurrected on the Sunday.

Other dedicated Christians who teach and practice observance of the seventh day Sabbath are a special target of Satan, and he carefully chooses his victims out of this group to trip them up on the commandment out of the ten that they appear most susceptible to. In this modern age of situational morality, Satan has found overwhelming success with Sabbath-keeping Christians who have troublesome marriages. The seventh commandment, Thou shalt not commit adultery, is so misunderstood that many Christians within this union willfully break it and steadfastly defend their actions as Biblically sound. Just as Sabbath reform was acutely mandatory, remarriage reform is mandatory also, to adhere to their proclamation of the Bible, and the Bible only, as their only rule of faith.

Companionship between a man and a woman is a gift from God. It is a natural desire in two people of the opposite sex to want to form a friendship that may lead to sexual involvement. However, God has placed strict limits on sexual intimacy, and commands that it may occur only within the bounds of marriage. "Marriage is honourable in all, and the bed undefiled: but whoremongers and adulterers God will judge." Hebrews 13:4.

And an intention to marry, itself, has safeguards to insure that obedient Christians do not violate the sanctity of marriage by marrying when they are ineligible to marry. Some Christians, however, wholly ignore the safeguards God has placed around marriage—and even if they are ineligible, they marry anyway. In many such cases, if they are aware of God's law, they hope in all honesty that God will look the other way, and understand why they *had* to get married instead of surrendering themselves to God's law, and remain unencumbered with a spouse.

The scenarios for unbiblical states of marriage are numerous, and although God expects total obedience to His seventh commandment, "Fear God, and keep His commandments: for this is the whole duty of man" Ecclesiastes 12:13, He understands that mankind is weak, and oftentimes some easily fall prey to the skillful deceptions of Satan. Indeed, within the plan of salvation, which included the death and resurrection of Jesus Christ, God has made provisions for His bountiful mercy to be shed upon those with good hearts who find themselves living their everyday lives under the condemnation of the law of God.

God's plan to redeem lost sinners did not end at the cross of Calvary with the suffering and death of Jesus, nor did it end after His resurrection and ascension to His throne in heaven. Besides His 3 1/2 years of public ministry on earth, Jesus, the eternal Son of God, still has an unfinished work to perform before the image of Himself can be perfectly restored in man, and He rewards sincere believers with eternal life. This work to be consummated by Jesus Christ, before His imminent return to receive His people, is the judgment.

Every human being must be judged by Jesus to determine if he is fit or unfit for eternal life in the presence of a holy God. In the judgment of every human being is where God's manifold mercy is brought to bear upon every sinner's case—whether to pardon, or condemn. No sinner is present in person at his or her judgment, but the unerring record of every individual's life on earth, faithfully recorded by the loyal angels of God, is the evidence that will attest to the eternal salvation or eternal lost of every person.

God perceives every thought, every motive, every word, and every action of every person who is living, or who has ever lived—"Neither is there any creature that is not manifest in His sight: but all things are naked and opened unto the eyes of Him with whom we have to do." Hebrews 4:13. And every nuance of everyone's personality is dutifully recorded by the heavenly angels, and stored in the books of heaven, to be faced by every individual when their time has arrived to be judged. No aspect of life escapes the compassionately discerning eye of God, and every sinner's sure destiny is judgment. A sinner may be living when he is judged, or he may have died; but the righteous (all who professed Christianity) dead will be judged first, and the living last. "For the time is come that judgment must *begin at the house of God*: and if it first begin at us, what shall the end be of them that obey not the gospel of God?" 1 Peter 4:17.

The Bible makes it strikingly clear when the judgment began with the record of the dead; but no one but God knows when it will close with those who are living. When the judgment is finished, Jesus will return the second time. "Watch therefore, for ye know neither the day nor the hour wherein the Son of man cometh." Matthew 25:13.

The Bible reveals much, and often, about the judgment. In His ministry Jesus found it to His advantage to teach about the non- visible judgment in parables. Oftentimes He used the phrase "kingdom of heaven," to denote the judgment—appealing to the mind of the common people regarding a final accounting they must give for their lives, while circumventing the error-filled doctrines of the scribes and Pharisees and leaving the deceitful teachers wondering about the underlying meaning of His stories. When the disciples asked Jesus, "Why speakest thou unto them in parables?" Jesus replied, "Because it is given unto you to know the mysteries of the kingdom of heaven, but to them it is not given. For whosoever hath, *to him shall be given*, and he shall have more abundance; but whosoever hath not *from him shall be taken away* even that he hath." Matthew 13:10-12.

In His answer Jesus painted a picture of a future time when a settling of all accounts would transpire, when persons would receive whatever they deserve—good or bad—in the judgment. Some receiving additional favoritism through eternal life; and some not having enough favor, having even that which they had taken away through eternal damnation.

In mankind's earthly existence it seems that evil prospers and goodness is downtrodden, and the whole system of justice is turned in favor of the wicked; but in the judgment of all who have ever been born, no one is spared the fair reward of their lifelong works. And in many of the parables where Jesus uses the phrase "kingdom of heaven," this scenario of reward and punishment is the message of the parable. In the judgment is where reward and punishment is meted out to all. "For he shall have judgment without mercy, that hath shewed no mercy; and mercy triumphs over judgment." James 2:13.

"Hear ye therefore the parable of the sower," Jesus said, as He continued teaching about the future judgment. And then, "Another parable put He forth unto them, saying, The kingdom of heaven is likened unto a man which sowed good seed in his field." Then Jesus told the story of an enemy who had planted weeds in the man's field. The weeds the enemy planted looked much like the good seed the man had planted, and the untrained eye could not tell the good seed from the weeds. Therefore, the man told His servants to let the weeds grow with the good seed.

"Let both grow together until the harvest: and in the time of the harvest I will say to the reapers, Gather ye together first the tares, and bind them in bundles to burn them: but gather the wheat into my barn." Matthew 13:30.

Later that day, after Jesus had finished teaching the people in parables—"and without a parable spake He not unto them: that it might be fulfilled which was spoken by the prophet, saying . . . I will utter things which have been kept secret from the foundation of the world." "His disciples came unto Him, saying, Declare unto us the parable of the tares of the field."

Jesus explained to His disciples that He Himself sowed the good seed. The devil planted the weeds. "The harvest is the end of the world; and the reapers are the angels. As therefore the tares are gathered and burned in the fire; so shall it be in *the end of this world.* The Son of man shall send forth His angels, and they shall gather out of His kingdom all things that offend, and them which do iniquity; and shall cast them into a furnace of fire: there shall be wailing and gnashing of teeth. Then shall the righteous shine forth as the sun in the kingdom of their Father. Who hath and ear to hear, let him hear." Matthew 13:34-43.

This answer that Jesus provided for His disciples could be nothing else but a lesson about the judgment, which could only occur "in the end of this world," and "which have been kept secret from the foundation of the world." Here is a gathering of God and the angels and a final separation of bad people from the good. The bad are cast "into a furnace of fire," and "then shall the righteous shine forth as the sun in the kingdom of their Father." All of this final settling of accounts occurs in the judgment, *in the end of this world,* and Jesus taught regarding it through the parable of the sower.

Again Jesus taught the people, saying, "For the kingdom of heaven is like unto a man that is an householder, which went out early in the morning to hire labourers into his vineyard." Matthew 20:1. And according to the parable the householder paid the laborers that he had hired the last hour of the day the same as the laborers who had worked a full day. The laborers who had worked a full day, in the heat of the sun, vehemently complained about the injustice of the householder who had paid everyone the same wages. But the householder reminded the all-day laborers that they had agreed beforehand to work for the same wages as he had paid to the one-hour workers; and their complaint was unjustified since they knew the conditions of their employment before they accepted the job. Then the householder sent the dissatisfied laborers away, saying, "Take that thine is, and go thy way: I will give unto this last, even as unto thee. Is it not lawful for me to do what I will with mine own? Is thine eye evil, because I am good? So the last shall be first, and the first last: for many be called, but few chosen." Matthew 20:14-16.

Here, again, is a summation of accounts at the end of the day (end of time) and a vital separation is in the works, "for many be called, *but few chosen.*" In the parable, the laborers were paid in full according to the terms of their employment, and the householder was completely within his rights, regardless of the time and hard conditions under which they had worked, to pay everyone what they had agreed to beforehand. In other words, it doesn't matter, in the judgment, how *long* one has lived—but *how* they've lived. Longevity is not nearly as important a factor as character. Many have professed to be the servants of God but in the judgment their character will be scrutinized and from the many professed, few will be chosen to receive eternal life. "So the last shall be first, and the first last," since someone could follow Jesus for one day, and be saved, while someone who has spent a lifetime being a Christian, in name only, could be lost. And Jesus Christ, who is the Householder, is completely within His rights to "reward every man according to his works" in the end of the world.

Likewise, "Whosoever therefore shall break one of these least commandments, and shall teach men so, he shall be called the least in the kingdom of heaven: but whosoever shall do and teach them, the same shall be called great in the kingdom of heaven." Matthew 5:19.

Here, an investigation is expected to shortly take place, and it involves two classes of *believers*—those who disobey the Ten Commandments and teach others to do so by their lifestyle and words, and those who observe all the Ten Commandments and teach others to do the same. The former class, who are disobedient, are looked upon with disfavor in the kingdom of heaven, which is the place where the investigation of their works will be carried out. The latter class, who are obedient to the Ten Commandments, "and teach men so," are congratulated, and they are called great in this place called the kingdom of heaven.

Truly, in order to even arrive in the kingdom of heaven and receive the privilege of being condemned or congratulated, the believer's character must outshine the scribes and Pharisees.

"For I say unto you, That except your righteousness shall exceed the righteousness of the scribes and Pharisees, ye shall in no case enter into the kingdom of heaven." Matthew 5:20. The ultimate character flaw of the scribes and Pharisees was their rejection of Jesus as the Messiah. Without recognizing Jesus as their Savior, they were not even worthy of *entrance* into the kingdom of heaven!

This insight into the "kingdom of heaven" must be a lesson on, in the disciples time, the future judgment for the Scriptures do not reveal that there is any kind of formal investigation of believers based on their keeping of the Ten Commandments except in the end of time—in the judgment.

"Let us hear the conclusion of the whole matter: Fear God, and keep His commandments: for this is the whole duty of man. For God shall bring every work into judgment, with every secret thing, whether it be good, or whether it be evil." Ecclesiastes 12:13, 14.

In the parable the ones who are investigated are believers in Jesus Christ. Hence, in this fashion, their righteousness has exceeded that of the scribes and Pharisees, and they have been allowed to enter the kingdom of heaven. But something further is required of them than simply believing—their faith must result in the keeping of His commandments. In the kingdom of heaven faith will get you there—but faith must be linked up with obedience to God's law in order to be called "great" in the kingdom of heaven. Indeed, since only believers in Jesus Christ are being investigated, persons who do not accept Jesus Christ as their Savior will not be investigated in this phase of the judgment. Nonbelievers are judged at another time—separate from believers.

"Do ye not know that the saints shall judge the world? . . . Know ye not that we shall judge angels?" 1 Corinthians 6:2, 3. "And I saw thrones, and they sat upon them, and judgment was given unto them . . . and they lived and reigned with Christ a thousand years." Revelation 20:4.

And so it is, parable after parable, the kingdom of heaven is presented within a framework of dividing one class of people from another—the worthy from the unworthy. This is exactly what takes place in the judgment of professed believers in the end of the world—the revealed character of every individual is closely examined and some are thus accepted according to their works, and some are rejected. The "kingdom of heaven," in the proper context, is synonymous with the judgment of believers, in the end of the world.

In the final judgment, as they appear in the unerring books of record, forgiveness of sin, confession of sin, and repentance from sin have a key role in determining the eternal future of the sinner. Confession, forgiveness, and repentance are aspects of salvation that must occur in the life of the sinner while he is still living. God and the sinner have distinct functions to fulfill—while the sinner lives—that are inseparably bound up with confession, forgiveness, and repentance; and the outcome of these functions are accurately recorded in the books of heaven, to bear witness, for or against the sinner, in the judgment.

Every sin that the sinner has committed has to appear in the books of heaven as forgiven. *Only the Creator God can forgive sin,* and this is an act of love that He has promised to perform when the sinner comes to Him seeking forgiveness. "If we confess our sins, He is faithful and just to forgive us our sins, and to cleanse us (in the judgment) from all unrighteousness." 1 John 1:9.

Without forgiveness of sin from Jehovah, the sinner has no

chance to receive eternal life. As often as the sinner commits sin, and asks forgiveness, God will keep His word and forgive the sinner. Forgiveness happens instantly, at the moment of asking, and forgiveness for that sin is recorded in the books of heaven to bear witness in the judgment.

God offers forgiveness of sin, and this is His sole prerogative, but forgiveness, independently, does not prepare the sinner to receive eternal life. The sinner must fulfill the conditions which God has assigned to him, which are confessing his sins and repenting of his confessed sins. Confession and repentance of sin are the sacred yoke of the sinner, and they must be united with God's forgiveness before sin can be forever removed from heaven's record, there awaiting investigation in the judgment.

Truly, the sinner, in his daily devotional, must remain aware of the climate of his behavior in word, thought, and action; and whether he has committed sins that must be presented to God for forgiveness. This process of remaining aware, and asking forgiveness for every sin, is a necessary ingredient in the transformation of the sinner's vile character into the pure and lovely character of God. It clears the path to overcoming every sin, and becomes a joy of worship as sins are laid aside and one is drawn into closer fellowship with Jesus Christ. "Remember therefore from whence thou art fallen, and repent . . . To him that overcometh will I give to eat of the tree of life, which is in the midst of the paradise of God." Revelation 2:5, 7.

To sincerely ask forgiveness for sin, the sinner must understand that sin is whatever words, thoughts, or actions that are at variance with God's law of Ten Commandments. In the judgment, where all forgiveness, confession, and repentance of sin is investigated, the standard for what constitutes sin is the Ten Commandments. Any act that violates the Ten Commandments is sin. "Whosoever committeth sin transgresseth also the law, for sin is the transgression of the law." 1 John 3:4. "Therefore to him that knoweth to do good, and doeth it not, to him it is sin." James 4:17.

Tell It Like It Is

In his prayer life, after the sinner has confessed, asked, and received immediate forgiveness for sin, he has submitted one of *his* character transforming responsibilities (confession) in favor of eternal salvation, to the record books in heaven. God utilizes three books, where the life history of every sinner is faithfully and unerringly recorded. There is the book of remembrance, where all the good deeds in every life experience is painstakingly placed into the record. "Then they that feared the Lord spake often one to another: and the Lord hearkened, and heard it, and a book of remembrance was written before Him for them that feared the Lord, and that thought upon His name." Malachi 3:16.

Only acts performed out of love for God, in accordance with His law, and acts performed out of love for one's fellowman, in harmony with God's law, are accounted worthy to be entered into the book of God's remembrance. Obedience to God and unselfish service to fellow human beings, especially those who cannot assist themselves, are the works of righteousness that pleases God the most, and are the outward indication of the image of God being created anew in the surrendered sinner.

Before God's book of remembrance can have one scribble of information entered therein, regarding the good deeds of the sinner, God's book, called the book of life, must contain the identifying name of the sinner. The only method by which an individual's name can be recorded in the book of life—which is the absolute beginning of the road to eternal salvation—is to accept Jesus Christ as his personal Savior. "Neither is there salvation in any other: for there is none other name under heaven given among men, whereby we must be saved." Acts 4:12. "He that hath the Son hath life; and he that hath not the Son of God hath not life." 1 John 5:12.

The moment a person enters into a saving relationship with Jesus Christ—recognizing Him as the "one mediator between God and men," and his name is entered into the book of life, and he is permanently on record in the heavenly sanctuary—his name resides there until his ultimate character, resulting from his lifelong relationship with Jesus Christ, comes up for investigation in the judgment. Only the names that still remain in the book of life, after the judgment, will be saved. "He that overcometh, the same shall be clothed in white raiment; and I will not blot out his name out of the book of life, but I will confess his name before my Father, and before his angels." Revelation 3:5.

In addition to God's book of remembrance, and book of life, God employs another book to faithfully keep a record of all the sins committed by professed Christians. Every evil thought, every surrender to the ways of Satan, every action in defiance of God's law, every secret motive to cause harm to another human being, are kept in store in the book of sin, to be weighted on the scale of life and death in the final judgment of the sinner. There is no small sin! "For God shall bring every work into judgment, with every secret thing, whether it be good, or whether it be evil." Ecclesiastes 12:14.

After the sinner has confessed his sin to God, he has fulfilled just one of the responsibilities assigned to him that sustains him on the right course to salvation. His confession, as with every act, good and bad, is recorded in the heavenly sanctuary in the dedicated book. But confession by the sinner, and forgiveness by God, will not suffice to recreate the image of God in man, and, therefore, the two deeds alone will not quality the sinner to pass successfully through the judgment, and receive eternal life.

In addition to confession and forgiveness, the sinner must have recorded in Jehovah's book of remembrance that he has repented of the sin he has confessed, and which God has forgiven. All the wrongs in his life that constitute sin, measured by the Ten Commandments, must be turned away from, and the sinner must begin to do that which is right in God's sight. Jesus taught a lesson of repentance in a few words, when He told the woman caught in adultery "go, and sin no more." Confession and forgiveness cannot stand alone in God's book of remembrance to clear the sinner of sin. Repentance must be recorded there, too, for that particular sin to be blotted out, and the sinner's name left recorded in the book of life.

God is merciful! His character is the essence of mercy. He manifests His loving-kindness in countless ways in the daily lives of His human creation. The terrible accident that should have caused the death of the unfortunate one—it was God's mercy that allowed him to live. It was the bountiful mercy of God that put into action the plan to redeem mankind from sin. So much mercy that God, Himself, gave up His life in terrible suffering to pay the penalty for sin for every human being. God's crowning act of mercy to save sinners is carried out in the judgment when every human being, who has ever pleaded the blood of Jesus to deliver him from sin, will appear before Jehovah through their faultless record to be judged—worthy, or unworthy, to receive eternal life.

God's awesome mercy will be displayed in its fullest splendor as He considers every name, with every breath that has been drawn by that name that has determined if confession, forgiveness, and repentance was assigned to every sin in the book of sin. If all three of the criteria for removal are there, that sin will be erased, and the sinner's name will survive in the book of life. The next sin in the book comes under investigation.

Every sin that the sinner has ever committed will fall into a category of evil that is determined by the transgression of the Ten Commandments. The seventh commandment—Thou shalt not commit adultery—covers all sin related to sexuality and marriage. All lies, evil surmising, masturbation, withholding of affection, secret affairs, brawls among spouses, and numerous others, are sins that fall under the seventh commandment.

Figuratively, under the seventh commandment, on the vows of marriage page, are the names of couples who have sustained a first marriage to their creation spouse. Sins were committed during this marriage that were sincerely confessed, faithfully forgiven by God, and repented of by the names. The sins committed under this union of marriage will not remain in the book of sin, but God will blot them out—and the marriage relationship will engender God's approval and He will, with joy, if all other entries of sin are blotted out, remember to reward the couple before all the company of the saved as He highlights their wonderful achievement in His book of remembrance.

Another creation marriage recorded under the seventh commandment reveal the names of persons who remained married for awhile, but due to circumstances that did not involve adultery, they obtained a divorce. God frowns in disapproval at the divorce since "The Lord, the God of Israel, saith that He hateth putting away (divorce)." Malachi 2:16. And divorce stirs up so many other carnal sins; but divorce, itself, for Biblical reasons (by, and upholding the Mosaic law), is not a sin so He bypasses this act. Then the record shows that the names in that marriage were obedient to the seventh commandment, and never married again. Their names are highlighted in God's book of remembrance, and should they pass successfully through the final judgment, their obedience to all of God's commandments will be rewarded with an eternal life of peace and happiness.

Another creation marriage that was entered into with vows of "until death do us part" ended in a violent, disappointing divorce because one party to the marriage regularly committed adultery. The heavenly record unerringly showed that the guilty spouse felt that God was too loving to require him/her to live the balance of their life, after their divorce, out of wedlock, committing the sin of fornication in singlehood, so they sought and found a love relationship, and married again.

In God's book of remembrance, since He had blessed it when it was consummated, was the entry for this creation marriage. And even though it had ended in divorce because of the sin of adultery, the record showed that both names had met all three criteria—confession, forgiveness, and repentance—for remaining in the book of life.

However, when the spouse who had previously committed adultery unwittingly married again, while their first marriage partner remained alive, they nullified the condition for their name to remain in the book of life (in the final judgment), and returned again to a sinner condemned by the law of the seventh commandment. Their second marriage removed repentance for the sin of adultery in their first marriage.

In addition to repentance for adultery in the first marriage being forfeited by the second marriage, the sinner has unlawfully entered into another marriage union where repentance, once again, is required for violation of the seventh commandment—he/she was not eligible to remarry, since their divorced spouse was still living.

If he is truly convicted of the unrepented sin that hangs over him, condemned by the law of the seventh commandment, he will confess the sin of his second marriage. As He has promised, Jehovah will immediately forgive his sin. But repentance of sin is mandatory, too, and until repentance is entered into for his second marriage, his sin of adultery, in his first marriage, will remain recorded in the book of sin as unrepented of. He cannot become clear of violating the seventh commandment, while continuing to violate it.

Since his second marriage is unlawful, his second spouse is also living under the condemnation of the seventh commandment; and repentance is required to have this violation of the moral law removed from the book of sin, and the sinner's name remain, after the judgment, in the book of life. Only names not blotted out of the book of life will be saved.

Marriage is a holy, lifelong commitment, and ones *first* marriage has precedence over all others. It forever sets the rules for what the parties to the marriage can and cannot do with respect to future opposite sex relationships. Since marriage is a bond that lasts until it is ended by death, and even though an innocent one, in certain cases, may choose to remarry without committing public sin, the vows of the first marriage are permanently etched in the books of heaven to be reckoned with in the judgment.

If an innocent spouse has occasion to marry more than once, each successive marriage, while any previous spouse is living, places both participants in the marriage as candidates for the justice of God. Then, in the final judgment, out of the book of remembrance, when all other occasions for obedience to God's law are considered, this spiritual transgression, recorded in the book of sin, is evaluated on the quality of the sinner's lifelong commitment to God. If compassion is warranted, God blots out this spiritual sin, and the sinner's name survives in the book of life. Therefore, the integrity of God's law is maintained; and by the sinner's true knowledge of the spiritual condition surrounding their marriage(s) they were able to submissively *ask* for, and become a recipient of God's mercy. Had other sins remained in the book of sin, their spiritual misconduct in marriage would have remained there, too.

Christian baptism is a gospel ordinance honoring the death, burial, and resurrection of Jesus Christ. Christians who are baptized by immersion (bodily, under water), the method by which Jesus was baptized, have been spiritually born again; and they are providing public testimony that they have turned from their ignorance of sin and have been duly crucified with Christ, buried with Him, and raised to a renewed life of dedication to Him. Therefore, any transgressions that occurred *before* their sincere repentance and baptism, and before they had a Biblical knowledge of truth, are not counted against them in the judgment. After baptism, the heavenly books of record are swept clean, and the believer is establishing a better life-history, beginning anew in Jesus Christ..

"Know ye not, that so many of us as were baptized into Jesus Christ were baptized into His death? Therefore we are buried with him by baptism into death: that like as Christ was raised up from the dead by the glory of the Father, even so we also should *walk in newness of life*. For if we have been planted together in the likeness of His death, we shall be also in the likeness of His resurrection." Romans 6:3, 4, 5.

A broken marriage where the spouses do not reunite, like the taking of a life by murder, cannot be undone to erase the event from having ever occurred; yet the need for repentance is still a condition for having the sin removed from the books of record in the judgment. A marriage once existed in the physical realm that now does not—similarly, a life once existed that now does not. A marriage and a human life once had a real, earthly existence, and since their existence was governed by the moral law of Ten Commandments, their demise was faithfully recorded in the heavenly books of record.

Murder cannot be repented of, unless the sinner who murdered utterly stops murdering. Adultery cannot be repented of, unless the sinner who commits adultery ceases to commit adultery. If a murderer murders again, he has surely forfeited his repentance for the previous crime. Likewise, for an adulterer. Repentance is called for again to amend the heavenly record in the sinner's favor.

Indeed, repentance is not simply the act of not committing the sin. Repentance occurs, first, in the heart, wherein, one is so committed not to commit the sin, and realizes his weakness, that he wholly avoids the opportunity to sin. A thief who does not steal cars, because he is incarcerated, has not repented—he doesn't presently steal cars because he can't. Therefore, when he is released from confinement, he steals cars again. He has not repented because in his heart he would regularly steal cars if only he had the opportunity.

True repentance is to hate the sin, and feel so ashamed that one will "Abstain from all appearance of evil." 1 Thessalonians 5:22. In true repentance he will "Enter not into the path of the wicked, and go not in the way of evil men; avoid it, pass not by it, *turn from it*, and pass away. . . . For they eat the bread of wickedness, and drink the wine of violence. But the path of the just is as the shining light, that shineth more and more unto the perfect day." Proverbs 4:14-18.

If an adulterer is ineligible to remarry—and does—he has turned the heavenly record, which he cannot see but believes by faith that it exists, against himself and until repentance is again assigned to his name he is living under the condemnation of the law of God, which will surely weigh against him in the judgment. No literal event in the day-to-day lives of believers that upholds, or violates, God's law of Ten Commandments ever vanishes in the spiritual realm until it is dealt with in the judgment, and the specific event is measured against the sinner's worthiness of salvation.

God is merciful! In the final judgment is when God's mercy and justice for the sinner are reconciled. Justice is treating the sinner with the utmost of fairness, and issuing to him the exact future that he deserves. Mercy is the manifestation of God's pity for the sinner who is undeserving and guilty.

The justice of God demands that His treatment of sin and sinners ensures that sin will never again arise in His creations. Truly, since love of God and obedience to His law are wholly voluntary, God's assurance that sin will *never* rise up again is that only those who demonstrate these willing qualities in their earthly life can pass through the final judgment. For Jehovah, voluntary love and obedience on earth, amidst the ever-present holocausts of sin, ensures voluntary love and obedience for all eternity, where there is no sin.

God not only applies His justice to the sinner, but to Himself, also. He has been accused by the foremost angel of all angels, Satan, of being unfair, and His law grossly unjust, and Satan vowed that none of the angels, including himself, could obey it.

In the final judgment Jehovah's character is forever vindicated by those whom He has redeemed from the earth by His own blood, and have been obedient to all His commandments out of love for their Creator.

In the judgment Satan is condemned by the pure character of the redeemed who have their "Father's name written in their foreheads" and His name (character) was put there by their obedience to all of God's commandments. Satan is proved a liar because God's law *can* be obeyed, and the redeemed are a witness against him that all God's creation can verify. Truly, Satan is condemned by his own works, when all the unfallen worlds deliberate the abysmal future that following Satan would have wrought, as they observe the devastating effect sin—disobedience to God's law—has had on the planet and the human race.

The sinner who has professed much faith in Jesus Christ, but their obedience to God's commandments has been sketchy, and willfully compromising, is steeped in unimaginable difficulty in the judgment since God's justice warrants his death, but God's mercy wants him to live.

"Have mercy upon me, O God, according to thy lovingkindness: according unto the multitude of thy tender mercies blot out my transgressions." Psalm 51:1

God's compassion for the guilty does not imply their release from guilt. In the judgment not only the sinner, but God, too, is now in a testy situation—someone is "there" without a wedding garment!

"The kingdom of heaven is like unto a certain king," Jesus said, as He spoke to the chief priests and Pharisees, "which made a marriage (wedding feast) for his son." Matthew 22:2. Then Jesus went on to tell the story of how the king sent out his servants to personally invite those to the wedding feast who were on the preferred guest list. But those persons refused to attend the feast.

Then the king, thinking that maybe his servants had not properly impressed the preferred guests, sent out other servants who were more sophisticated when it came to conversing with important people. And to make the invitation practically impossible to refuse, the king told these servants to describe to the preferred guests how lavish a dinner he had prepared; and on top of that, the table was set, the white candles were burning, and his best chefs were ready to serve his best meats hot. "Tell them to please, without delay, come to the feast!" the king said..

But when the sophisticated servants went and told all of this to the preferred guests, the guests sneered at the servants, and belly laughed at the king, and made fun of his silly dinner. They especially didn't want to purchase that ridiculous white robe the king wanted them to wear in honor of his son. Then some of the preferred guests jovially went off to take care of their private affairs, but some of them were so recklessly indifferent that they killed the king's sophisticated servants.

When the king heard what had happened he was enraged—and sent forth his armies, and they destroyed those murderers, and utterly burned down their city (justice). Then the king sent out more servants, and told them to invite anybody that they could find, good and bad, to come to the feast.

Indeed, the king's only son was getting nervous, and the king, himself, was embarrassed that no one thought enough of him to come to a lavish feast in honor of his son. If nobody showed up real soon, he would have to reschedule the dinner. All that fine preparation would have been for nothing!

The king told his servants to inform the new invitees that he wanted guests so bad that he would provide everything they needed to attend his dinner: a paid day off from work; a good job later, if they didn't have one; transportation; he would even provide the special clothes that they needed, free, to look their best at the wedding feast for his son. Then the king anxiously waited for the response to his new invitation.

When the news came to him, he was overjoyed—because his servants had told him that the banquet hall was packed with guests! The king could hardly wait to see all the finely attired guests, and the broad smile on his son's face because the marriage was going ahead as planned.

When the king arrived at the hall he was highly pleased at the good response to his invitation. Just as his servants had said, the banquet hall was packed—But then, he saw someone there who looked odd, out of place, acting nervously; and the king was amazed, even taken aback, because this outlandish guy wasn't even dressed for the dinner! He didn't have on the special wedding garment that was required for the feast!

That foolish man is wearing a business suit, the king thought to himself. He looks intelligent, so I'm sure he understood the rules of dress. I'm the king, it's my feast, I ought to at least be able to tell my guests how I want them to dress. But it looks as though this fellow didn't care what I wanted. Look at him, he's trying hard to fit in, butting in the pleasant conversations of the other guests; quite a talkative fellow, I see; but he's making the other guests uneasy. I don't blame them for not wanting to have anything to do with him. The way he's carrying on, he could accidentally soil their spotless white robe. I'd better get him out of here, before something terrible happens!

But wait a minute, the king abruptly thought, it would sure please my son, if I could squeeze in one more guest! Maybe I ran out of white robes, and that's the reason he's not dressed for my dinner. The robe was totally free, so not being able to afford one couldn't have been his reason. I ran out of robes—that has to be it! If I ran short of robes, I could let him stay. Then it wouldn't be his fault that he's not dressed—but mine! If it's my fault, then I will earnestly apologize to him, and have my tailors make him a special white robe with a blue border on the hem, to show him, and everyone, how sorry I am that I didn't have enough robes.

Then the king saw ten of his best wardrobe servants hurriedly exiting through a side door with their arms over-loaded with extra, one-size-fits-all, long white robes. The king deliberately looked back at the man—and kept staring at him, until the man looked up, and caught the king's eye.

I tried not to look at him, the untidy man thought to himself, but he kept staring at me. I could feel seven eyes peeling off my clothes, making me appear naked. I had to look at him, hoping he'd stop making me feel so wretched.

I've never met the king, I've just heard about him through his son. I didn't like his son, at all—too perfect for my taste. Not anybody I'd want to hang out with. His dad put on a fabulous feast for him, though. I'd sure like to stay, but I'd have to stay on my own terms—pretending I'm one of them—the way I got in here. No way I'm ever going to put on that white robe that everyone else is wearing. When the feast is over, I'll tell all my close friends what a wimp the king is, just like his son. And you can dress any way you want to, and still attend any gig the king throws. I did it—that proves he doesn't mean what he says.

Uh, oh, he's coming this way! And he doesn't look too happy about something! I think it's the way I'm dressed, since I look so different from everyone else. I think I can handle the ole king simply by not saying anything, act dumb, maybe he'll have a little pity on me, and let me stay. But, logically, what can I say, for not dressing like everyone else? Everything here, including the white robe in honor of the king's son, is *free!*

When the king arrived, accompanied by his personal attendants, at the place where the man was sitting in someone else's seat, the man stood up, and bowed from the waist toward the king.

"Friend," the king coldly said, "how camest thou in hither not having a wedding garment?"

The man, boldly sticking to his plan, acted as though he hadn't understood the king's question. "And he was speechless."

I addressed him as my friend, the king thought as he keenly observed the man absentmindedly not respond to his question, hoping he would see that although I'm displeased, I really want him to remain at my feast—If he can provide me with just two *reasonable* explanations as to why he's not dressed properly!

He's not going to answer me, I see; knowing that confession and repentance is what I want to hear. And by his dumb silence, he's playing me for a fool, expecting that I need only forgive his transgressions, and him do nothing, because he's heard all his life what a nice guy I am. That my wrath is just a myth.

He's never seen me, but he's seen my son, and I know my son told him—if he's seen the son, he's seen the father, also. He saw with his own eyes the compassionate side of my son—suffering the way he did—and my son only *told* him about my justice. He should have read about both, in the books about me circulated all over town, especially the last part of rule number two. That's the way I apply my justice, and compassion:

"I the Lord thy God am a jealous God, visiting the iniquity of the fathers upon the children unto the third and fourth generation of *them that hate me* (justice). And showing mercy unto thousands of them that love me, and *keep my commandments* (compassion)." Exodus 20:5.

He's never seen my compassion and my justice in action side by side. And because my justice is equal to my compassion, I apply them equally to everyone. All compassion for the obedient to my rules who have *repented*—

"Know ye not that the unrighteous shall not inherit the kingdom of God. Be not deceived: neither fornicators, nor idolaters, nor adulterers, nor effeminate, nor abusers of themselves with mankind, nor thieves, nor covetous, nor drunkards, nor revilers, nor extortioners, shall inherit the kingdom of God. And such *were some of you*: but ye are washed, but ye are sanctified, but ye are justified in the name of the Lord Jesus, and by the Spirit of our God." 1 Corinthians 6:9-11.

Yes! All justice for the disobedient who will *not* repent, the king thought. Justice demands that I certainly cannot allow this *disobedient* man to remain at my dinner. He's conniving, and disrespectful of my position as king. He'll never confess, *and repent.* He'll only make trouble here!

Then the king emphatically said to his strongest personal attendants, "Bind him hand and foot, and take him away, and cast him into outer darkness (justice); there shall be weeping and gnashing of teeth. For many are called, but few are chosen!" Matthew 22:13, 14.

The present day is the most dreadful, yet most promising time in planet earth's history. For those who intend to make heaven their home, today corresponds to the time in the history of ancient Israel, before the birth of Jesus Christ, when the people of the nation were penitently preparing for Yom Kippur—the Day of Atonement. This was the most sacred time of the year for the Hebrews, for it was a special ritual ordained by God to instruct the nation of Israel on the final stage in God's plan of redemption for the human race.

Indeed, God's whole plan of redemption—from the sacrifice of Jesus Christ for the transgressions of the world, typified by the sacrifice of an innocent lamb in the sanctuary service, to the Day of Atonement, when the "cleansing of the sanctuary" took place just prior to the second coming of Jesus—was, for over fifteen hundred years, a daily and yearly lesson in how sin and sinners were to be dealt with to eradicate the blight of sin from God's creation.

The sanctuary services for the whole year pointed to the grand Day of Atonement—the judgment—when all the people, who had all year long sincerely confessed and repented of their sins, were gathered into one company around the tabernacle to witness the removal of their sins from the sanctuary; and witness Satan, charged with all their sins, led out of the camp into the wilderness, never to be seen again.

The indelible lesson concerning sin and the Messiah that the children of Israel were instructed in, through the daily and yearly sanctuary services, was a pattern of the course of future events in heaven. Including Christ's ascension to His Father to finish the work of redemption—the judgment—after the cross.

Daniel, in the longest time prophecy in the Bible, foretold the exact year when the heavenly, antitypical judgment would begin. To emphasize the unfailing truthfulness of his prophecy he also foretold, within the same time span of 2300 years, the exact year when Jesus would formally begin His ministry; also the exact year of His death on the cross; and the exact year that the gospel was to be taken to the Gentiles. Daniel's prophecy, given 600 years beforehand, concerning Jesus and the gospel are a matter of factually recorded history; and the judgment, although commencing in heaven, and out of sight of human vision, is also a Biblical fact and a present day occurrence that impacts upon the life of *every* human being.

The angel Gabriel told Daniel, while Daniel was in vision, concerning the end-time judgment, that "Unto two thousand and three hundred days; then shall the sanctuary be cleansed." Then sometime later, while Daniel was still puzzled as to what the whole dream meant, and was awaiting an explanation from Gabriel, the angel himself returned to Daniel, and said to him, "Understand, O son of man: for at the t*ime of the end* shall be the vision." Daniel 8:14, 17. Gabriel then proceeded to explain to Daniel the events that had symbolically transpired in the vision that were to take place near the end of time, and were dramatized in his vision by a dirty fight between a rough and tumble ram, with two horns, and a strongly fierce he-goat with one large horn between his eyes. But Gabriel decidedly left out of his explanation of the vision the meaning of the 2300 years (in Bible prophecy a day equals a year) to the "cleansing of the sanctuary."

Then while Daniel was "praying and confessing my sin . . . and presenting my supplication before the Lord my God," Gabriel again came to Daniel, and said to him, "O Daniel, I am now come to give thee skill and understanding. . . . Therefore understand the matter and consider the vision." Daniel 9:20, 22, 23.

Gabriel explained to Daniel, regarding the time in his vision, "Unto two thousand and three hundred days; then shall the sanctuary be cleansed," that seventy weeks (490 years) of the 2300 years was set aside for Israel "to finish the transgression, and to make an end of sins, and to make reconciliation for iniquity, and to bring in everlasting righteousness, and to seal up the vision and prophecy, and to anoint the most Holy." Daniel 9:24. And the starting point of the 490 years that was set aside for Israel to accomplish the prophecy was the same as the starting point for the 2300 years—which, extending over many centuries, reached to the "cleansing of the sanctuary."

Gabriel knew that for Daniel to fully comprehend and identify the series of events that would certainly occur during the 490 years cut off for Israel that he also had to be told when both the 490 and 2300 years would begin. Gabriel made it known to Daniel that two historically significant events would mark the *time*—one at the beginning, and one 483 years after the beginning. "From the going forth of the commandment to restore and to build Jerusalem" would signify the beginning, and "the Messiah the Prince" would mark the termination of exactly 483 years. (Daniel 9:25)

Scholarly Bible study and archeology have determined that the "going forth of the command to restore and to build Jerusalem," occurred in 457 B.C., and this date is the factual beginning of the 2300 years. (See Ezra 7) The first landmark given by Gabriel to firmly establish 457 B.C. as the correct date was that 483 years after 457 "the Messiah the Prince" would make Himself known to Israel. In A.D. 27 Jesus Christ exactly fulfilled the prophecy when He encountered John the Baptist preaching and baptizing in the wilderness.

"Then cometh Jesus from Galilee to Jordan unto John, to be baptized of him . . . and Jesus, when He was baptized, went up straightway out of the water: and , lo, the heavens were opened unto Him, and He saw the Spirit of God descending like a dove, and lighting upon Him: And lo a voice from heaven, saying, This is my beloved Son, in whom I am well pleased." Matthew 3:13, 16, 17. And Christ, Himself, testified to the validity of the occasion saying, "The *time* is fulfilled, and the kingdom of God is at hand: repent ye, and believe the gospel." Mark 1:15.

Another definite landmark that Gabriel gave, confirming 457 B.C. as the date commencing 2300 years to the cleansing of the sanctuary, was he foretold the exact year and season of the crucifixion of Christ, saying, first, "And after threescore and two weeks (434 years) shall Messiah be cut off . . ." Daniel 9:26.

Four hundred thirty four years *toward* the seventieth week, after the ancient prophecy was fulfilled "to restore and to build Jerusalem," in A.D. 31, in the spring of the year, Jesus Christ was crucified on the cross of Calvary. By His death He was "cut off" from the living; then continuing, Gabriel said, "and in the midst (middle) of the week He shall cause the sacrifice and the oblation to cease." Daniel 9:27.

"The midst of the week" was 3 and 1/2 years into the final seven years (seventieth week) immediately following the 483 years to Christ's baptism by John. Upon the death of Jesus the temple services that had, for many centuries, pointed to His death were rendered obsolete, and of no more value as a means to engender faith in a coming Messiah. Just as Gabriel had said, "the midst of the week" foretold A.D. 31 as the year, and spring as the season of the year, when the Son of God was crucified. Today, the exact fulfillment of this prophecy is an undisputed fact of history.

Among the list of landmarks, two more events, one earthly and one heavenly, were to be consummated to mark the *close* of the 490 years prophecy allotted to the Jews, and pointing back to 457 B.C. as the starting date. Since the public ministry of Christ continued for 3 and 1/2 years, at which time His crucifixion occurred, there remained 3 and 1/2 years to complete the last 7 (70th week) "and to seal up the vision and prophecy."

The earthly close of the seventy weeks occurred with the persecution and stoning to death of Stephen, an apostle of Jesus Christ, in A.D. 34. (Acts 7:54-60) The martyrdom of Stephen marked the formal rejection of Christ as the Messiah by the Jewish Sanhedrin and commenced the "times of the Gentiles," which was the taking of the gospel to the world.

When the earthly temple services carried no more spiritual significance, coinciding with the death of Christ, and just 3 and 1/2 years remained to the end of the seventy weeks prophecy, it was during this period that the temple services, which the Bible says was a "pattern," was transferred to the antitypical, real services in the heavenly sanctuary. Just as the Jewish priests on earth had ministered in the holy and most holy apartments of the earthly, typical sanctuary, so Jesus began His ministry as High Priest of the heavenly sanctuary. The 490 years prophecy foretold this initiation of Christ's work, as High Priest, in the heavenly sanctuary, by declaring what had always occurred before the priests were allowed to begin their ministry in the earthly—"to anoint the most Holy." Daniel 9:24.

The phrase "most holy" is frequently used in Scripture to characterize things and places, never *persons*, and consistent with its use in this prophecy it is referring to *things* and *places* connected with the tabernacle services. (See Exodus 29:37; 30:10, 29, 36; Leviticus 6:17, 29; 7:1; 27:28.)

Since the earthly sanctuary services had lost their significance, "to anoint the most Holy" could not be a prophecy that referred to anything having to do with earthly things and places. Indeed, the earthly sanctuary services were a pattern of heavenly things. "Let them make me a sanctuary," God said to Moses in the wilderness, "that I may dwell among them." Then God proceeded to show Moses, exactly, how He wanted the sanctuary and its furnishings made; and He said to construct it "According to all that I shew thee, after the *pattern* of the tabernacle (in heaven), and the pattern of all the instruments thereof, even so shall ye make it." Exodus 25:8, 9.

Since the earthly service was a pattern, or copy, of the heavenly, and all the earthly vessels connected with the sanctuary service had to be anointed, it is more than reasonable to conclude that the heavenly sanctuary, and all its holy vessels, must also be anointed for service. "And thou shalt take the anointing oil, and anoint the tabernacle, and all that is therein, and shalt hallow it, and all the vessels thereof: and it shall be holy." Exodus 40:9. (See also verses 10-16)

By the anointing of the most holy things and places connected with the heavenly sanctuary Christ, as High Priest, after His ascension, began His ministration there. His continuing work on behalf of sinners would take place in heaven—in the real heavenly sanctuary—and comprise the balance of 1810 years of the 2300 years prophecy (2300 minus 490 leaves 1810), and culminate with "the cleansing of the sanctuary" at the close of the 2300 years.

"Now of the things which we have spoken this is the sum: We have such an high priest, who is set on the right hand of the throne of the Majesty *in the heavens; A minister of the sanctuary,* and of the true tabernacle, *which the Lord pitched,* and not man." Hebrews 8:1, 2.

The following is a partial summation of the prophecies fulfilled during the period from 457 B.C. to A.D. 34, the time span of the 490 years (seventy weeks) of Daniel 9:24. By these events the prophecy is thoroughly tested, and a definite indication that the remaining *heavenly* events to the close of 2300 years will also surely be fulfilled.

"To finish the transgression."

Fulfillment: Crucifixion of Christ.

"Make an end of sins (sin offerings)."

Fulfillment: Offering of Christ on Calvary.

"Reconciliation for iniquity."

Fulfillment: Sacrificial death of the Son of God.

"Bring in everlasting righteousness."

Fulfillment: The sinless life of Jesus Christ.

"Going forth of the commandment to restore and to build Jerusalem."

Fulfillment: Decree executed by King Artaxerxes in 457 B.C. Beginning of the seventy weeks (490 years); and 2300 years of Daniel 8:14.

"Unto the Messiah the Prince shall be seven weeks, and threescore and two weeks (483 years)."

Fulfillment: In A.D. 27, 483 years subsequent to 457 B.C., Christ began His formal ministry, which was marked by His baptism by John the Baptist in the Jordan River, and His anointing by the Holy Spirit.

"And He shall confirm the covenant with many for one week (7 literal years)."

Fulfillment: This is the very last seven years of the 490 years which began in A.D. 27, and ended in A.D. 34. During this time first Christ, before His crucifixion, and His disciples, after His crucifixion, openly preached the gospel of the new covenant (as opposed to the first covenant) to the Jews, which is all salvation is dependent upon the blood of Christ, and not by the works of the law alone.

"And in the midst of the week (middle of the last seven years) He shall cause the sacrifice and the oblation to cease."

Fulfillment: The middle of the last seven years of the 490 years was A.D. 31, which was 3 and 1/2 years after A.D. 27. In A.D. 31 ("midst of the week") Christ was crucified—which put an end to the need for the Jewish *ceremonial* laws pointing to the death of Christ. Although the Jews kept up the obsolete sacrifices until the vast destruction of Jerusalem by the Romans in A.D. 70 ("the overspreading of abominations").

"And after threescore and two weeks (434 years) shall Messiah be cut off."

Fulfillment: 434 years after the completion of the restoration and rebuilding of Jerusalem in 408 B.C., and leading up to, *but not to*, A.D. 31 when Christ was crucified (cut off).

"To anoint the most Holy."

Fulfillment: The anointing of the heavenly sanctuary by Christ after His resurrection and ascension, when the earthly sanctuary was replaced by the heavenly, and Christ entered upon His work of ministering on behalf of sinners in preparation for the judgment.

The historical events that have occurred during the seventy weeks prophecy have tested the prophecy, and proven it to be accurate and dependable to the letter, therefore, the cleansing of the sanctuary—the judgment—at the end of the 2300 years, must also bear the weight of investigation and fulfillment, and take place in heaven where Christ is ministering as High Priest.

Since the earthly tabernacle service was a true pattern of the heavenly service, and exemplified the plan of salvation, the cleansing of the sanctuary in the earthly service on the Day of Atonement must be a lesson in type of what was to take place in the heavenly cleansing of the sanctuary.

The Bible makes it quite clear that there is an antitypical, real sanctuary in heaven. This view is supported by the fact that the sanctuary Moses built was not an originally designed structure, but it was precisely constructed after a pattern of a building, and its unique furniture, already in existence somewhere else. After His resurrection, when Christ ascended to the throne of His Father, He became High Priest for the finishing of the work of salvation in the heavenly sanctuary.

"But Christ being come an high priest of *good thing to come,* by a greater and more perfect tabernacle, *not made with hands,* that is to say, not of this building." Hebrews 9:11.

In His role as High Priest, through the shedding of His own blood for the sins of the world, Christ "purified" the heavenly sanctuary in readiness for His "daily" ministration, including the cleansing of the sanctuary.

"It was therefore necessary that the *patterns* (on earth) of things in the heavens should be purified with these (blood of calves and goats); but the *heavenly things themselves* with better sacrifices than these. For Christ is not entered into the holy places made with hands, *which are the figures of the true;* but into heaven itself, now to appear in the presence of God for us." Hebrews 9:23, 24.

While in prophetic vision, more than sixty years after the ascension of Christ, John was given the privilege of looking into the heavenly sanctuary. "After this I looked, and behold, a door was opened in heaven," and as he beheld the splendor of Jehovah, and those attending Him, he saw also the furniture round about the throne of God, and holy vessels that were associated *only* with the ministration of high priests in the services of the earthly sanctuary.

"And out of the throne proceeded lightings and thunderings and voices: and there were *seven lamps of fire* burning before the throne, which are the seven Spirits of God." Revelation 4:1, 5.

"And when he had opened the seventh seal, there was silence in heaven about the space of half an hour. . . . And another angel came and stood at the altar, having a *golden censer;* and there was given unto him much *incense*, that he should offer it with the prayers of all saints upon the *golden altar* which was before the throne." Revelation 8:1, 3.

As John saw these objects that owe their existence to the sanctuary, and are confined only to the holy ministration of priests, he beheld also the furniture that represented the continual presence of God in the earthly sanctuary—for within it was enshrined the Ten Commandments—and wherever this most sacred object of God's presence was found one may know that there *must* also be a sanctuary, whether on earth, or in heaven.

"And the temple of God was opened in heaven, and there was seen in His temple *the ark of His testament:* and there were lightings, and voices, and thunderings, and an earthquake, and great hail." Revelation 11:19. By the testimonies of Paul and John there is valid proof that there is a sanctuary in heaven, and these holy spokesmen of God were permitted to substantiate its reality.

The cleansing of the typical sanctuary on earth, which was a model of the heavenly, took place once a year, and ended the daily ministration of priests in the tabernacle. The cleansing of the sanctuary was celebrated on the Day of Atonement, and it was the most sacred Jewish celebration of the year. In preparation for the solitary Day of Atonement, or cleansing of the sanctuary, once a year—which was not a cleansing from physical uncleanness or invisible germs, but a cleansing from sin—the humble, repentant sinner, all other days of the year, brought a sacrificial offering to the door of the tabernacle. He had expressed his faith in the coming Messiah by selecting a lamb "without spot or blemish" to represent his Savior. There, in the outer court of the tabernacle, in the presence of the priest, he confessed his sins over the lamb; then the penitent one, himself, sacrificed the lamb, ending its life by shedding its blood. Then the priest took the blood of the lamb into the first apartment of the sanctuary, called the holy place, and sprinkled it before the curtain that separated the holy place from the second apartment, the most holy place.

By this solemn ceremony of confession, slaying, and sprinkling of blood the participant understood that under God the vileness of sin demanded the life of the sinner to purge the sin from the congregation. And by confessing over, and killing the lamb, he had transferred his sins and its guilt from himself to the lamb. When he slew the lamb, he understood by faith that the innocent lamb represented the Messiah to come, and that Messiah would substitute His own life—as the living Lamb—for the life of the sinner. Then the participant saw the temple priest take the blood of the lamb into the sanctuary, and he understood this to mean that his sins, by the blood of the lamb, had been transferred to the sanctuary. And until the Day of Atonement, when the sanctuary would be cleansed of sin, his, and the all accumulated sins of all the nation of Israel, would remain in the sanctuary. Then the believer returned to his place of abode, free of his sins—but not entirely free—for his sins were still in the sanctuary, until the only day of the year when the sanctuary would be cleansed. Then he would be entirely freed of his sins, for that year!

This was the religious service that was carried out at the tabernacle every day of the year except the Day of Atonement. All the other days all the confessed sins of the people, that had been transferred to the sanctuary through the blood of a lamb, remained in the first apartment of the sanctuary, the holy place, until the Day of Atonement. The cleansing of the sanctuary, on the Day of Atonement, was the final step in separating the people from their sincerely confessed and repented sins—and removing their sins (for that particular year), forever, from the congregation of Israel.

This most sacred and eternally significant Hebrew observance of the year, the venerable Day of Atonement, commenced "in the seventh month, on the tenth day of the month," and the Hebrews were to humble themselves and, " ye shall afflict your souls, and do no work at all, whether it be one of your own country, or a stranger that sojourneth among you: For on that day shall the priest make an atonement for you, to cleanse you, that ye may be clean from all your sins before the Lord." Leviticus 16:29, 30.

For ten days leading up to the Day of Atonement, and particularly on the day itself, the people of Israel were in a high state of preparation. During which time they were to fast; search their hearts for unconfessed sins; mend all relationships with their neighbors; prayerfully reveal their wicked souls before God for His mercy, and thoroughly place all their faith in His lovingkindness to accept the ministration of the high priest in the most holy place of the sanctuary.

When the fearful Day of Atonement had arrived, and all Israel was focused upon the sanctuary, two goats were brought to the door of the tabernacle. The high priest, dressed in the "holy garments" of the atonement, consecrated the two goats for the service of the cleansing of the sanctuary. "And Aaron shall cast lots upon the two goats; one lot for the Lord, and the other lot for the scapegoat." Leviticus 16:8. Then the high priest confessed the sins of all Israel over the goat which by chance had become the Lord's goat. "Then shall he kill the goat of the sin offering, that is for the people, and bring his blood within the veil . . . and sprinkle it upon the mercy seat, and before the mercy seat." Leviticus 16:15.

When the congregation of Israel saw the high priest confessing over the Lord's goat, and then kill the Lord's goat, they understood, just as they had all year with their own sins and their lamb, that the sins of the whole nation of Israel had been placed upon the Lord's goat. Then they saw the high priest take the blood of the Lord's goat into the sanctuary, out of their sight, and they knew that through the blood of the goat their sins had been transferred to the sanctuary.

Indeed, they had learned from the beginning that the Day of Atonement was a summation of the year-long daily tabernacle service. And since the Messiah was to shed His blood only *once* for their sins, and there would never be another sacrifice after Him, their lamb had been symbolic of His one-time offering. He could not be sacrificed again on the Day of Atonement, therefore, a goat was used to represent the Messiah's blood.

"Nor yet that He should offer Himself often, as the high priest entereth into the holy place every year with blood of others: For then must He often have suffered since the foundation of the world: but now *once in the end of the world* hath He appeared to put away sin by the sacrifice of Himself." Hebrews 9:25, 26.

While the high priest remained in the sanctuary, "within the veil" in the most holy place and administered the blood of the Lord's goat "upon the mercy seat, and before the mercy seat" the people outside awaited his return in reverent silence, their hearts uplifted in earnest prayer for God's divine blessing. If the high priest remained in the sanctuary, in the most holy place in the presence of God, beyond the accustomed time the people became highly fearful, lest the high priest, because of their sins, or his own, had been killed by the glory of the Lord and they were doomed to an existence apart from God, in the hostile wilderness, with no eternal salvation awaiting them.

As the high priest emerged from the sanctuary, minus the blood of the sacrificial goat, a long cry of silent relief went up throughout the congregation. Their judgment in the most holy place, in the presence of an awesome God, had, once again, been successful, and He had consented to remain in their congregation and be their God.

But their joy was not complete—since they knew that until

the final phase of the cleansing of the sanctuary was finished, they remained under the condemnation of their sins. Anything could still happen, to interrupt the cleansing of the sanctuary, and leave them bound by the burden of all their sins: The high priest could collapse, and die, from the awful stress of being in the presence of God; or Jehovah could wholly change His mind, because someone in the congregation was not truly repentant. Anything could still happen! And they waited with bated breath as the live goat was brought before the high priest.

"And when he hath made an end of reconciling the holy place, and the tabernacle of the congregation, and the altar, he shall bring the live goat: And Aaron shall lay both his hands upon the head of the live goat, and confess over him all the iniquities of the children of Israel, and all their transgressions in all their sins, putting them upon the head of the goat, and shall send him away by the hand of a fit man into the wilderness: And the goat shall bear upon him all their iniquities unto a land not inhabited: and he shall let go the goat in the wilderness." Leviticus 16:20-22.

While in the presence of God, in the most holy place of the sanctuary, the high priest had been the mediator between God and the people. In his role as mediator, he took the blood of the sacrificial goat and sprinkled it upon the mercy seat that was the gold-layered cover of the ark, above the stone tablets of the Ten Commandments that lay within the ark. By the sprinkling of the blood on the mercy seat, the claims of the law, which demanded the life of the sinner, were satisfied. Then the high priest, in his character of mediator, took all the sins of Israel upon himself and as he completed his ministration, and left the sanctuary, he bore with him all the sins of Israel, and Israel's guilt, *out of the sanctuary.* Then at the door of the tabernacle, as he confessed over the "scapegoat," he transferred all the transgressions of Israel from himself to the goat. And the scapegoat, bearing the sins of Israel, was led away into the wilderness, to perish there.

Thus the vile sins of Israel were forever separated from the people. And the congregation then celebrated with over-joyous relief, hand clapping and loud cheering, as they watched the scapegoat, which represented Satan, the devil, the instigator and originator and precipitator of their sins, being led away into the wilderness to suffer the slow death that he deserved for all their transgressions. Such was the cleansing of the sanctuary on the Day of Atonement performed "unto the shadow and example of heavenly things." Hebrews 8:5.

As a means to instruct Israel (and all mankind) God used the yearly cleansing of the sanctuary to dramatize the *real* judgment to take place in heaven, where the final destiny of every human being will be decided. In his deceit, Satan, *to bypass the judgment,* introduced the false doctrine of immortality of the soul—that man has an immortal spirit that survives death, and eventually enters eternal bliss after the demise of his physical body.

Nearly the whole world believes Satan's lie, and he knows that if he can continue to successfully deceive the masses, they will live their lives ignorant that *not everyone* receives eternal life—and they will have to give an accounting of their lawless works in the judgment—and be destroyed with him when he is "sent away by the hand of a fit man into the wilderness" to perish.

The truth about life after death is: "the living know that they shall die: *but the dead know not anything.* . . . Also their love, and their hatred, and their envy, is now perished; neither have they anymore a portion forever in *anything* that is done under the sun." Ecclesiastes 9:5, 6.

"His breath goeth forth, he returneth to his earth; in that very day his thoughts perish." Psalm 146:4.

Indeed, the Creator God is "the blessed and only Potentate, the King of kings, and Lord of lords; Who *only* hath immortality." 1 Timothy 6:15, 16.

And until the King returns, all the dead remain dead in their graves, and when He comes "the coming of the Lord shall not prevent them which are *asleep* (dead). For the Lord himself shall descend from heaven with a shout, with the voice of the archangel, and with the trump of God: and the *dead in Christ* shall rise first: Then we which are alive and remain shall be caught up together with them in the clouds, to meet the Lord in the air: and so shall we ever be with the Lord." 1 Thessalonians 4:15, 16, 17. "This is the first resurrection." Revelation 20:5.

Where there exists a first of anything, there is at least one more of the same thing, therefore, "Marvel not at this: for the hour is coming, in the which *all that are in the graves* shall hear His voice, and shall come forth; they that have done good, unto the resurrection of life (first resurrection); and they that have done evil, unto the resurrection of damnation (second resurrection)." John 5:28, 29.

If one believes Satan's lie, with no Scriptural foundation—that an immortal spirit survives death—then one who believes Satan is grossly deceived, and will owe an answer in the judgment with respect to why they willfully chose to believe God's *adversary,* who communicates directly to the unwary through UFOs, disembodied voices, mediums, and apparitions, rather than God, Himself. When they cannot answer ("And he was speechless."), God answers for them—"And this is the condemnation, that light is come into the world, and men loved darkness rather than light, because their deeds were evil." John 3:19. "Depart from me, ye that work iniquity!"

Practically all, believers and nonbelievers alike, would agree that a catastrophic event is poised to disrupt the common order of life on earth. Biblical research reveals that this disruption, after the plagues, will be the second coming of Jesus to set up His kingdom of eternal peace. The Scriptures teach, also, that before Jesus departs from His heavenly throne to appear before His believers on earth, He will *finish* the judgment of believers to determine who, of the living, will be changed into their eternal bodies; and who, of the dead, will rise up in the first resurrection in their eternal bodies and both happily fellowship with Him for eternity.

"And, behold, I come quickly; *and my reward is with me*, to give every man according as his work shall be." Revelation 22:12.

Not all believers will be saved; their judgment will decide who is. "Many will say to me in that day (in the judgment, by their explicit record), Lord, Lord, have we not prophesied *in thy name?* And in thy name cast out devils? And in thy name done many wonderful works? And then will I (Christ) profess unto them, I never knew you: depart from me, ye that work iniquity." Matthew 7:22, 23.

The law of God, contained in His Ten Commandments, is the standard by which all will be judged. When John saw the ark of the testament in heaven, he immediately recognized it as the *real* furniture that Moses had been commanded to make a copy of for the sanctuary in the wilderness. Had John been permitted to wonderfully gaze within the ark, he would have beheld the Ten Commandments—for it's the law within that provides the heavenly ark with its eternally enduring significance. Although it was worded for comprehension by a fallen race, it is the same law in heaven as on earth. And, like earth, all God's other intelligent creations are obligated to obey it.

In the earthly sanctuary the ark of the testament resided in the most holy place, the second apartment of the sanctuary. On the Day of Atonement, every tenth day of every seventh month, when the sanctuary was to be cleansed of the sins of the people, the high priest entered the most holy place. Immediately upon entering with the blood of the Lord's goat, his eyes fell upon the ark of the testament. Moses had built the ark exactly according to the pattern that God had given him in the mount; and the ark on earth was a gold-layered replica of the real ark in heaven.

In the most holy place, the high priest was immediately dumbfounded by the majesty of God—His presence manifested by the Shekinah, a brilliant cloud of light, suspended over the ark of the testament, centered above the mercy seat. Standing on each end of the ark, in shining solid gold, the high priest beheld the splendid cherubim with their farthest outstretched wings extended heavenward, and their other wing reverently folded over their body and their angelic faces toward one another, looking down upon the golden mercy seat of the ark.

As the high priest approached the presence of Jehovah, suspended above the ark between the cherubim, the light of God's presence cast its hallowed glow over him, and majestically illuminated the deep royal colors of the hanging curtains that provided the room of the most holy place.

As the high priest ventured before the ark, he bowed on his knees, and prayed a humble prayer of confession and repentance for himself and the congregation of Israel. Then he rose from his humble prayer, and placing his fingers into the golden laver, containing the blood of the offering, he then sprinkled the blood upon the cover of the ark, which is the mercy seat, thereby accepting the authority of the sacred law within the ark, and satisfying it claims upon himself and Israel to obey it. In the presence of God, in the most holy place, the high priest heard the voice of Jehovah emanating from the brilliant cloud above the ark, speaking to him as he reverently sprinkled the blood, approving or rejecting mercy for each transgression of Israel to be placed upon the high priest.

All year long, subsequent to the Day of Atonement, in the first apartment of the sanctuary, the holy place, the high priest had offered incense, which represented the prayers of Israel, with the blood of the sacrificial lamb as he sprinkled its blood before the curtain that separated the holy place from the most holy place. So, on the Day of Atonement, all the individual prayers of Israel had already ascended into the presence of God, represented by the smoke of the incense, filling the whole sanctuary with its sweet fragrance.

In his role as mediator, the high priest, on the Day of

Atonement, ventured into the most holy place without incense, to plead before God, on behalf of the year-long prayers of the penitent that had come to Him, forgiveness of their sins and recognition of the single offering of the sacrificial blood that the high priest sprinkled upon the mercy seat. By the daily and once yearly services of the Jewish tabernacle, and later in the permanent, magnificent temple built by Solomon, the plan of redemption for the human race was dutifully played out.

The apostle Paul, a Jew of the highest caliber, "a Pharisee, the son of a Pharisee," "born in Tarsus . . . yet brought up in this city at the feet of Gamaliel, and taught according to the perfect manner of the law of the fathers, and was zealous toward God," Acts 23:6; 22:3, and an A-student of the Law and the Prophets (the Old Testament) was thoroughly rehearsed in the meaning of the rites carried out in the sanctuary. And that the violated law of God was at the center of the services, and the sole reason for the necessity of a Messiah, and a sanctuary. It was only after his miraculous conversion to Christianity that he was able to apply all the Old testament prophecies of the coming Messiah to Jesus Christ.

After his conversion, his heart burned within him in sincere admiration for Jehovah, that He would not only reveal the past relating to Jesus, but the present and the *future* plan of redemption, as well. And not only to know the past, present and future, but to have two reliable sources of knowledge to establish a firm, unshakable foundation upon which to build his new faith—the Scriptures, and the temple services.

He was permitted to know by the holy Scriptures that Jesus, the blessed Messiah, would not return in his lifetime to reward His saints with their eternal bodies; but this event was *far* in the future from his day.

As he curiously calculated the time, based upon his thorough knowledge of the temple services, and particularly the incredible prophecy of Daniel, which said, "Unto two thousand and three hundred days; then shall the sanctuary be cleansed,"

Daniel 8:14, he was able to arrive at the nearest date possible for the second coming of his beloved Jesus, and it could *only* occur after 2300 years had expired.

He knew by his study of the Old Testament book of Ezra, that the beginning of Daniel's prophecy of the "time" was 457 B.C., and he, himself, was present 490 years later at its conclusion. He knew for a certainty, from personal experience, that the "cleansing of the sanctuary" that Daniel spoke of, that would occur at the end of the 2300 years, was a *real* manifestation in heaven of the pattern that had been dramatized on earth all his life; and all of his ancestors, in their generations, had taken part in, too. Just as the sanctuary on earth had to be cleansed of sin, so it must be that, *true to the pattern*, the sanctuary in heaven must be cleansed of sin. And as Daniel had stated, this cleansing must take place at the termination of 2300 years.

His calculation now to determine when the sanctuary in heaven must be cleansed was simply to subtract 490 years from 2300. Then add that figure to the year that he himself had assisted in the murder of Stephen. And, waal-lah! he had the exact year that the *real* sanctuary in heaven would be cleansed.

He knew, from his sincere participation in the earthly Day of Atonement, that the cleansing of the sanctuary meant that God was performing a thorough investigation of Israel, ridding the sanctuary of their accumulated sins, and finally charging Satan with all their sins and sending him away to perish in the wilderness. This dramatized, final eradication of Satan, and those who follow him, both angels and humans, marked the end of sin—and the end of God's dealings with sin and sinners.

Paul knew, from the Scriptures and centuries of Jewish ceremonial rites, that the cleansing of the sanctuary, on the Day of Atonement, was a figure of the judgment of all believers who relied on a Savior. And this figure *must* become a reality—just as all the other figures had become a reality in Jesus—in the real heavenly sanctuary; and the real judgment must be fulfilled before the final destruction of Satan and sinners—Again, in purpose and sequence of events, *true to the figure on earth.*

By his studied application of Old Testament prophecy, and what was then recent history, Paul determined that A.D. 1844 was the exact year that the heavenly sanctuary must be cleansed. And since the ministry of the high priest in the first apartment of the earthly sanctuary, the holy place, consumed a whole year of transferring sins to the sanctuary, likewise, the cleansing of the real sanctuary in heaven, true to the single Day of Atonement figure, must, too, require a much *shorter* time.

Indeed, the ministry of Jesus Christ, the *real* High Priest, after His ascension, must have anointed the heavenly sanctuary and transferred with Him—through His shed blood—the sins of believers to the heavenly sanctuary. And until the cleansing of the heavenly sanctuary of sin—the judgment—His work was pleading the virtue of His blood for their sins before His Father. True to the prophecy of Daniel this work of Jesus in the first apartment of the heavenly sanctuary would consume 1810 years, and close in A.D. 1844, when the cleansing of the sanctuary would begin. And after the heavenly cleansing, which is the *real* final judgment (only God knows its duration from A.D. 1844), Jesus Christ will return the second time (in figure when the high priest emerged from the sanctuary on the sacred Day of Atonement) to resurrect the dead who survived the judgment, and change the living.

And while the wicked dead remain in their graves, and the wicked living are killed by the power in Christ's coming, all the redeemed are taken up with Christ to spend a thousand years with Him in heaven. Satan and his demons will be confined to the desolate earth for the thousand years (in figure, the scapegoat was led into the wilderness to perish). At the conclusion of the thousand years Christ, and all of the redeemed, will return, and the wicked will be resurrected, receive their sentence of punishment and death, and then they are burned up in the lake of fire along with Satan and his demons. Then Christ will return the earth to its pristine beauty, as the Garden of Eden was before the entrance of sin, and the renewed earth will be the eternal home of the redeemed. (For an in-depth Bible study on the foregoing, go online to www.visionpublishers.com for a special link to printed studies.)

Paul frankly knew by the prophecy of Daniel, and its partial fulfillment during the "time" (490 years beginning in 457 B.C.), that the second coming of Jesus was a long ways off from his day. And the judgment must be *finished* before Jesus can return.

It was the privilege of John the Revelator to pick up where Paul left off, and include in the Scriptures all that Daniel was denied knowledge of about the events at the end of time. John, like Paul, was an ardent A-student of the Old Testament book of Daniel.

Daniel received instructions directly from the angel Gabriel regarding his book, saying, "Go thy way, Daniel: for the words are closed up and sealed till *the time of the end.*" Daniel 12:9. Then, more than 600 years later, Jesus Christ communicated to John, saying, "Go and take the little book (book of Daniel) which is open in the hand of the angel . . . And I took the little book out of the angel's hand, and ate it up (earnestly studied it); and it was in my mouth sweet as honey: and as soon as I had eaten it, my belly was bitter." Revelation 10:8, 10.

John was describing in symbolic language of a time near the conclusion of the 2300 years when the previously sealed book of Daniel, particularly the prophecy "Unto two thousand and three hundred days; then shall the sanctuary be cleansed," would be clearly opened, and those who wanted to understand the prophecy, could understand it.

Precisely this prediction was fulfilled shortly before and after A.D. 1844 when the "little book" was revealed to a small body of Christians; and when they thought they understood it, it was "sweet as honey" to their understanding; but the experience of falsely applying the prophecy to the second coming of Jesus, and not the judgment, was a grossly disappointing ordeal and their "belly was bitter." Thus by the trial of those Christians, from all denominations, both the prophecies of Daniel and John were fulfilled—the judgment commenced on schedule, and the book of Daniel was unsealed.

John arrived at the year 1844, for the cleansing of the sanctuary, using the same lessons from the temple services, history of fulfilled prophecies and numeric calculations as Paul had; and John prophesied of the worldwide proclamation of the judgment gospel, saying, "And I saw another angel fly in the midst of heaven, having the everlasting gospel to preach unto them that dwell on the earth, *and to every nation, and kindred, and tongue, and people,* saying with a loud voice, Fear God, and give glory to Him; for the *hour of His judgment* (1844 and following) *is come:* and worship Him that made heaven, and earth, and the sea, and the fountains of waters." Revelation 14:6, 7.

Here John stresses the unfathomable importance of worship of the only true God, Jehovah, Who created everything that exists, because in the time of the end, after A.D. 1844, the final judgment of all the earth would be in progress. It is impossible to worship the only true God, "in righteousness and in truth," "and give glory to Him," without loving obedience to all of His Ten Commandments. Truly, the whole creation of God on earth was plunged into sin because the first humans transgressed God's law of Ten Commandments.

John, the end-time spokesman of God, said, "And hereby we do know that we know Him, if we keep His commandments. He that saith, I know Him, and keepeth not His commandments, is a liar, and the truth is not in him. But whoso keepeth His word, in him verily is the love of God *perfected:* hereby know we that we are in Him. He that saith he abideth in Him ought himself also so to walk, even as *He walked.*" 1 John 2:3-6.

Jesus Christ was obedient, without exception, to all of His Father's commandments. He was the eternal God, Who lived in human flesh, and felt the sting of temptation to sin that all humans feel. "For we have not an High Priest which cannot be touched with the feeling of our infirmities; but was in all points tempted like as we are, yet without sin." Hebrews 4:15. And He has promised His followers who walk "as He walked," that through His grace (power) and their desire to be like Him they, too, can obey His Ten Commandments and "He that overcometh (sin) shall inherit all things; and I will be His God, and he shall be my son." Revelation 21:7.

After the judgment in heaven, that is in progress today (and it is a shortened work, just as the figure was a once-a-year Day of Atonement), Christ will return the second time. When He returns He will find believers in Him who are living, which the Bible symbolically refers to as the 144,000, and they have "His Father's name written in their foreheads," since their sinful characters have been "washed in the blood of the Lamb."

"These are they which were not defiled with women; for they are virgins." Revelation 14:4.

Here John cloaks the language of the "Revelation of Jesus Christ" using the female gender to describe a wayward church that has the capability to defile her members. (See Revelation 17 for a description of this wealthy woman who is an end-time church, a blaspheming whore, and a sovereign government.) However, the 144,000 have *not* been defiled by her falsified teachings.

When she supported evolution as a plausible explanation for the existence of man, the 144,000 said, No—"In six days, the Lord made the heavens and the earth." Exodus 20:11. When she said that she stood in the place of God, and could forgive sins, the 144,000 said, No—"Thou shalt have no other gods before me." Exodus 20: 3. When she, and her daughters, joined forces with the world's superpower to openly enforce Sunday worship, the 144,000 said, No—"Remember the Sabbath day, to keep it holy . . . the seventh day is the Sabbath of the Lord thy God." Exodus 20:8, 10.

Since the 144,000 were obedient to all the commandments of

God, it was impossible for them to receive the mark of the beast. Even if they had not known what the mark was, obedience to all of the Ten Commandments would have protected them—shielded them from the awful wrath of God upon those who yielded to the mark. But they were steadfast in their obedience, and immovable in their dedication to walk as Jesus walked. On the opposing side of God's law were the disobedient, who received the mark; but on the favored side were the 144,000, and "Here is the patience (steadfastness) of the saints: here are they that keep the commandments of God, and the faith of Jesus." Revelation 14:12. They had a twofold dedication to God—total obedience to His law, and faith in Jesus Christ as their Savior.

"These are they which follow the Lamb whithersoever he goeth. These were redeemed from among men, being the first-fruits unto God and to the Lamb. And in their mouth was found not guile: for they are without fault before the throne of God." Revelation 14:4, 5.

Those who are living and translated when Jesus comes, symbolized in Revelation by the 144,000, have survived the final judgment of the righteous, and their Christ-likeness does not surpass the redeemed who are resurrected. Their place in end-time history was simply a matter of who was alive, and who was dead, when Jesus returned. The refinement of character in each company must be the same to pass through the judgment. God does not have two standards of righteousness. All sinners are weighed on the same scale—the Ten Commandments—and all must have their transgressions of the law blotted out in the judgment through confession, forgiveness, and repentance.

The seventh commandment—Thou shalt not commit adultery—is of no less importance than the other nine. And simply because one feels entitled to the satisfaction that sex may bring, or the companionship of marriage, to gain these amenities in violation of God's law is a very foolish decision—for this life is short, disruptive, and temporary; while God's reward is long, peaceful, and permanent.

"Except"

As Moses pleaded with God on behalf of Israel for their sins, he used the final judgment of himself as a means of appealing to God's mercy. He said, "Yet now, if thou wilt forgive their sin—; and if not, blot *me,* I pray thee, out of thy book which thou hast written. And the Lord said unto Moses, Whosoever hath sinned against me, *him* will I blot out of my book." Exodus 32:32, 33.

"I beheld till thrones were cast down, and the Ancient of days did sit, whose garment was white as snow, and the hair of His head like the pure wool: His throne was like the fiery flame, and His wheels as burning fire. A fiery stream issued and came forth from before Him: thousand thousands ministered unto Him, and ten thousand times ten thousand stood before Him: *the judgment was set,* and the books were opened." Daniel 7:9, 10.

It began in A.D.1844—When will it end? Today, all the signs are apparent!

In the earthly service, while the high priest was in the most holy place performing the ceremonial rites for the cleansing of the sanctuary, the congregation of Israel was outside the tabernacle, morally prepared for his coming forth.

Likewise, in the heavenly sanctuary, the real High Priest, Jesus Christ, is performing the sacred rites of the investigative judgment—surely deciding the eternal future of every Christian. Soon, His work will be done and after that His coming forth, too, is imminent. His followers themselves must be morally prepared, being prayerfully mindful to put all their faith in His sacrifice for their sins, and bodily and spiritually obey all of His Ten Commandments. Indeed, remembering, co-diligently, the seventh commandment—Thou shalt not commit adultery—and although His compassion is overflowing for those who repent, He "will by no means clear the guilty." Exodus 34:7

13

Divorce: Episode Three

ADON sat in the waiting room of the rental car company for one and a half hours after Jewel had gone. After she left, his conscience immediately began to torment him for the spiteful lie he had told to Jewel. In a moment of anger at Jewel he had rebelled against God, and received the tongue of Satan in his mouth. He had committed the same spur of the heated moment sin that Moses had when "Moses lifted up his hand, and with his rod he smote the rock twice," and God was no less displeased with Adon as He was with Moses—sin is sin, and who commits it is of no significance, since "God is no respecter of persons."

But Adon stubbornly fought against his conscience, seeking to justify his actions by recounting all the evil that Jewel had plotted against him. He felt, in all seriousness, that he deserved an act of revenge toward her. How else could he find any relief from his desire to see her suffer without doing actual physical harm to her. He had looked forward to many days of inward satisfaction at knowing that he had initiated the destruction of Jewel and her scurrilous lover without having to provide a clue to her, or anyone else, of his vulgar deed. He had desperately wanted to give her the Bible study on divorce, to prevent her from falling prey to the sin of adultery, but now he hoped that she would never have occasion to learn the truth, and somehow slip out of his quiet trap by not marrying, divorcing after marriage, or himself preceding one of them in death.

From that day forward he planned to give special attention to his health, so that his living longer than Jewel or her slum-rat husband was greatly enhanced. He wanted to be there, at both their funerals, when their family and friends were placing them in the coming heavenly kingdom, to secretly gloat over where their journey through life, at his expense, had really ended up. This was his self-indulgent revenge on Jewel and Brian and he was thoroughly reluctant to let go of it by confession to God, and informing Jewel that he had lied.

After he had wrested some devilish satisfaction for himself with respect to Jewel, he removed the letter from his shirt pocket that Jewel had given to him from Princess. He tore open the envelope, and read:

"Dear Daddy: I received your last email. I've been real busy with school, so that's why I haven't written you back. Mom said that she was going to see you, so I'm writing this short note for you. Hope you get it.

"Thanks for the money you sent me.

"Anyway, Dad, I met a very nice man at school (boy to you), his name is Roderick. I won't be vague here. We're in love, and we want to get married during the Thanksgiving break. We don't see any reason to wait, since we're both mature adults who have experienced, since high school and into college, most of what there is to life, except marriage.

"Our minds are made up. What I'm asking you to do is make sure that you start making plans now to attend my wedding. It'll be a small wedding because we don't have any money right now, except for school. I would like for you not to miss my wedding, the most important event in my life (so far) the way you have all the other important events in my life because of that business.

"I'll let you know the exact date as soon as we know when Roderick's parents can be out of the house during the TG break, so that we can spend our honeymoon at home—alone. Love, Princess."

Adon threw up his arms in disgust, sending the one page letter flying toward the ceiling, and then it wafted down on the movement of air from the air conditioning to the floor in front of him. As he was reaching around the coffee-table to pick it up, the door to the waiting room was opened, and Ms. Wade, the airline stewardess who had been in the waiting room most of the time that he and Jewel were talking, and overheard a great deal of their conversation, came back into the room. After she had closed the door behind her, she went across the room to where she had previously sat, before moving closer to Adon and Jewel. Adon watched her for a moment, looking through the cushions of a green love-seat.

"Can I help you find anything?" Adon asked, seated again and putting the letter back into the envelope.

"I've misplaced my keys." she said, "They must have fallen out of my purse while I was sitting here. You haven't seen any keys, have you?"

"No. I haven't been anywhere but here. Maybe they dropped out while you were sitting over there."

She stopped poking behind the cushions of the sofa where she was, and moved to the circular seating arrangement that was closer to where Adon was sitting. "You're right, I did sit here, too, didn't I?"

Adon rose, and went to help her search through the circular sofa. He removed the cushions, and she stuck her hand in the frame space under the cushions.

"Isn't that strange?" she said, "I know I had them when I came in here."

"That's the unsolved mystery of losing things," Adon replied. "You know you had it—now you don't."

She removed her hand from the last crevice in the seat and stood erect again, looking concerned. "It was just two keys on a ring. I guess I could have dropped them anywhere."

Adon took notice her outward appearance. She was clean-cut, closely cropped dark hair, but not attractive facial features, her smeller being too long and predominant for her round face, like a Halloween pumpkin with a paper nose. Her pants style stewardess uniform did a great deal to enhance her figure which was shaped like a trash can, too big at the top, and much smaller at the bottom. He began replacing the cushions.

"Did you look under the other one?" he asked. "Maybe they dropped on the floor, and you kicked them underneath."

"I had my shoes off all the time I was in here. If I had moved anything, I would have felt it. Being on my feet all the time, it's just a habit to kick them off, whenever I sit down."

After all the cushions were put back, Adon got down on his hands and knees and ran his hand on the floor around the bottom edge of the sofa, and visually checked underneath. "Well, it doesn't hurt to look," he said from the floor. Then, finding nothing, he stood up again, and started toward the love-seat. She stopped him with the intonation of her voice.

"Listen! You don't have to look around the other one. You've been more than helpful, already. I'll just call ahead, and make sure my roommate is there before I go home." She paused for a moment to recommence her thoughts, and then said, "Why are you still here? Can't they find you a car?"

"My wife . . . the person that was here and I just came here to talk. Neither of us rented a car."

Ms. Wade sat down on the circular sofa, and kicked off her shoes. "How did that turn out? I couldn't help but overhear some of your conversation."

Adon sat down, too. "Oh, that's over for good! Anyway, we're divorced already—have been for a long time."

"That's too bad. I'm divorced, too. It leaves a hole in your life that never seems to heal. I was fortunate, though, I knew way ahead of time that it was going to happen, so I was ready when it finally did. Seems you didn't find out, until it was too late. I'm just assuming that, from some of the things you said."

"I can do you one better than that—I didn't know until it was done!

She was sympathetic toward Adon. "Yes. That is unfortunate." She offered her hand. "My name is Heidi, with two i's. What's yours?"

Adon shook her hand. "Glad to meet you, Heidi. I'm Adon." They completed their handshake. Adon added, "Are you flying out again, tonight?"

"No. I have four days off. That's why I rented a car. This is not my home base, but it's a regular stop-over for me. I try to get around and meet as many people as I can when I'm not flying. I have to take the initiative in that. As you can see, I'm no Halle Berry."

"Who is?"

She slipped her feet back into her shoes. "Well, I guess I'd better be leaving. I left my purse and my flight bag at the cocktail lounge, down the way. I always stop in there when I'm in town. . . . If you've got a minute, why don't you have a drink with me? You could probably stand one, after your meeting with your ex."

"Thanks, for the invitation, but I don't drink."

She stood up. "I'll tell you what, then! You can't spend the night here, so why don't you leave now, and walk me back there. You don't have to drink, but I'd like for you to go in and meet a friend of mine, who can let you know what to expect for the next few months. You'd like to know that, wouldn't you? No more surprises—uh?"

Adon stood, too. "If you're talking about a psychic reader, I don't do that, either."

"My friend's not really a psychic; she just does it for fun. For instance, she never tells passengers not to fly, because she's in an airline terminal—That makes sense, doesn't it?"

Adon laughed. "It sure does." Then added, "I suppose you get your fortune told, too?"

"Yes, I have to admit, I do."

"But if you know you can't believe her, why bother?"

"Well, I guess it's because a lot of the time, many times, she's right. Do you remember that I said I knew about my divorce, way ahead of time?" Adon affirmatively nodded. "Well, she's the person who told me. She's been right about a lot of other things, too. President Reagan had a psychic. It's just fun!"

"It's *not* fun! That's Satan's way of misleading people."

"I guess you could say that, if she was in a dark room with black curtains, and candles. But she uses tarot cards, in plenty of light."

"No, it's not for me!"

"Well, come and watch her do a reading for me. I get one every time I'm here. It's just fun. Something to start off my free time."

Adon moved toward the door. Heidi followed. "I'll be glad to walk you back," Adon said, "but I'll be leaving after that."

Adon arrived at the door, and with his hand on the doorknob, he looked back at Heidi. He heard her next words, and plainly saw her lips moving, but the voice he heard was that of a man, which said, "Don't you want to know what's going to happen to your ex?"

The voice was so clear, and it seemed to be inside and outside of his head, and it fit in perfectly with his evil thoughts of Jewel. It actually made him feel better! Without hesitation he replied to Heidi, "I can go in for a minute. Maybe I can stop her from doing it. And, maybe it'll be your last time, too." Then he heard Heidi's usual voice saying—

"It'll be fun!"

Adon opened the door, and let Heidi leave the room ahead of him. As they had walked a little pass the car rental counter, the customer service person called out to Heidi, "Ms. Wade, don't forget your keys!"

Heidi heard her, stopped, and glanced at Adon for his reaction. Seeing none, she returned to the counter and received her two keys on a ring. "Thanks, but I was coming back for them."

Then she met up with Adon again, and they resumed walking in the direction of the cocktail lounge.

On the way, Heidi was telling Adon about an incident of air turbulence on her flight coming in that was rougher than usual, and what was required of her, as a stewardess, to be of calming assistance to the passengers under those circumstances. She was talking, but Adon wasn't really listening to what she was saying, just giving her an affirmative, "Yeah; Um, uh; Yeah;" every now and then so as not to indicate that he wasn't listening. His subjective intellect was wrestling with the eerie feeling he was carrying with him, since he had heard the man's voice in the waiting room. He hadn't mentioned hearing it to Heidi. It was too personal to mention to her; someone who wouldn't understand the dire implications of hearing a demonic utterance, and would probably be influenced to fall even deeper into a satanic lifestyle of fortune telling, séances, apparitions and other varied forms of evil spirit communication.

But he was acutely aware, although he was temporarily mesmerized by the voice, that he was in Satan's cross hairs, and apt, at any moment, to lose his privileged gift of faith in God which gave him his believability of the Scriptures. He remembered Eve, in the idyllic Garden of Eden, who, in an instance of curiosity brought on by Satan through the serpent, had begun the process to cause the whole world to be thrown into sin. And Saul, the first king of Israel, who, through disobedience to God, eventually lost his faith in God, and turned to satanic spiritualism for direction in his life. Both willfully committed the great transgression, believing there is such a thing as insignificant sin, but the outcome of their "little" transgression was tragic for themselves and mankind.

Adon knew from his study of the Bible that Satan will attack in a person's weakest moment, and in an area where he is likely to gain a foothold to their mind, and then manipulate their reasoning to his own destructive ends.

Satan was there, in the waiting room, and witnessed his lie to

Jewel and his murderous motivation behind his lie; and then Satan sought to increase his curiosity by allowing him to hear the demonic voice through Heidi, intensely tempting him in an area that Satan knew was a weakness for him at that moment. Satan's subtle question regarding his "ex" was the live bait, and now Satan's plan was to further reel him in by meeting Heidi's friend in a fortune telling session.

Adon knew that Satan was not toying with him, in a light game of curiosity, but Satan was out to kill him! If he went in that cocktail lounge with Heidi he would likely not come out, alive! Indeed, Satan is not too particular about wooing persons who do not believe the whole gospel, he already has them in his grasp, he's not passionately interested in them anymore, except to find pleasure in their present and future torment. The people he wants to kill, and where his greatest efforts to deceive are concentrated, are on Christians who know the truth. These are the ones he wants dead—as soon as possible—to stop their true witnessing about Jesus, and revealing Satan's own character of constant evil.

Adon and Heidi arrived at the recessed entrance to the cocktail lounge. Heidi started in ahead of Adon, but she stopped, just inside the door, when she saw that Adon was not coming in behind her.

"I'm not going in with you!" Adon said.

Heidi looked puzzled. "It won't take long for her to do my reading, then you can go. Please, you promised."

"Heidi, I'm a Christian, and I don't go to places like this, or get involved in fortune telling. In the dark—or in the light."

"Well, okay. I guess I could have one before my flight out. Can you wait a minute, until I get my things, and then walk me to my car? The car rental spaces are close by. But the light's pretty bad over there at night."

"Alright, but hurry up. I'm ready to get out of here."

"I'll just be a minute," Heidi replied, and went on into the cocktail lounge. The door closed behind her.

Divorce: Episode Three

True to her word, Heidi returned in about a minute, and met Adon outside of the door carrying her purse on her shoulder and pulling a small black flight bag with wheels. She let Adon take the flight bag. "Okay, I'm ready!" She started off ahead of Adon, then she stopped before Adon had started following her, and turned back to him. "Oh, my friend said to give you this message—'Someone you know, will *die,* real soon!'"

Adon abruptly let go of the handle to the flight bag, allowing the bag to tip back onto its legs, and solidly pushed the handle back into its receptacle—"I think you can manage this by yourself. Have a good evening!" he said , and walked off toward the terminal entrances.

After Adon had arrived at his car, from walking some distance to the long-term parking lot, he discovered that he had two flat tires—both on the passenger side. He briefly looked at them, and then got into the car in the driver's seat. With his hands in his lap, he bowed his head, and prayed. In his prayer he first praised God for His sole sovereignty in the earth, and that he himself was a created creature, a sinner too, owing his present and future life to the unmerited love of God. Then he praised God for allowing him to have a desire to pray. That the Holy Spirit had not departed from him, and left him without an awareness of his need to seek God in prayer. He confessed his sin of lying to Jewel, and his sin of murder, in hoping that she and Brian would meet their fate of eternal death through the sin of adultery. He went on praying, emptying his heart to God, until he was assured, through the Holy Spirit, that God had heard his prayer. He concluded in Jesus' name, and amen.

Then he got out of his car, and inspected his tires again. He determined that the car next to him was parked too close for him to get his jack under the frame of the car in the position that it was designed for. Besides, he had two flats, and one spare tire, and changing one would do him no good in driving his car. He decided to leave the car where it was, walk back to the terminal, and take a taxi home. He would have a towing company, tomorrow, change a tire and fix one flat. Then he'd pick the car up after work, and pay for the parking. He'd tell the towing company where he kept his spare key to the ignition and trunk.

As soon as the taxi had dropped him off at home, and he was inside the door, he went immediately to his computer and typed off an email to Jewel. He confessed to her that he had lied about his adultery, and then he gave her a written Holy Bible study on divorce and remarriage. After his very serious letter to Jewel, he typed another letter to Princess, telling her that he wanted to talk to her and Roderick about their plans for marriage, and that he would be in Maryland in four weeks, nearly a month before Thanksgiving when they planned to marry. After he had written to Princess, he made a telephone call to Jewel, knowing that she had not had time to arrive home from her trip to see him, and left a message on her answering machine, confessing again that he had blatantly lied to her, and to take special note of his Bible study in his email.

The next day, Adon called Jewel from his work. At her job, she had him waiting on hold for fifteen minutes, and when she finally came on the line, already knowing that it was Adon, she hung up in his face without talking to him. He called her three times that day, with the same scene played over each time—he waited on hold for an extended period of time, then she hung up. He called her the day after that, and the day after that, and on many other days, until she had his work, home and cell numbers blocked from her office telephone system. At her home he could only leave messages on her answering machine, phone calls that she never returned. After she saw an unfamiliar number but then heard his voice on her cell phone—she hung up.

Adon arrived on an early morning flight at an airport that served the multitudes in the Washington, D.C. metropolitan area. Upon arrival, he went to the rental car company with the vivd green decor, now being one of their loyal customers, and picked up his rental car. He had arranged with Princess to meet with her and Roderick on campus at the university where they both attended school.

When he had previously made arrangements with Princess, she was reluctant to meet with him, since she knew that her dad would probably make an ardent attempt to dissuade herself and her boyfriend from getting married. But Adon had threatened her with not attending her wedding, if she and Roderick did not agree to discuss their marriage with him, prior to the ceremony. Princess finally gave in, fearing that her dad would adhere to his threat, and she would be left, again, with that feeling of neglect that she had learned to hate so much, when her dad was absent from events where she had desired his presence.

They met in the student lounge, when Princess had a three-hour break between 10:00 A.M. and 1:00 P.M., and Roderick was without a class from 10:00 A.M. to 11:00 A.M. They luckily found a corner table which afforded them some relief from the heavy chatter and busy shifting about within the room.

After Adon was introduced to Roderick (as his future son-in-law) by Princess, they sat down to talk. From Roderick's outward appearance, Adon thought that he was a pleasant looking young man, clean shaven, pants up that fit him, and his verbal skills seemed to be at a college level. He seemed a little nervous, but Adon could understand that. He remembered his first encounter with Princess' mother's parents.

Adon attempted to get Roderick to relax some, by asking him questions about his interests. As Adon listened to his replies he noticed that Roderick hadn't mentioned sports as one of his interests, but Adon didn't pursue that matter, and continued persuading him to talk. Princess was unusually quiet, too, which for her was totally out of character from her strike you in the gut with a barrage of frankness from the outset personality. Quickly, Adon determined that they were using the old—if you don't ask me, I won't tell you—strategy to skim through their meeting with him. He cut to the chase—

"So, Roderick, are you a Christian?" Adon asked, switching

to a completely different category of inquiry than his prior conversation. Before Roderick could answer, Princess chimed in—

"Of course he is, Dad! He was raised in the church, just like me. We go together, all the time."

Adon kindly replied, "That's good, Sweetcake, but when I address Roderick, I want *him* to answer, not you."

"Yes, sir. I'm a Christian,"

"Rod—in the Garden of Gethsemane," Adon said, "when Jesus was under terrible, terrible stress, and the Bible says that Jesus sweat drops of blood, was that real blood, or just a figure of speech?"

Roderick paused, visibly considering his answer. But before he spoke, Princess chimed in again—

"That was real blood! Modern medicine has proven that it's possible to sweat blood, if your level of stress is high enough."

Adon decided against following up on Princess' true but unsolicited answer, since she had quickly provided him with the evidence that he needed to further pursue his line of reasoning. So he asked, point-blank—

"Tell me, Roderick—what is it that you don't like about Princess? And, Princess, I want you to be thinking about what you don't like about Roderick, because I'm going to ask you the same thing—after I hear from *him.*"

"That I *don't* like, sir?" Roderick replied, thinking that was a strange question.

"Yes. That you don't like," Adon said matter-of-factly. "I know that you could go on all day telling me all the great things about her, but we don't have that much time. So, I want you to tell me one, maybe two—if you can possibly think of two—things you don't like about her."

Princess moved her body over closer to Roderick, and put her arm through his—"You can't think of anything, can you, Pooky?"

"Not really!"

"There must be something—she's not perfect, you know."

"I can't think of anything, sir."

"Well, let me see if I can help you," Adon said. "What about the way she always cuts you off, and won't let you talk, as though you don't have a healthy mind of your own? And, what about that nickname she just called you—Pooky—do you like being called that, in public? See, I just gave you an example of two things you may not like about her. So, surely, you can come up with *something.*"

"Well, I guess she does have a habit of interrupting me, when I'm talking; and, a lot of the time, just rudely butting in when nobody was even talking to her."

"How does that make you feel?" Adon asked Roderick.

"Well, like you said, stupid, I guess. And I don't like it!"

Princess removed her arm from under Roderick's and moved her body away from his, looking at him in amazement—"This is the first I've heard of this. You've never mentioned anything like this!"

"Well, you never let me talk," Roderick replied defensively, "so how could I ever say anything? You wouldn't listen, anyway! My parents don't like it either—the way you butt in all the time."

"I don't like some of the things your parents always do, but I don't go around discussing it with other people, the way they *evidently* have done."

"What are you trying to insinuate about my parents—that you don't like them?"

"I'm not crazy about your parents—in case you thought I was—your mother eats like a pig, and she's always claiming to be on a diet!"

"Well, at least my parents aren't divorced!"

"Whoa! Princess. Now he's really getting personal! What have you got to say to that?"

"Well, I don't like the way you look at other women. Like you can't wait to get rid of me, so you can go and be with them! What about that *bitch,* Teneshia!—Oops!" Princess clasped her hand over her mouth, and then quickly removed it. "Sorry, Dad. I didn't mean to say that!"

"Yeah! I hope I don't hear you misapply that word again. I accept your apology. But what about Roderick, don't you need to apologize to him, too?"

"Hell no! I'm not apologizing to him! He doesn't deserve any apology, after what he's said about me."

Right then, Adon thought about how much his Princess was just like her mother; and poor Roderick didn't know it, but he would likely never get an apology out of Princess. He saw that Princess and Roderick were now sitting with their heads turned away from each other, their bodies too, apparently too disgusted to look at one another, or say anything else. Adon broke the silence.

"Listen, you guys, you are *not* ready to get married! Both of you are barely into your twenties, and you don't know anything about what marriage is really about. The little spat, you had just now, was just sweet candy compared to the sour grapes arguments you're headed for. And look at the way you're acting. Your chances for staying married, if you do it now, are practically nil! Do you know that if you marry now, and get divorced, you can never marry again while one of you is living? Did you know that?! That's not something I made up. That's God's law, and there's nothing you can do to change it. If you marry now, you will be married until one of you is dead! You can *never* marry anyone else! Do you believe, Roderick, that you want to spend, possibly, another sixty or so years with Princess? Think about how you're feeling right now; all the anger and frustration inside; then—consider how you will feel after fifty years of being rudely cut off, with her butting in, constantly embarrassing you around the guys, without the possibly of dumping her and marrying someone else without going to hell if you die in that second marriage while Princess is still living. Women usually live longer than men, so until you die, you will be *married* to Princess! That's God's law! There's nothing you can do about it—but accept it—or lose your eternal salvation!"

Roderick pushed his chair back, and stood up—without looking at Princess. He extended his hand over the table toward her dad. Adon responded, likewise, and shook his hand. "Thanks, Mr. Johnson," Roderick sincerely said. "I'm not getting married for a long, long time. I don't want to spend fifty years with *anybody!"* They released their resolute handshake. Then he said to Princess, without making any eye contact with her, "See you around, I've got to get ready for my next class." Then he walked away.

Adon sat observing Princess, who was sitting slouched in her chair, with her body turned away from him—sulking.

"I know you can't see it now," Adon said, "but someday you'll thank me for what just happened. I'm sorry, you're feeling so hurt, and probably mad, too—at me. I wouldn't blame you, if you never spoke to me again."

Princess turned her body back toward Adon, not making eye contact with him, but looking at her fingers while she subconsciously picked at her fingernails. ". . . I'm not angry with you. Everything you said is true. I don't think he was the *last* person I ever wanted to marry. It just seemed like the right thing to do, right now, since I thought he loved me. . . . I love him, too. But I'm not sure if he's the only person in this world I'll *ever* want to marry."

Adon leaned toward her, taking both of her hands in his. He spoke from his heart. "Honey, until you are absolutely sure of who that person is—do not get married!"

Princess looked up at him. "I won't, Daddy. But you didn't have to make me sound so bad, did you?" she said, quietly laughing through a loving smile.

"He left, before I could get to *him*," Adon replied. They understandingly laughed and hugged one another across the table. Then they both sat back in their chairs again.

"I want to see your mother, before I go back," Adon said.

"I don't think she wants to see you. She won't even let me

mention you to her, anymore. What happened, since she went to see you?"

"We had a little disagreement. She'll get over it. Does she know that I'm in town?"

"No!" Princess adamantly replied. "She told me don't mention you to her—and I haven't!"

"What if I go by her job—unannounced. What do you think she'd do?"

"Nothing, because she's not at work. She's at home, packing. She's moving into Brian's house. They just got back from their honeymoon . . ."

Adon's mouth dropped open. "Honeymoon! She's married?"

"Yes. You didn't know that? She said she told you that she was getting married."

"Yes, she told me that. But I didn't think it would happen so quickly."

Princess moved in closer to the table. "For some reason, the day after she went to see you, she suddenly got in a big hurry. She couldn't wait—any longer. Brian was surprised, too. They were supposed to have the wedding in late February. But they went ahead, and did it. And they just returned from their honeymoon."

Adon was trying to hide his total shock from Princess, as he asked her, with a forced natural look on his face, "Did they get married in the church?"

"Yes. Our pastor married them. But it wasn't the kind of big wedding that they were planning. I was her only bridesmaid. It was small, and quick!" Princess had noticed her dad's change of mood from genial satisfaction, at her wedding being off, to one of somber introspection. "What's the matter, Dad. Are you having a bad heart attack?" she asked, purposely exaggerating her question to lighten his dark mood, but it was a sincere inquiry to learn the cause of his abrupt change of outlook.

"I'm okay," Adon haply replied, aware of Princess' genuine concern. "I was hoping that I could talk to her before she got married. But I guess, it's too late for that."

"Yep! It's too late to talk to her, they're good and married!" Princess paused a moment, gathering her thoughts, then added, "What you just told Roderick and I, about never being able to remarry, while one of us is alive, does that apply to Mommy and Brian, too?"

Adon answered frankly—"Today, it equally applies to everybody. There are no exceptions!"

Princess withdrew into a period of silence, then asked, "Did Mommy know that, when she got married?"

Adon saw that Princess was burdened by her concern for her mom, and he was tender with his reply. "I don't know, Honey, I tried to warn her. But she won't talk to me."

Princess sought for some reassurance from her dad. "She must not have known it, or she wouldn't have gotten married. I'm sure she's aware, that *you're* still living."

"To be honest with you, I think she knew it, but she doesn't believe it. I told her at our meeting." Adon was introspectively silent for a moment, then he continued, "Princess, I'm going to tell you something that I've recently done, that I'm not proud of—I regret it tremendously. And I've been trying to make it right again since it happened." Princess listened patiently, while Adon chose his words. "At our meeting, I lied to your mother. I was angry at her, and I wanted to know that she was going to hurt, the way I've been hurting over our divorce. I wanted to get revenge, so I lied to her. I told her what she wanted to hear, when I knew it was a lie."

"What did you tell her, Dad? That was so terrible, that she *wanted* to hear?"

"Well, Honey, she was looking for grounds to get married to Brian. But she wasn't sure if she had Biblical grounds—well, she was sure, but Brian wasn't—and she wanted me to admit to her, in a way that would convince Brian, that I had committed adultery during our marriage. Or, since we've been divorced. To her understanding, and according to what our church has condoned that would provide her with the grounds to remarry, since I had committed adultery, first, and she was the innocent one. Well, the Bible doesn't teach that, and I know the Bible doesn't teach that. But I lied to her, and told her that I had committed adultery since our divorce . . ."

"But you haven't?"

"No. I haven't. I've never been with another woman since I've known your mother. But I told her that I had, since our divorce, so that she would go ahead and marry Brian, and live in adultery. . . . And, Honey, I hoped that she would die, living in adultery . . . and be lost."

Princess was somewhat shamefully affected by her dad's confession, but, at that moment, she was more concerned about her mom's excuse. "But Mommy was glad to hear your lie, not *knowing* it was a lie, that's why she went ahead, and married Brian?"

"That's right. And I'm the cause of her and Brian living in adultery. That's why I've got to talk to her, and tell her what I've done. I've tried repeatedly to reach her, but she won't talk to me."

Princess thought for a moment, then said, "But it won't do any real good to tell her what you've done, because she already believed, before you lied to her that you had committed adultery. So what good is telling her, now, going to do? Her mind's made up, especially after she's already married. Brian is the one that wanted you to admit it, so that he could be sure."

"Yes, that's true, now. But I just found out from you that she's *already* married. I thought I could tell her before she got married, and stop her from getting married, and living in adultery. I thought if she knew that I had lied to her, she wouldn't get married because she didn't have grounds. That's what she thinks the Bible teaches."

"But, Dad, if the Bible doesn't teach that, why does Mommy think that it does?" Princess asked, with an attitude of sincere inquiry with respect to her mom, and gloomily suspicious of her dad's newfangled beliefs. In the back of her mind wondering if she had done the right thing by agreeing with her dad, so quickly, and letting Roderick go.

"The best answer I can give you to that question is that she's never been taught anything else. And she hasn't studied her Bible closely enough to learn it on her own. But it's there, and can't be denied!"

"Today, is the first time I've heard of that, too. Since you've been so honest with me, I'm going to be honest with you."

"I don't know how much more honesty I can take, but go ahead."

"Well, I had never planned on staying married to Roderick for a whole *lifetime*. I loved him enough to marry him, and give up my virginity to him, but I knew, after that, at some point we would get a divorce. And, I would have perfect grounds because he already plays around on me, a lot. I knew, eventually, I could claim the best grounds for our divorce, and, then, I could marry someone else. But I would have had a lot of fun with Roderick in the meantime. He is cute—don't you think?"

Adon was in shock, again, but pleasantly so, unlike the first lightening strike of bad news about Jewel and Brian. He already knew how strike you in the gut frank Princess was, but still he could only manage to say, "I'm sure glad you're still a virgin!"

Princess went on, "I want you to show me in the Bible, where I can never marry *again,* as long as my husband is alive. Or, I'm going to get Roderick back—marry him—and do like I had planned to do in the first place." She unzipped her book bag that was lying on the floor, and took out her Bible. She laid it open on the table in front of her dad—"Show me!"

Adon was glad, then, that he had prayed before meeting with Princess and Roderick, and he felt doubly blessed that everything he believed about divorce and remarriage, he could show Princess from the Bible; for he knew she would do exactly as she had said with Roderick, if he couldn't show it to her. She was frank that way!

"Okay, I'm glad that you want me to show it to you from the Bible. That's the best rule you can follow when it involves your faith. If it's not in the Bible—forget it! If it is—do it! I'll start by showing you why some people get the false idea, basically by focusing on the little word 'except,' that there's grounds for remarriage in Matthew 19:9. Then I'll explain to you what the text really teaches, and then show you, from the Bible, that what it teaches is in agreement with the whole Bible."

Adon took forty minutes to show Princess from the Bible his Bible study on divorce and remarriage. She listened intensely, her young mind clicking, critically reasoning out what he was saying, interjecting a sincere question, where one was called for, until he had concluded the study in First Corinthians.

Adon closed Princess' Bible. "Do you have anymore questions," he asked.

Princess relaxed some, and sat slightly slouched in her chair. "No. But I feel like the disciples—if *that* be the case, it's better not to marry!"

"There's nothing wrong with getting married. In fact, I highly recommend it. Just don't plan on marrying, *again.* You get one shot, and you had better make it count—because after that you're out of bullets, unless your husband dies."

"I had planned on being a virgin, anyway, whenever I got married. But, now, I'm certain that I will, since fornication is considered as much a sin as adultery. If you're married, or been married, it's the same thing."

"I'm glad to hear you say you intend to keep your virginity. That shows a measure of wisdom way beyond your young years."

Princess sat up straight again, with her elbows on the table. "But what about Mommy, and Brian, they're living in adultery? What if one of them suddenly dies?"

"We don't want to think about one of them dying—because then it would be too late for us to do anything."

"What can we do, they're already married? The only thing

they can do, is get a divorce." Then she added jokingly, "What if *you* died, that would solve everything!—Just kidding, Dad!"

Adon playfully thumped her on her forehead. "All of that wisdom is leaking out of your ears! Which reminds me, when did you start using that kind of foul language, like I heard when Roderick was here?"

"I have some friends that I hang out with sometimes. We cuss like that, when we're together, because it's fun. But I don't do it around other people. But I've noticed, lately, that it's starting to slip out, when I don't want it to. That's what happened, it came out, twice, when I wasn't expecting it."

"That should be a warning to you! You've allowed the devil access to a weakness in you. He'll infrequently embarrass you with it, just to keep you available, and thinking it's not a big deal, and you can control it. Then, somehow, he'll kill you with it! Maybe involved in road rage. He already knows how he plans to do it, he's just subtly leading you up to it. *It may take years*. The way to beat the devil is to stop playing his game; whatever sin it is, stop doing it—and stay on the Lord's side. He can't touch you as long as you abide in Jesus' ways. As a Christian, who knows the truth, when you venture onto Satan's ground, he'll eventually kill you."

"I'm finding that out—the way I can't seem to control my mouth."

"You've got to make it a point of serious study and prayer, and stop running around with those friends who make it fun to commit sin. Sin is sometimes fun, but it's always leading to eternal death."

"I promise you, I'm going to do whatever it takes to stop cursing—What about Mommy, and Brian?"

"Well, Honey, like you said, it probably won't do any good to talk to your mother. Since she went ahead and got married, anyway. I'm sure she read my email with the Bible study, at least part of it, and rejected it, that's why she suddenly got in such a big rush to get married. Before Brian got knowledge of what the Bible says. Since he was the one, in the first place, seeking proof of her availability to marry."

"Since they just got married, maybe Brian is still open to hearing what the Bible says, and do something about it."

"That's what I'm thinking. . . . Do you know where his medical office is?"

"Sure. I've been there with Mommy, plenty of times. If you're thinking about going by there, you'd better call, first. He spends a lot of time in hospitals. I have his phone number, and my cell phone, right here, if you want to call him." She quickly reached in her book bag, took out her cell phone, and handed it to her dad. "The number's in auto-dial, under Brian."

Adon refused the cell phone, backing it off with his hand. "Hold on a minute, Princess. Let me think a moment!"

"You've already thought about it, Dad! What if one of them dies!? If he's not in his office, I have his cell phone number, too, under Brian-1. Here, I'll call his office for you. Try there, first." She fingered the auto-dial, held the phone to her ear, and then handed it back to her dad. "It's ringing!"

Adon received the phone, and put it to his ear. Presently, he said, "Good morning. My name is Adon Johnson. I would like to speak to Doctor . . . what's his last name?"

"Sparks!"

"Doctor Sparks, please." (Listens.) "No, no I don't, it's a very personal matter." (Listens.) "Well, tell him that I'm Jewel's first husband, and it's a friendly call."

Princess still had plenty of time before her next class, so she accompanied her dad to Brian's office, giving her dad precise directions as he drove. Brian's office was a twenty-five minute drive from the university campus. As soon as they had arrived, and Brian was notified that they were in his waiting room, he had his receptionist escort them to his private office. The receptionist opened the door, and Adon let Princess walk through first, and he followed. The receptionist quietly closed the door.

Brian was seated behind a large desk that was cluttered with papers, but he stood up when Princess and her dad walked in. He was wearing a white lab coat over a blue shirt and tie. He appeared to be roughly ten years older that Adon, shorter, too, with a softer muscular build and a midsection spread slightly showing underneath his lab coat. He greeted Princess, first, coming from behind his desk and meeting her in the middle of the room.

"Hello, Miss Johnson. I'm sparks-ling to see you. Although, it's only been a few hours," he said lightheartedly, placing both hands on Princess' shoulders. Then Princess turned to her dad, who was standing behind her.

"Brian, I'd like for you to meet my dad," she said, moving from between them. The two men made eye contact, evaluating the strength of one another—if this meeting was going to be a contest of determining a winner, or of beating "their swords into plowshares." Brian offered his hand, first.

"Mr. Johnson, glad you took time out of your schedule to stop by."

Adon shook his hand, a hard grip, Adon noticed, which he appreciated. One thing he disliked in a man was a weak, girlish handshake. They released their physical greeting. "I was in town, so I though I'd better take this opportunity to meet you. Princess showed me the way here, with no problems."

"Well, I'm glad to see both of you," Brian said. Then he directed them toward a brown leather sofa that was turned from the plaque covered wall, at an angle, to face his desk. Behind the sofa was a wedge shaped credenza, designed to fit between the custom-made sofa and the wall. The office was expensively furnished, indicative of a successful medical practice. Adon and Princess sat on the sofa, and Brian sat in a single arm-chair that was facing them, at a precisely conversational distance.

"I'm between classes," Princess said, "and my dad wanted to meet you, so here we are."

"I'm a bit taken aback," Brian replied, "since I usually know ahead of time who I'm meeting with here, but it's good that you and your dad took the time to come by."

"I realize you must be very busy, this time of the day," Adon said, "and I appreciate you taking this time to see me. Besides wanting to meet you, as a matter of friendship, I have an important issue that I need to discuss with you."

"I'll admit to you that I was quite apprehensive, after we spoke on the phone," Brian replied, "and it hasn't completely vanished. Right now, I'm still slightly that way—*nervous* is probably a better word. Which, in my field of medicine, is not easily accomplished."

"Princess said jokingly, "Relax! My dad left his gun in the car!" Adon and Brian mannerly laughed, for Princess' sake, but her humor was timely, and provided space for both of them to loosen up, and set aside badly preconceived notions of one another.

"I had hoped that I could speak with Jewel before the two of you were married," Adon said, "but Princess tells me that you're husband and wife, already."

"That's right," Brian replied, "two weeks ago. But I thought that Jewel went to see you, about a month ago?"

"She did. But I meant that I wanted to talk to her again, since then. But she's been hard to reach, and I haven't spoken to her."

"Mommy doesn't know that my dad's in town. You didn't tell her, did you?"

"Noo! I thought about calling her. But she's been adamant about keeping you out of our conversations. After she told me what you said, at your meeting, she said that there was no need to *ever* mention you again. So, I decided not to call her."

"Brian," Adon said, uncrossing his legs and moving to the edge of the sofa, "mine and Jewel's meeting is what I need to talk to you about. . . . You see, there's been a big misunderstanding regarding what I said to Jewel. . . . I lied to her. . . ."

"All she told me was that you admitted, to her, that you had a sexual affair, since your divorce. Anything else you told her is none of my business. And, please, if you don't mind, I don't care to know."

"I think you need to know this!" Princess said.

"What is it, Adon? What is it that I need to know?"

"Alright, I won't mince words—Jewel is still my wife!"

Brian stood up, his face wroth, his body half turned toward the door, his words biting—"I've never asked anyone to leave my office, but I'm about to make an exception! I'm busy. I don't have time for foolishness! And Princess, did you know that's what he came here to say?"

Princess stood, too, defensive of her dad. "Yes. I knew that's what he wanted to say. And I agree with him. I think you need to listen, to all he has to say."

"Princess, Honey, sit down," Adon calmly said, still seated. "I don't blame him for being upset. I would be, too." Princess sat down again, relaxed against the back of the sofa. "Brian, if you don't mind, I'd like for you to sit down, too."

Brian reluctantly sat down. "You've got five minutes!"

Princess surged forward again—"It's going to take longer than that if . . ."

"Princess, please!" Adon kindly reprimanded Princess, "I'll take care of it." Princess relaxed again, leaning back on the sofa.

"Brian, this is not easy for me to say. It's not easy for me being here. . . . While Jewel and I were married . . ."

"I thought you just said that she was *still* your wife!" Brian roughly interjected.

"Let him finish!" Princess blurted out. Adon gave Princess a fatherly, what did I just tell you, stern look, and she faked a smile back at him, in recognition of his reminding her.

Adon continued. "While Jewel and I were together, I read a letter from you, to Jewel. I didn't know who you were until Jewel told me at our recent meeting."

Brian suddenly lost a great deal of his angry pomposity, from just learning that Adon knew of his illicit involvement with Jewel, subsequent to their divorce. He shamefacedly looked away from Adon. Adon waited, in an uncomfortable silence, until Brian could look at him again, and then he was about to speak, but Brian spoke, first—

"Adon, I . . . I've been struggling with the guilt of my affair with Jewel, while she was married to you. . . . Princess—should you be hearing this?"

"Mommy told me that she knew you before her divorce," Princess nonchalantly replied. "I could figure out the rest. I wasn't born yesterday, you know."

"Well, that's when it started, but we didn't, I should say that she didn't, get serious until after her divorce. We never had sexual intercourse, until after we were married. Jewel made sure of that. But still, I took advantage of problems she was having in her marriage, and aided in causing her divorce. I acted selfishly, and irresponsibly, on occasions when I might have been of some assistance. I wanted her for myself, and at the time, I didn't care who was hurt. Adon . . . I don't have any acceptable excuse for what I've done. But I need for you to forgive me. I am sincerely sorry, for what I've done to you."

Adon hung his head, in final recognition of Jewel's conduct during their marriage, and now facing the man whom she was involved with. Presently, he looked up at Brian. "I suspected that she was having an affair, while we were married," Adon sorrowfully said, "but I refused to believe it, until a month ago, when she told me, out of anger, that she had. You've contritely asked for my forgiveness, and as a Christian, I want to forgive you, and I have no choice but to forgive you." Adon paused a moment, then added, "Jewel told me that you've been baptized, since our divorce, is that true?"

"Yes. I've accepted Jesus Christ as my personal Savior, and I've been baptized, over a year ago."

"Well, what you've done before your baptism, God has forgiven you for. And, He would be very displeased with me, if I didn't do as He has done. As a brother in the Lord . . . I forgive you, too."

Divorce: Episode Three

"Thank you, Adon. I can finally lay that guilt to rest.

Princess saw that Brian was searching through the pockets of his lab coat. She rose from the sofa, went to his cluttered desk, pulled three white napkins from the dispenser box on his desk, and then returned to Brian, gave him one, gave her dad one, and kept one for herself. She sat down again, and dabbed her eyes, along with her dad and Brian.

"That statement you made about Jewel, being your wife, worked," Brian said. "It certainly got my attention. But it was worth it, to get that off of my chest."

"He's not finished!" Princess said.

"Brian, God has forgiven you, for everything you've done with Jewel, *before* your baptism—but since you've married her, you've got another problem that you'll need to take to the Lord. When I said that Jewel was *still* my wife, I wasn't just trying to get your attention."

The creeping fear of bad news began to overtake Brian's grateful demeanor. He peered questioningly at Adon—"Adon, you're not making good sense. I saw Jewel's divorce papers. Irreconcilable differences was what they said. No property was contested. You gave everything you owned to her, except your car, and your truck. Unless those documents were fraudulent, she is *not* your wife!"

"When you took your vows, before baptism," Adon replied, "you agreed that you would hold the Bible as your only rule of faith. And, you understood that you are not saved by works, but by acceptance of the righteousness of Jesus Christ to atone for your sins; and His giving of His life, because of His love for you, was to pay the debt of death for your sins, so that by your faith in Jesus you would not have to pay for your sins with your own life. And, because of your love for Jesus, you accepted His saving grace that allows you to keep His commandments. And, because of His love, for settling a debt that you yourself can never repay, you *want* to keep His commandments, because this is His reward and desire for your life on earth.

"I'm saying this, before I say what I'm about to say, so that you would know, by a recollection of your own vows, what manner of Christian I am. I am not one who believes that I am saved by keeping all of the commandments, but I am one who believes that I obey the commandments because I am saved—and I'm doing God's will in my life, to obtain victory over sin, according to the Bible.

"Before your baptism, what you learned from Jewel, and I suppose from someone else who gave you good Bible studies, was that all that was needed for you, or Jewel, to remarry was the death of a spouse, or that I had committed adultery, first. I understand that your wife is deceased, so you were okay there. And, Jewel had informed you that I had admitted to committing adultery, so you thought you were in the clear there, too. The truth is, I lied to Jewel. I am not guilty of adultery. . . ."

"So what's the big problem?" Brian suspiciously asked. "We married on what we took for granted was a true statement from you. God's not going to hold us accountable for that. We didn't know! It seems to me that you're the one that's in violation of the commandments here."

"He's not finished!" Princess said.

You're right, Brian, I have sinned, and I've asked God's forgiveness for it. I know He has forgiven me, but my repentance is not done, until I confess what I know about your marriage to you. What you need to know is, that as far as your marriage to Jewel is concerned, it doesn't matter if I lied, or did not lie—Your marriage to Jewel, in God's eyes, and according to the Bible, which you vowed to study and follow, is not valid. You and Jewel are living in adultery! Because I, her first husband, am still alive, your marriage to Jewel, according to the seventh commandment, is invalid. And until you get out of it, you are committing the sin of adultery—Without fail!"

"I've been a bearer of adverse information for many people," Brian replied, deeply concerned and leaning toward Adon, "and I've appreciated it when my patients have made sure of what I've said, by repeating it back to me. Now, I'm going to do the same thing for you—for *my* clear understanding of what you're telling me.

"You're saying, that my wife and I are committing adultery, even though we're married, because the Bible says that she is *still* married to you. Adon, is that what you're telling me?"

"Brian, that's, absolutely, what I'm telling you!"

Brian slowly rose from his chair, and walked around the back of it, and stood, with his head bowed, with his back toward Adon and Princess. Presently, he turned to face them again. "Adon, that's ridiculous! I don't believe that's what the Bible says—at all. I think you've got a hidden, deep-seated grudge against my wife that you're not admitting to; and you're out to break up our marriage, because she doesn't want you. If that's the kind of vindictive Christian you are, I can see why my wife never wants to hear your name again. Princess, you can stay, but Adon—I'm asking you to leave!"

Adon reluctantly stood up; Princess, too.

"I didn't come here to convince you," Adon said, "to do anything about what I've told you regarding Jewel and I. What you do about what I've said, is a matter between you and God. But you greatly jeopardize your future salvation, if you don't know what the Bible teaches about divorce and remarriage—which you can't do anything about, but accept it. If I don't show it to you, before you force me to leave, I won't feel that I've accomplished anything by coming here. What you do with the information is out of my hands, but God is going to hold me accountable, if I don't make a sincere effort to show it to you. Princess told me that you have a Bible here." Princess left her dad's side and went to Brian's desk, opened the middle drawer, took out Brian's Bible, returned to her dad, and handed the Bible to him. Adon took the Bible, and held it in the palm of one hand that he extended toward Brian—"May I?"

Brian slowly walked over to a small conference table with six chairs. He pulled one chair away from the table. "Princess, you can sit here. Adon, I suppose, whether she wants to hear it or not, I'll have to tell Jewel that I, at least, tried to let you show it to me. You can sit next to Princess. I have another Bible that I mark in, that I want to use to follow along with you—unless this is one of those *one* verse studies, in which case I won't need it. Which is it?"

Adon and Princess walked over to the conference table. Princess sat down in the chair that Brian had positioned for her. Before Adon had sat down next to Princess he said to Brian, "You'd be smart to get your *marking* Bible." Then he sat down, and Brian went to a floor to ceiling book case and removed his Bible from a shelf at eye level. He returned to the table, and sat down across from Adon and Princess. He removed a yellow felt-tipped marker from the pencil holder on the table. Adon opened his borrowed Bible to Matthew 19:9. He shared the Bible with Princess. "Before we begin, I want to pray that the Holy Spirit will give us understanding of His Word." Everyone bowed their head.

Adon spent forty-five minutes revealing from the Bible Brian's dilemma in being married to Jewel. During the study Brain objected, at first, many times, but as the evidence mounted in favor of his unbiblical connubial relationship, he began to accept that maybe he deserved the dire report he was receiving, because of the way he had aided in destroying the inner sanctum of Adon's marriage. Under his circumstances of guilt, he became more inclined to believe the Bible since he could readily see the reasoning behind God's rule of never tampering with another man's wife. His conviction of himself, perpetrating the great sin of adultery, and then marrying into it, made his resolve to rid himself of it, thereby redeeming himself and Jewel, even deeper, and surely more immediate than someone who may not have premeditatedly married into an adulterous sequel relationship.

During the study Princess had been studiously quiet, but at the conclusion, when Adon and Brian had closed their Bibles and

Brian had replaced the yellow felt-tipped marker in the pencil holder, she leaned back in her chair, and said—

"Now, he's finished!"

"This has certainly been a big eye-opener! Adon, I owe you one," Brian said.

"Now, what are you going to do about it?" Princess asked. "Hurry, because I've got to get back to school."

"Well, I don't know how I'm going to accomplish it," Brian replied, "but I'm going to get a divorce. I can't do this adultery to myself, or Jewel, and have any semblance of a peaceful marriage. I couldn't bear the guilt of that. This marriage began in the wrong direction, I'm not totally surprised that it's ending up this way. If I get my attorneys moving on it right away, since we've been married such a short time and I haven't changed any facts of my estate, it shouldn't be too much of a problem to annul the marriage."

"You've got a great deal to think and pray about," Adon said, "but it's something you must do. The sooner, the better."

"How are you going to tell Mommy? She's been happy as a canary, to be finally married to you."

"I haven't figured that out, yet. This isn't the kind of thing you can smooth over with flowers. With that said, I don't think I'm going to tell her—until I have all the paperwork, ready for her signature."

"What goes around, comes around!"

"What was that, you said, Adon?" Brian asked.

"Oh, nothing! I was just thinking out loud." Adon resolutely pushed his chair back, and stood up. "We had better get going, Princess. You've got to get back for your afternoon classes." Brian and Princess stood also. "Honey, I wonder if you wouldn't mind meeting me at the car? I want to say a word or two to Brian, before I leave. Here are the keys. Get in, relax, and wait for me."

"Okay, but hurry, Dad. We don't have much time!" Princess replied, receiving the car keys from Adon. Then she went out the door.

Adon moved a few steps toward the door, then turned toward Brian. Brian remained standing beside his chair, wondering what Adon could have to say to him in private, since they had, all along, been so candid in front of Princess. He attempted to make it easier for Adon to initiate their conversation. "This has taken longer than I expected; now I've got to rearrange my schedule, to allow for our meeting."

"Brian, I would like to know something. I don't know quite how to ask you this, and you don't have to give me an answer, if you feel my question is too personal."

"I'll answer it, if I can. Is this a medical question?"

"No, it's not. But I would appreciate it, if you would answer it for me."

"I'll try. What is it?"

"Well, as I said, I suspected some time ago that Jewel was having an affair. And, the thought crossed my mind, of the guy she could be involved with, what must he look like? Then, after she told me, herself, that she was in love with another man, I was really bothered, being a man, too, by what she could have seen in another man that persuaded her to leave *me.* Don't take this personal, but after seeing you, you're not who I expected you to be. I mean, you're not tall, athletic, or anything. You're not bad looking, but you're not what I would call handsome, either. You're just a regular looking guy. Granted, you appear to be financially well-off. But, you're certainly no stud, or the like. I guess what I want to know is, why did Jewel choose you, over me? What did you do to win her over to you?"

"Well, I guess that's a fair question, and one that deserves an honest answer, seeing as how I was successful at stealing your wife—I'm not that bad looking, though!"

Adon smiled, and came back toward the table and stood opposite of Brian. "What was it, that you did? I need to know."

Brian seriously thought for a moment—

"Well, I think that you didn't realize, nor recognize that

Jewel was a woman with deep feelings, and she needed an outlet for those feelings. She couldn't break through to you, and communicate with your soul, is the best way that I can put it. Jewel is like most women. The more a man is like a woman, in his temperament, without being a woman—the more they like it. They don't want a woman, they want a real man, not anyone effeminate, either; but they want a man to have kind, responsive feelings like a woman. They want the gentleness of understanding from a man that women seem to possess naturally, and they get that from other women. But it's something, and I believe it's because of sin, that a man has to learn, and it usually only happens between a man and his wife.

"I don't think that it ever happened with you and Jewel. I saw in Jewel that that was what she needed, and I only gave her the possibility of it occurring with me, but that was enough to steal her from you. Had she known the lifelong permanence of marriage, the way you've shown me, today, she more than likely would have never even considered leaving you to attempt to find it with another man. Had she made up her mind, to stay with you, made a definite commitment to honor her marriage vows, God would have rewarded her with wisdom, to grow in her marriage.

"But once Jewel allowed the devil to access her thinking with divorce, which he used me to bring about, and began to view her marriage as a temporary union, that could be broken—if she came up with the right excuse—it was just a matter of time before Satan, with me as his pawn, had wrecked another home. Jewel loved you. She probably still does. But I gave her the promise of receiving that important element of deep-soul communication that she couldn't get from you. Being a fairly good looking man, you've never had to make up for not having good looks, as I have, so you couldn't see in Jewel what she desperately needed from you. I did, and I gave it to her. That's why you lost her."

"Thanks, Brian," Adon said, shaking Brian's hand with a

firm grip. "Let's stay in touch. I hope I've made a friend today." Brian smiled, nodded his head in agreement, and Adon walked out of the office.

That selfsame day, Brian called his personal attorney, and had him to begin the legal process of annulling his marriage to Jewel. A month after their marriage had ended, Brian was dead!

He had gone on an African safari, caught malaria in Kenya, and died in a hospital in Nairobi. His body was brought back to the United States, and Adon attended his funeral. Adon sat with Princess, but Jewel sat with Brian's two sobbing children, and other members of Brian's family.

It was never mentioned, prior to the large funeral, by Brian, Princess, or Adon that Brian had received his knowledge of Biblical divorce and remarriage from Adon. So far as Jewel knew, Brian had just recently discovered the information from someone else, and was moved to seek a divorce because of his renewed awareness. She bitterly wept when Brian broke the news to her that he loved her, but according to the Bible, they could not remain married.

He gave her the Bible study that Adon had given to him, that he had highlighted in his Bible. She was hard pressed to accept what the Bible actually said, and lose her husband, but Brian made it clear that if they wanted to see each other in heaven, they had better follow the undeniable teachings of the Bible. So Jewel signed the divorce papers, without contesting them, and shortly, thereafter, their divorce was final. Brian provided her with a lifelong, generous income from his estate, that if she chose to, she could quit her job and live comfortably on. At the time of Brian's funeral she was still working, and had no plans, at that time, of relinquishing her job.

Adon and Princess were divided on whether Jewel should ever know that the both of them were instrumental in Brian wanting a divorce because of what he had learned from Adon. Adon wanted to tell her, but Princess did not. Princess' reasoning was in keeping with her strike you in the gut frankness—what good would it do, for her to know? It was not a gross sin to keep it secret.

However, Adon felt that anything that was held in secret, which could, at some point in time, be found out by an involved party, was just ammunition for Satan to use to someone's detriment. He told Princess that he well-intended to tell Jewel where Brian had received the information, but he would not inform Jewel that Princess was there, too. He would leave that decision up to Princess, whether she ever wanted to tell her mother that she was present at the meeting—and she was wholeheartedly in favor of Brian knowing, and seeking a divorce.

After Brian's elaborate grave side ceremony, Jewel invited Adon to accompany Princess to Brian's home, where Brian's family had prepared a special meal for members of the family, and their guests, to seek repose after a trying and difficult day. A relaxing environment to talk with out-of-town family, some who had traveled long distances to attend Brian's funeral.

As the members of Brian's large family and guests milled about his spacious home, eating, and engaging one another in friendly conversation, Adon made himself continually aware of where Jewel was, for he was looking for an opportunity, when she was alone, that he could approach her, and talk with her. They had not talked again since their unsettling meeting in the airport, roughly three months ago. Princess had called Adon, and informed him of Brian's death, and the time and date of the funeral. He had arrived for the funeral that morning.

Presently, Adon saw Jewel leave an acquaintance of hers and Brian and go out of sight to another part of the house. He kept an eye on the direction in which she had gone, and, presently, he saw her return to the family room wearing her coat and long wool scarf. He watched her wrap her scarf tightly around her neck, lifting her hair with one hand to layer it underneath, and then open a sliding glass door, and go outside onto the terrace.

He got up and went to the entrance of the house, removed his coat from the guest closet, and returned to the family room, putting his coat on as he went. When he arrived at the terrace doors where Jewel had gone out, he went out, too, onto the balcony that served the family room and a half-kitchen area of the house, where most of the guests were gathered. He saw Jewel at the far end of the balcony, leaning on the decorative wrought iron railing, looking out over the patio and pool area one story below. She was the only other person on the balcony.

He walked up to her, standing at the railing. He leaned on the railing, not talking, but just letting her know that he was there in case she wanted to say anything. He was not going to presume that he knew what to say to her; and by his silence he wanted her to know that he respected her right to accept his presence, or to move away, and leave, if she felt that was what she wanted to do. He was not going to pass judgment on her, by assuming that he understood her state of mind at a crucial crossroad in both of their lives, probably more crucial than any heated argument that they had ever had. More crucial than his calling her indecent names, and accusing her of premeditated adultery. More crucial, even, than their hurtful divorce, for their divorce was the end of a chaotic, earthly episode; but his standing there, close beside her, was the beginning of what could never end, a new beginning of a union that could not be broken by all the past diversities that they had faced, and a beginning that would take them into their eternal existence with God.

He stood there beside her for what seemed to him like a lifetime, waiting to see if she would accept, or reject him. Then she put her arm through his, and all the hatred and hurts of the past left him, and he felt that he could finally speak.

"That pool, so clean, and crisp looking, makes you feel that you could dive from this balcony, doesn't it?"

"I guess someone took the cover all the way off, and turned the heater on, to melt the ice that was over it yesterday, when I was here, visiting the kids."

"How are they taking this?"

"They seem to be dealing with it, okay. But losing both of

your parents, by the time you're their young age, has to be totally devastating. It should make us aware of how blessed we are, to still have both of our parents. I think now that if Mom or Dad died, I could take it so much better, knowing how, for so many years, the Lord has blessed me with them."

"How are you taking this, Jewel? I know that this has been a terrible lost for you. And, I want you to know that I'm sorry, that Brian's passing has happened."

"Thanks, Adon. I appreciate your sympathy, and caring, and for coming out here in the cold, and standing with me."

"I've been keeping my eye on you all afternoon, hoping I could get a chance to speak to you alone. It could not have been cold enough to stop me from coming out here."

He felt her forearm strengthening her snug hold on his arm, and she leaned her head over onto his shoulder. "Adon, I've really made a mess of things, haven't I?"

"We can't see it, right now. But we have to always remember what Jesus told us in His Word: 'And we know that all things work together for good to them that love God, to them who are the called according to His purpose.' We can't ever forget that."

She raised her head from off of his shoulder. "I don't know how people can make it in this world without Jesus, without the comfort of His promises to us. Life is so hard, sometimes. Without Jesus, it would make good sense, to just give up. But He gives us so much hope for the future, if we keep trusting in Him. I couldn't live another day, without Jesus." She removed her arm from inside of his, and turned her body slightly, so that she could look at him. He looked at her, briefly, into her soft eyes, but he couldn't hold that intimacy with her, seeing that she was about to say something to him, and for fear of embarrassing her, by holding her in his arms, so he looked away again, and he heard her speaking—

"Adon . . . I've done some terrible, awful things to you. Some things I've done on purpose, and some, I let happen, which I could have prevented. . . . I've lied to you. I've worked against you, without your knowledge. . . . I've slandered your name. I've accused you of adultery, when I was the one that was the adulteress. I've even talked about you badly, to our child. . . . There's nothing I can do now to repair all that I've done to you. You've apologized to me, and I purposely didn't apologize to you, when I just knew that it was the right thing to do. But I purposely didn't do it, because I wanted to hurt you. What I've done to you has not been your fault, and I take full responsibility for my actions against you. If I had to give a reason for what I've done, or if you ask me for a reason, I would just have to say that I was deeply angry with you. I was very angry with you, for letting me stop loving you. You saw me slipping away, and you didn't seem to care. You were leaving it all up to me to stop my withdrawal from you, but I couldn't stop myself, I needed you to help me to stop. But you didn't, you let me go. And, I was so angry with you. You let me go, and I didn't really want to go. And, I was angry with you.

"Adon, I apologize to you, for all I've done. I'm asking that if you can find room in your heart to forgive me, Adon, please, forgive me?"

Adon had given up hope of ever hearing an apology from Jewel; a recognition of her own contribution to the failure of their marriage, and the grief that she had heaped upon him. He had thought many times in the past that if she would apologize to him, his own offensive conduct toward her would be vindicated, and he would feel that he had won a victory. But, then, hearing Jewel, he felt no such victory! His heart was aching for Jewel, and the sounds of suffering in her voice had brought back to the surface of his consciousness every desire that he had ever possessed to protect her from all harm and hardship—his very spirit was telling him that he had caused every pain in her life, that he was the complete cause of her every unhappiness since she had known him. He felt completely at her mercy, and he desperately wanted her to forgive him, for all he'd done to her.

"Jewel . . . first, I want you to know, that I forgive you,

without lingering doubt, or reservation. With all the forgiveness that is within my power to give, I give it to you. But my forgiving you, makes me in no way guiltless of all the wrongs that I've done to you. I find no position of superiority over you, because of the wrongs you've done to me. I am to blame for violating my sacred vows to God, to do everything possible, every day, to increase your happiness. Instead, I've turned your life into one of sorrow, and pain, and I am deeply regretful for what I've so foolishly done to you. I am a conniving rascal, and a selfish scoundrel, and I need you to help me, if you possibly can, to see some value in myself again, so that I can continue to go on living with this guilt from day to day. I'm asking you, Jewel, to please, if you can find it in your heart, forgive me?"

"Hold me, Adon, I'm cold," Jewel said. A timely reality? An inspiration for mending of hearts? A longing desire to feel the comfort of her husband's protection? A naked realization that she could now turn to this man in her weakest emotional state without condemnation, or rejection? Adon turned to her, and opened his topcoat, and she placed her arms around his body and he covered her in close to himself with his coat and arms embracing her. He felt her crying on his chest, releasing the years of torment, letting go of the enmity and shame and enslaving revenge, gathering the strength to go on another day in joyful recognition that this is not all there is to life. He held her, knowing that this was all that he was capable of doing in the life of his wife; to be a part of her existence, that element outside of her body that she could count on for understanding, comfort, and protection. He held her without words, until he felt her gently moving away from his body.

After she was free, he looked down at her face, and it was tear-soaked, her eyes were still brimming and she seemed faintly embarrassed. He took his handkerchief out of his suit coat pocket, tilted her head up with the tips of his fingers under her chin, and dried her face with his handkerchief. He was gentle with her, touching her lightly here and there with his fingertip wrapped in his handkerchief. When he was done, he removed his fingers from under her chin. He wanted to kiss her—but he didn't.

"I must look a mess," she said.

"I've known you a long time, under every circumstance, and I've never seen you look a mess."

"Not even when Princess was born?"

"Especially not when Princess was born—Speaking of Princess. Where is she? I haven't seen her since we ate."

"She's with Edward, and Tangela," Jewel replied. She heard his pause. She looked at him, and saw that he had a question on his face. She added, "Those are Brian's children. They became fond of one another, and they were looking forward to being brother and sisters. But I've noticed, and it started the day after Brian and I returned from our honeymoon that she's been acting strangely. Not at all like herself. Not *talkative*, you know what I mean? Like something's bothering her."

Adon thought that this was a good time to tell Jewel that he was the one who gave Brian his Bible study, that led to their divorce. "Um, Jewel, there's . . ." He saw that Jewel was attempting to adjust her scarf for a closer fit around her neck, under her coat, and he paused in what he was about to say to help her. After he had assisted her with her scarf, she turned her coat collar up, and held it in place under her chin. "Are you still cold?" he asked, instead. "Do you want to go inside?"

"No. I'm okay. I want to stay out here. I started not to wear my boots to the funeral. But, now I'm glad that I did. . . . Brian was a fine man. I wish that you could have met him."

"Um, Jewel, listen, there's something that I need to tell you about . . ."

"Just let me say this, first, before I forget it!" She giggled a little, in a cute, girlish way. "It's funny now, when I think about it. But it wasn't when it happened. Brian was about to give me a Bible study, on divorce, but I didn't know what he was going to say yet, because he hadn't told me anything about our own divorce. But I suspected what he was going to show me in the Bible, because I had read part of your email the day after I came back from seeing you. So, I didn't want him to get started on that. But we were married, and I had no idea of what he was thinking about doing. But I didn't want to hear it, and ruin our Sunday morning. So, to get him to stop, I stood up, then I just collapsed to the floor—pretending that I had fainted—the back of my hand over my forehead, the whole stage drama! Isn't that funny?" she asked, embarrassingly laughing as she said it. Adon laughed with her. Then she said, "That was so immature of me, but it worked! He should have known, being a doctor, that I was faking. But he didn't. I let him call an ambulance, and everything, until I couldn't take those smelling salts he was holding under my nose. Then I stood up—like nothing had happened! He brought me flowers, and gave me a present that day.

"That wasn't out of the ordinary, he always let me know that I was special to him. He was the kindest man I ever met. I'm not sad about our divorce. I'm glad that he did it. I agreed with what the Bible said. We were living in adultery, there was no getting around it. And, I'm very appreciative of the person who showed him our condition of adultery in the Bible. He never told me who it was, just another Christian that he met in his office, he said, but I would like to thank them, if I ever find out who it was.

"He had been planning to go on the African safari for a long time. What if he hadn't found out first, and died while we were still married? I'm so glad that he got the divorce, first, now I know that I will see him again. But, it could have been that I would've never been in heaven with him. And maybe I wouldn't have been there, either. So, if I find out who gave him the Bible study, I want to thank them from the bottom of my heart! No. I'm not sad about the divorce, I'm sad, today, because he's dead, and I won't get to see him today, or tomorrow, or the next day—

"I just go on, and on, don't I? I'm sorry, I didn't know that I was going to say all of that." She snuggled up closer beside Adon, looking up at him. "Now, what was it that you were going to tell me? Quick! I want to know!"

Adon fumbled for an answer. "Oh . . . it was nothing, I guess. It'll come to me, again."

"Well, when it does, I want to hear it."

"Princess told me about part of Brian's estate, that he left for you in trust. . . ."

"I see she's talkative, about some things!"

"I'm glad he did that, now you won't have to keep working until you're sixty-seven. Is it enough for you, in case you want to quit?"

"Brian was generous. Yes. It will be enough. I'm planning to keep working until Princess finishes college. She'll probably go on to graduate school, too. She's thinking about becoming a lawyer. I told her that she had better make up her mind before next school year, so that she won't miss out on those prerequisite courses."

"She'd make an excellent attorney. She has a sharp mind."

"But after she graduates, then I'm going to quit my job, and go into full-time counseling. Since my pastor, who married Brian and I, learned what the Scriptures really say about divorce and remarriage, we've started a new counseling ministry, for couples who may want to dissolve their marriage because they're living in adultery. It's not the right course for everyone, depending on their situation when they married. It was, without a doubt, the right thing for Brian and I. It's not a small matter to God to break up a marriage. Some will just have to confess it, and totally rely on God's mercy in the judgment to pardon them. But they have to know—first! But especially our young people, who are considering marriage, need advice; they need to know all that God requires of Christians who marry, before they get into it. I haven't been long at knowing, myself. But who is more qualified to counsel them than me—or you?"

"I guess we're two qualified people all right!"

Divorce: Episode Three

"I've met another couple in the church who've divorced for the same reasons that Brian and I did. We have a special kind of Christian friendship. We know that we are willing to sacrifice everything, because we love Jesus, therefore we have a trust in one another's sincere commitment to God. We are truly Christian singles, who have dedicated our lives to serving God, and we are not concerned about finding someone to marry as our motivation for associating together. We have placed all of our faith in God, to allow us to lead pure lives, free of fornication. We can associate with our minds centered on serving God, rather than being preoccupied with hopes of finding a mate. It's a freedom of companionship and love that I believe God is expecting from His church before He returns. As couples learn the whole Bible truth about adultery, and some divorce, we intend to expand our group, and become a real force for proclaiming the love of Jesus in our community."

"Jewel, I've never heard any better future plans from anyone. You will be an instrument in the hands of God to help couples to remain married, for a lifetime, rather than trying to produce an innocent party who can remarry. Your role as a faith counselor is Biblically defined, and success has to come from that."

"But, Adon, since we can never remarry . . ."

"You know about the rule of abomination?"

"Yes. Whoever taught Brian, did a good job. But I've studied it for my own self, since then. And I've totally accepted it in our special situation. The Bible clearly shows that whatever God has declared as an abomination, remains an abomination forever. When I studied it, I found that all God had called an abomination in the Bible, is still an abomination today. Since that's true, I don't believe that God has recently changed His mind, and made an exception for modern spouses who divorce and marry someone else; and then, for whatever reason, want to marry a previous spouse again. Even if their last husband or wife has died, like Brian, they can't remarry a previous husband or wife. If they do—in Deuteronomy 24, God plainly calls that an abomination, and I've accepted it as God's commandment under sexual sins.

"If I hadn't married Brian, then you and I could have started anew today, with hopes of legally marrying again. But because of the rule of abomination—now that can never happen. And, I'm at peace with that, because God loves me, and He would never ask me to do anything that wasn't good for me. I'm doing no more now, regarding remarriage, than He's asked me to do in eating healthy, or observing the Bible Sabbath. It's all for my own good. He's just teaching me obedience to all of His commandments, that I'll gladly obey, again, for eternity."

"Jewel, the Lord has a great work for you to do, today, and He's taken His time in preparing you for it."

"But, Adon, you've been kind of wandering around from place to place, since our divorce, and you've told Princess that you don't have any roots anywhere . . ."

"She is talkative, isn't she?"

"Since you don't *seem* to have any roots anywhere, why don't you move here, and join our church, and our singles ministry, and we could even do counseling together—what a great witness that would be—and you could be close to Princess, and to me. I want you to be my best friend, from now on, until Jesus comes. Would you think about doing that?"

"I don't need to think about it, Jewel. That's what I'm going to do—That's what I want to do! I'll start making arrangements as soon as I get home."

Princess came out of the house onto the balcony not wearing a coat, and approached her mom and dad standing at the railing. They hadn't seen her coming toward them, until they heard her voice as she came near.

"Are you guys going to stay out here all day?" Princess said. Adon and Jewel turned toward Princess, and saw her walking toward them with her arms tightly wrapped across her chest for warmth. "It's cold out here! I've been watching you guys from Tangela's window, up there." She turned, pointing up toward her observation bay window on the second level from the main floor of the house.

"Princess, why didn't you put your coat on, before coming out here?" Jewel said. "You're going to get sick, and be out of school for a month!"

Adon opened his top coat, and Princess squeezed in between her mom and dad as Adon placed his arm and top coat over her body.

"So, how long have you been up there, keeping an eye on us?" Adon asked.

"Since Mommy came out here. Then she wasn't out here for two minutes, then you came out—Who's keeping an eye on whom?" Princess knowingly asked.

"Yeah! Come to think of it," Jewel said lightheartedly, "you came out here mighty fast. I wasn't gone long enough for you to miss me."

"I'm planning to be around both of you, if you want me to, for a long time," Adon replied, bringing Princess in closer to him. Jewel pressed in close to Princess. Adon added, "Princess, your mom and I were just discussing me moving here. What do you think about that?"

"What's there to discuss?" You're still married—You just can't do it legally, or have sex, or live together. But you can love us, and you can do that much better if you live where we live. What's there to decide? God knows what He's doing. He's not finished!"

"I guess that settles it then," Adon said.

"I'm ready to go in now," Jewel said. "I don't want my baby to get sick—out here with no coat on!"

They turned from the railing, with Princess still under her dad's coat, and walked together back toward the entrance into the family room.

Index

Followed by

Synoptic Bible Study

Index

Index

Index

Index

Index

Index

Synoptic Study on Divorce and Remarriage

Synoptic Study on Divorce and Remarriage

This Holy Bible study is an attempt to condense the message of this book into a concise and informative format. It provides many key Bible texts but omits the contextual details that may be found in the book. It is structured in question and answer form to facilitate the posing of relative questions and to pin-point Bible and author supplied answers to those questions. Of course, every aspect of the book cannot be covered here, but the reader will find much to receive, contemplate and obey. Read Matthew 19:1-12 to refresh your memory, and then begin the study.

1. Why did the Pharisees question Jesus regarding the legality of divorcing their wives?

"The Pharisees also came unto Him, ***tempting Him,*** and saying unto Him, Is it lawful for a man to put away his wife for every cause?" Matt. 19:3

Answer: The Pharisees and their spies placed themselves in the company of Jesus with one sinister goal in mind, to disprove His claim of being the Jew's Messiah. Their plan was to consistently harass Jesus with thought provoking questions until He somehow in His replies conflicted with the law of Moses. Then they could say to the people that He could not possibly be the Messiah since He had denied Moses, and thereby guilty of blasphemy, and worthy of death.

2. On this occasion how did Jesus avoid the snare of the Pharisees?

"And He answered and said unto them, Have ye not read, that He that made them at the beginning made them male and female, and said, For this cause shall a man leave father and mother, and shall cleave to his wife, and they twain shall be one flesh? Wherefore they are no more twain, but one flesh. What therefore God hath joined together, let not man put asunder." Matt. 19:4-6

Answer: In all of Jesus' interactions with the testy Pharisees His goal was to persuade them to acknowledge the magnitude of their sinful lives, and repent. At every opportunity He pointed out to them their gross enmity against God and His law. Since they had sought to trap Him with respect to divorce, He replied to their question with a question, and then continued with an informative, repentance driven explanation that told them that they were in continual violation of God's law by engaging in divorcing their wives. In His counsel He did not mention Moses, or his law, nor contradict Moses in any way, but adhered to what God's eternal commandments required, which was no divorce.

3. How did the Pharisees show their rejection of God's law and further pursue their objective to entrap Jesus with the law of Moses?

"They say unto Him, why did ***Moses then command*** to give a writing of divorcement, and to put her away?" Matt. 19:7

Answer: Jesus had prefaced His statement on God's law regarding divorce with the phrase "have ye not read," knowing that the Pharisees claim to religious prominence was based on their knowledge of the Hebrew scriptures; thus revealing to them that they were learned enough to not dispute what He was about to say. The Pharisees, after hearing Jesus' pure appeal to their conscience, did not discard their original intent, face their error, and repent, but returned to the decrees of Moses in an attempt to show Jesus that He was in contempt of Moses' law by emphasizing God's law and not the Mosaic. Their question was insincere, and meant only to smoke Jesus out into the open with His, to them, readily apparent blasphemy of Moses. They were engaging in an incriminating doctrinal bout with Jesus over the issue of which law would prevail, Jehovah and divorce or Moses and divorce.

4. Without condemning Moses, what was the reason Jesus gave that caused Moses to allow them to divorce their wives?

"He saith unto them, Moses because of the ***hardness of your hearts*** suffered you to put away your wives: but from the beginning it was not so." Matt. 19:8

Answer: Jesus repeated again that from the beginning, or from the creation of the world, divorce was not a part of God's plan to terminate a marriage; but because the hard-hearted Jews had been abusing their wives, and they sought a legal means to change wives, God allowed Moses, to mitigate transgression, to provide a way for the loud rebels to separate from their wives with the stipulation that they could divorce for only *one* cause. Up until Jesus came, and began to re-educate on divorce, the custom among the hard-hearted was to divorce their wives for *any* cause. This was in stark violation of the Mosaic law which provided for only one cause for legal divorce i.e. sexual immorality.

5. How did Jesus show that God's law cannot change and He had the authority to speak as God, and uphold or dispense with Moses?

"And I say unto you . . ." Matt. 19:9

Answer: Before this encounter with the Pharisees Jesus had used the phrase "And I say unto you" many times to indicate that He was overriding any and all previous conclusions with respect to what conduct was acceptable or not acceptable with God. He never gave the impression that He was not in complete agreement with

God, and the counsel He gave was to be regarded as coming from the mind of God, further building upon the sure foundation of God's commandments. Because He always spoke with such unequivocal authority was the reason the Pharisees continually sought to kill Him, since they had assumed the role of speaking for God and Jesus was seriously diluting their self-imposed authority. They knew that when Jesus prefaced a statement with "And I say unto you" that He was wiping out all that had transpired before that was not in absolute harmony with His present counsel.

6. How did Jesus solidly dispel the Pharisees plan to charge Him with blasphemy, and plainly indicate that He had not forgotten, nor was he avoiding their original entrapment question regarding causes for divorcing their wives?

"And I say unto you, Whosoever shall put away his wife, ***except it be for fornication . . .*** *"* Matt. 19:9

Answer: In Jesus' complete statement to the Pharisees He had a greater lesson for them to learn than responding to their insincere inquiry regarding ***cause*** for divorce, which they already knew; but on the way to His urgent point He disarmed their strategy to charge Him with blasphemy by agreeing with Moses that divorce was still permissible, but with the same concrete rule that Moses had given, "***except it be for fornication.***" After making it clear what the only cause for divorce was, in agreement with Moses, He went on to the pertinent counsel that He really wanted them to grasp, and that was what were they to do ***after*** they had escaped the condemnation of God (owing to Moses) as a result of divorcing their wives.

7. Subsequent to upholding Moses, thereby fouling up their strategy, what was the urgent message that Jesus wanted to communicate to the Pharisees that was re-enacting God's unchangeable law of "Thou shalt not commit adultery?"

"Whosoever shall put away his wife . . . ***and shall marry another, committeth adultery:*** and whoso marrieth her which is put away doth commit adultery." Matt. 19:9

Answer: The ultimate motivation for Jesus' interaction with the Pharisees over divorce is embodied in His final counsel to them regarding what they should do *after* legally divorcing their wives. Should they, under any circumstances, marry again? No! Why should they not marry again? Doing so would plunge *both* spouses into the sin of adultery.

8. What did the disciples say that clearly showed that they remained focused on and understood what Jesus had said with respect to a single cause for divorce?

"His disciples say unto Him, If the case of the man be so with his wife, ***it is not good to marry."*** Matt. 19:10

Answer: Notice that the disciples response to Jesus was "it is not good to *marry,"* and not, it is not good to divorce. Their primary concern, at this point, was the great difficulty in divorcing their wives if fornication was truly the *only* cause. Thus they concluded that if divorcing their wives was so restricted, it was better not to *marry* in the first place!

9. Since a common mistake made by Christians, who insert grounds for *remarriage* in Matthew 19:9, is to overlook the question Jesus is responding to that was asked by the Pharisees, what if

Matthew had recorded only the Pharisees question and Jesus' answer, would this then clearly show that Jesus is *not* giving grounds for remarriage when He said, "Except it be for fornication?"

Matthew 19:3, the Pharisees question: "The Pharisees also came unto Him, tempting Him, and saying unto Him, Is it lawful for a man to put away his wife for ***every*** cause?"

Matthew 19:9, Jesus' answer to the Pharisees: "Whosoever shall put away his wife, ***except it be for fornication,*** and shall marry another, committeth adultery: and whoso marrieth her which is put away doth commit adultery."

Answer: Very clearly. Without a doubt. Jesus is simply addressing the Pharisees question, and answering that there is only *one cause* for divorce, "fornication," and as His style of answering questions was He included an important lesson associated with their question in His answer i.e. how divorcing their wives for fornication would lead to adultery if they remarried. There is nothing in His answer that minutely sanctions remarriage after divorce. No innocent party survives the divorce. (Maybe the one doing the putting away fornicated, too?) No innocent party and no remarriage is in complete harmony with the whole Bible except for the concession in the Mosaic law which permitted women to remarry (Deut. 24:2), and Jesus is overriding the Mosaic law, and re-enacting God's law, for those who desire to be in perfect harmony with His will through keeping all of His commandments.

10. The twelve disciples were present and overheard all of Jesus' lengthy encounter with the Pharisees, including His clarification of what constituted adultery after divorce. However, were the disciples fully convinced that *all* remarriage was adultery?

"And in the house His disciples asked Him ***again of the same matter.***" Mark 10:10

Answer: Evidently, from Mark's Gospel of the same occasion, after concluding with the Pharisees, the disciples remained troubled by Jesus' remarks linking divorce, remarriage and adultery and they sought for additional information to permanently set the matter to rest. Therefore, in the house, where they could talk without constant interruptions, they asked Jesus to make it plain what His instructions to them were. Previously, outside, they had made it quite clear that they had fully grasp the Mosaic law of a single cause for divorce (except it be for fornication) and so the only item left for their complete understanding was how to *avoid sin after divorce.*

11. Inside, in the privacy of the house, after escaping from being charged with blasphemy by the Pharisees, what did Jesus plainly and *directly* say to His disciples that cast aside all doubt about getting married again after a *Moses sanctioned* divorce?

"And He saith unto them, Whosoever shall put away his wife, and ***marry another, committeth adultery*** against her." Mark 10:11

Answer: In Mark's record of Jesus' encounter with the Pharisees, which ultimately led to the conversation in the house, Mark supplies the essence of Jesus' urgent counsel to both the Pharisees and His troubled disciples. Remember, the Pharisees had inquired of Jesus for causes for divorcing their wives, and Jesus had given them the only cause. However, since cause was not the central issue in His counsel He does not address it again in His private conversation with His disciples.

Outside, Mark must have realized the true emphasis of Jesus' communication to His hearers, and, although Mark wrote about the same occasion as Matthew, he does not further cloud Jesus' point with cause for divorce, therefore, he left out cause (fornication), and focused all of his Gospel report on remarriage, which is sin, and dismisses divorce, which is not.

In Matthew's Gospel "except it be for fornication" is included in Jesus' reply solely to agree with Moses and address the Pharisees sly question of causes for divorce and, grammatically, the main point of His complete reply would survive in its essential meaning without its insertion. This essence of meaning is what the Gospel of Mark has clarified by leaving out the words "except it be for fornication" in His indoors counsel to His disciples. They are not consequential to His primary point.

12. Although the Mosaic law governing divorce and remarriage applied mainly to men, since they were the perpetrators for legalizing disobedience to God's law, how did Jesus make it clear that from then on, when it came to remarriage, women were equally guilty of adultery?

"And if a woman shall put away her husband, ***and be married to another, she committeth adultery."*** Mark 10:12

Answer: God's Ten Commandments law does not allow for divorce, it was permitted only under the Mosaic law as a concession to the hard-hearted. So Jesus is saying to His disciples that under the Mosaic law (which all modern Christian divorces owe their existence to) if a woman obtains a divorce, and remarries, she has likewise committed adultery the same as her husband.

In Moses' time the Mosaic law addressing public adultery applied only to men if they remarried after divorce, and not to women. But Jesus is upholding both the Mosaic law and God's eternal law so He does not show any special favor to protect women from public adultery, as was done in the past, and supersedes the Mosaic law and re-enacts God's law which shows no respect for gender; thus women are equally guilty of adultery if they divorce and then remarry.

13. In the Gospel of Luke, when Jesus is teaching on another occasion apart from the accounts in Matthew and Mark, what does Luke record that further proves that Mark was correct by placing the emphasis of Jesus' instruction, regarding divorce and remarriage, on obedience to God's law and sin, and not cause for divorce?

"And it is easier for heaven and earth to pass, than one tittle of the law to fail. Whosoever putteth away his wife, ***and marrieth another, committeth adultery:*** and whosoever marrieth her that is put away from her husband committeth adultery." Luke 16:17, 18

Answer: Taking into account that Jesus, once again, as in Mark's Gospel, has taught on divorce and remarriage without even mentioning causes for divorce provides assurance that divorce, although a highly important issue, is not comparable to obedience to God's law by *refraining from remarriage after divorce.*

14. Along with prayerful study and guidance by the Holy Spirit how may a Christian be certain that Jesus is not providing grounds for remarriage in His Sermon on the Mount?

"Think not that I am come to destroy the law, or the prophets: I am not come to destroy, but to fulfill. For verily I say unto you, Till heaven and earth pass, one jot or one tittle shall in no wise pass from the law, till all be fulfilled. . . . It hath been said, Whosoever ***shall put away his wife,*** let him give her a writing of divorcement: But I say unto you, That whosoever ***shall put away his wife,*** saving for the cause of fornication, causeth her to commit adultery: and whosoever shall marry her that is ***divorced*** committeth adultery." Matt. 5:17, 18, 31, 32

Answer: With direct reference to marriage, Jesus' core subjects are the permanence of God's law and divorce, not qualified remarriage. The only marriage that is mentioned is of another incidental person who marries someone who is divorced, in which case *both* are then guilty of adultery. The thrust of Jesus' admonition is the ungodly state of mind of persons who would selfishly and unreasonably divorce their wives and *cause* them to commit adultery. In supplying meaning to Jesus' words the phrase "saving for the cause of fornication" serves two purposes i. e. to state lawful cause for divorce; and to release the instigator of divorce from causing her fornication if she had committed it before he divorced her. Christ cannot fulfill the law (demonstrate obedience to it) and then advocate breaking it by sanctioning remarriage—all in the same verse.

15. Surely Jesus must have realized that there was a flaw in His teachings by overriding the Mosaic law and not providing *any* grounds for remarriage after divorce. Therefore, didn't Jesus, after He returned to heaven, seek to correct His mistake by communicating to the apostle Paul, through the Holy Spirit that abandonment and adultery were legitimate

grounds for the innocent spouse to remarry?
"The wife is bound by the law so long as her husband liveth; but if ***her husband be dead***, she is at liberty to be married to whom she will; only in the Lord." 1 Cor. 7:39

Answer: No! In all of the epistles of Paul, written for instruction in righteousness for the young Christian church, and the Christian church today, he agrees totally with Jesus Christ that divorce, for any cause, does not entitle either spouse to remarry. Apart from the Mosaic law, which was provided for the ill will hard-hearted and permits an innocent spouse to remarry, *if the guilty spouse divorces them,* the only grounds for obedience centered remarriage is that there is no previous spouse who is still living to spiritually void the marriage. In other words, only widows and widowers are biblically eligible for remarriage.

16. When Paul wrote to the church with respect to divorce and remarriage, what prior knowledge must the members possess, and to what extent must they be governed by that knowledge?

"Know ye not , brethen, (for I speak to them that ***know the law)*** how that the law hath dominion over a man ***as long as he liveth?"*** Romans 7:1

Answer: The basic knowledge that Paul expected the church members to have was a respect for and obedience to God's Ten Commandments; for only God's law must take possession ("dominion") of a persons life, and *all* of their decisions are guided by it, as long as they have the breath of life.

17. Since Paul's inspired counsel to the church is consistent, guided by God's Ten Commandments, has he self-imposed deviation from the demands of the law and made concessions for divorce and remarriage that Jesus Christ Himself did not teach?

"For the woman which hath an husband is bound by the law to her husband so long as he liveth; but if ***the husband be dead,*** she is loosed from the law of her husband. So then if, ***while her husband liveth, she be married to another man, she shall be called an adulteress:*** but if her husband be ***dead,*** she is free from that law; so that she is no adulteress, though she be married to another man." Romans 7:2, 3

Answer: No! Jesus and Paul are in complete harmony regarding their teachings on divorce and remarriage. Jesus and Paul acknowledge that unfortunate circumstances in a marriage may lead to divorce, and divorce for biblical cause is not a sin. However, neither Jesus nor Paul relinquishes their firm hold on remarriage for everyone, other than widows and widowers, produces the sin of adultery.

18. Well—what's a "burning" person to do if they can't marry again, until their previous spouse is dead?!

"Ye have not yet resisted unto blood, ***striving against sin."*** Heb. 12:4

"Then said Jesus unto His disciples, If any man will come after me, ***let him deny himself,*** and take up his cross, and ***follow Me."*** Matt. 16:24

"Not every one that saith unto me, Lord, Lord, shall enter into the kingdom of heaven; but he that ***doeth the will of my Father*** which is in heaven." Matt. 7:21

"He that saith, I know Him, and keepeth not His commandments, is a liar, and the truth is not in him." 1 John 2:4

"He that ***overcometh*** shall

inherit all things; and I will be his God, and he shall be my son." Rev. 21:7

"Let us hear the conclusion of the whole matter: Fear God, and keep His commandments: ***for this is the whole duty of man."*** Eccl.12:13

Answer: God, not man, is in charge of eternal salvation. Mankind may establish governments and conduct wars and populate the earth and travel into outer space and care for the poor, but man cannot save himself from eternal damnation. God has set the rules, and unless mankind submits to the rules, he has no other means of saving himself from eternal death. God's law, "Thou shalt not commit adultery," only requires what is best for mankind because God is love. He has, beyond comprehension, proven that He is love by relinquishing His exalted position as Creator and taking on the debased form of a man, forever thereafter to be associated with man as both God and man. Out of pure love He suffered the crucifixion, the cruelest instigation to quit that Satan could implement, to save mankind from paying the penalty of eternal death for its own sins.

Mankind, which has never been anything more than base sinners, cannot complain when the Creator God requires, for its own benefit that human beings do not remarry until their spouse is dead. When Paul admonished, "It is better to marry than to burn" (1 Corinthians 7:9), he meant that it is better for those who are *eligible* to marry i.e. widows and the never married, to marry than to burn with sexual passion.

Who knows better than Jehovah God what is best for humanity? Within the book of Job, God clearly delineates to Job the infinitude of His wisdom and power.

19. Why is remarriage before a previous spouse has died a sin?

"But He answered and said, It is written, Man shall not live by bread alone, ***but by every word that proceedeth out of the mouth of God."*** Matt. 4:4

"Therefore shall a ***man*** leave his father and his mother, and shall cleave (be joined) unto his ***wife:*** and they shall be ***one flesh."*** Genesis 2:24

"Wherefore they are no more twain (two), but ***one flesh***. What therefore ***God hath joined together, let not man put asunder"*** Matthew 19:6

"For the woman which hath an husband is bound by the law to her husband ***so long as he liveth;*** but if the husband be ***dead,*** she is loosed from the law of her husband. So then if, while her husband ***liveth,*** she be ***married to another man,*** she shall be called an ***adulteress:*** but if her husband be ***dead,*** she is free from that law; so that she is no adulteress, though she be married to another man." Rom. 7:2, 3

Answer: Because God said it is. Truly, a first, and any subsequent marriages, cannot be terminated except by death.

20. After learning the truth about divorce and remarriage will God automatically condemn those who are already remarried, and a previous spouse(s) is still alive?

"For God shall bring every work into judgment, with every secret thing, ***whether it be good, or whether it be evil."*** Eccl. 12:14

"Know ye not, that so many of us as were baptized into Jesus Christ were baptized into His death? Therefore we are buried with him by baptism into death: that like as Christ was raised up from the dead by the glory of the

Father, even so we also should walk ***in newness of life."*** Romans 6:3, 4

Answer: No! God does not condemn persons who commit sin in ignorance and their desire is to confess and repent of their sins. Anyone who has remarried and another spouse is still alive, and they remarried in ignorance of God's law governing divorce and remarriage, may confess their sin and be born again through baptism (by immersion). As with all manner of sins committed before baptism, the sin of unlawful remarriage may be removed from the sinners heavenly record, and baptism is counted as repentance and the marriage may remain intact. If divorced from a living spouse and still single, he or she who has discovered and accepted the truth may choose, after baptism, to remarry.

On the other hand, if a Christian remarries in violation of God's law and he or she ***did or had the opportunity to have*** knowledge of God's law ["To him that knoweth to do good, and doeth it not, to him it is sin." James 4:17] their repentance will be manifested by ending the marriage. Or, they might choose to remain married, confess their sin and totally depend on God's specific mercy in the judgment to pardon their *unrepented* sin.

God's sole desire is to redeem sinners from sin, and those who come to Him with contrite hearts, willing to practice obedient to all of His commandments "He will in no wise cast out."

ABOUT THE AUTHOR

Preston Bradley is a Christian who studies his Holy Bible, and he is expecting the immediate return of Jesus Christ. He has a university degree and lives and writes in Huntsville, Alabama. He believes the Bible messages he has presented in this book. He is divorced with two adult children and living a chaste lifestyle. Contact him through the publisher:

www.visionpublishers.com

ALSO BY PRESTON BRADLEY

THE FINAL WARNING
(PROPHETIC BIBLE BASED NOVEL)

Book One in the series—*HOW THE WORLD WILL END.* Revelation 14:6-12 vividly erupts in today's world. Fascinating characters realistically experience all of the final prophecies leading up to Revelation 13: 13, "And he doeth great wonders, so that he maketh fire come down from heaven on the earth in the sight of men . . ." and the fierce reign of the land beast engulfs the inhabitants of the world.

THE LOUDEST ALARM
(PROPHETIC BIBLE BASED NOVEL)

Book Two in the series—*HOW THE WORLD WILL.END.* A continuation of *THE FINAL WARNING:* The Christians who refuse to accept the mark of the beast struggle in perilous and eroding times to warn the world of the wrath of God poured out upon those who succumb to receiving the mark, and the imminent return of Jesus Christ will end all opportunities to receive eternal life in God's kingdom. The gripping story unfolds into the millennium and culminates in the earth made new for the home of the saved.

GOSPEL OF JUDGMENT
(HISTORIC BIBLE BASED NOVEL)

"And I beheld when he had opened the sixth seal, and, lo, there was a great earthquake; and the sun became black as sackcloth of hair, and the moon became as blood; and the stars of heaven fell unto the earth . . ." Revelation 6:12, 13

Those Bible prophecies, which were to occur before the second coming of Jesus Christ, are factually recorded phenomena in American and world history:

Their fulfillment:

Lisbon Earthquake (4 million square miles) November, 1755.

Dark Day, May 19, 1780.

Moon became as blood, May 19, 1780.

Stars of heaven fell (unique grand display of meteoric showers) November 13, 1833.

Circa A.D. 1844, a turbulent epoch of American slavery, a worldwide movement arose announcing the very next fulfillment of Bible prophecy, and a date for the return of Jesus Christ ["And the heaven departed as a scroll . . . and hide us from the face of Him that sitteth on the throne. and from the wrath of the Lamb." Rev. 6:14, 16], which some have proclaimed led to the greatest disappointment in the Christian Dispensation. However, while many believers discarded their faith, a few clung to belief in their Bibles and "prophesied again," of the final judgment and *then* the imminent return of Jesus Christ, embodying a literal fulfillment of Revelation 10:8-11.

www.visionpublishers.com